Therapeutic Songwriting

Therapeutic Songwriting

Developments in Theory, Methods, and Practice

Felicity A. Baker
University of Melbourne, Australia

First published 2015 by
PALGRAVE MACMILLAN

Palgrave Macmillan in the UK is an imprint of Macmillan Publishers Limited,
registered in England, company number 785998, of Houndmills,
Basingstoke, Hampshire RG21 6XS.

Palgrave Macmillan in the US is a division of St Martin's Press LLC,
175 Fifth Avenue, New York, NY 10010.

Palgrave Macmillan is the global academic imprint of the above companies
and has companies and representatives throughout the world.

Palgrave® and Macmillan® are registered trademarks in the United States,
the United Kingdom, Europe and other countries.

ISBN: 978–1–137–49921–9 hardback
ISBN: 978–1–137–49922–6 paperback

This book is printed on paper suitable for recycling and made from fully
managed and sustained forest sources. Logging, pulping and manufacturing
processes are expected to conform to the environmental regulations
of the country of origin.

A catalogue record for this book is available from the British Library.

A catalog record for this book is available from the Library of Congress.

Contents

List of Tables

List of Figures

Acknowledgments

Writing this book has been perhaps the biggest academic challenge in my life to date. It has pushed me to expand my views on practice, shifted my thinking about possibilities, and enabled me to grow and deepen my appreciation for songwriting as a method. It has been an absolute privilege to work on this book over the past four and a half years and I thank Nicola Jones and Eleanor Christie and their team at Palgrave Macmillan for agreeing to publish it. I also want to thank the Australia Research Council for funding my research fellowship (ARC Future Fellowship FT100100022). Without the ARC's support, I could not imagine undertaking a project of this scale.

While I am very close to the contents of this book and have poured my heart and soul into it, what has been communicated in the ensuing pages has unquestionably come about because of the interviews and interactions with 45 experienced clinicians and researchers. As you read the book, their varied perspectives are represented in every chapter. My thanks to all of them for finding space in their busy lives to share their work with me. Many allowed me to visit their workplaces, watch sessions, and share examples of songs. They have all been very generous with their time and I thank them for the privilege of being able to hear (and now represent) their work.

I want to acknowledge the intellectual contributions of Michael Viega, Helen Short, and Kimberly Khare, whose approaches and perspectives on songwriting have greatly impacted my thinking. Our numerous dialogues and your sharing of powerful stories have opened me to possibilities and perspectives I was not aware of, and your critical feedback of this entire draft has challenged my thinking; your voices are very much present in this book. My thanks to the three of you for your generosity over the years. A special thanks also to Jinah Kim, Helle Lund, Hanna Hakomaki, Neils Hannibal, Randi Rolvsjord, Brynjulf Stige, Lucy Bolger, Amy Clement-Cortes, and Ken Aigen, who all read early developed models and drafts of the analysis and provided invaluable feedback. I also want to recognize the contributions of my long-term collaborator and friend Jeanette Tamplin. Having worked closely as clinicians and co-researchers for almost 20 years, I hold a great deal of admiration and respect for her work. Her voice and perspectives on songwriting are present in this book.

I want to thank Professor Kenneth Bruscia here. I attended his Sear's lecture at the American Music Therapy conference in Atlanta in

2011 where he mapped out his integral thinking – outcome-oriented, experience-oriented, and context-oriented thinking. This keynote address had a profound effect on me. It helped me to find a way to frame the development of the models presented in this book.

While not specific to this book, I cannot write an acknowledgment section without paying tribute to my mentors: Denise Grocke, Tony Wigram, Cheryl Dileo, and Barbara Wheeler. You have offered me varied forms of support over the years. If I ever asked for help, you never refused (despite how busy you all were), and have afforded me opportunities I once only dreamed about. I also want to say a special thank you to my friend and colleague Katrina McFerran. We have known each other a long time and share a common lust for life and a sense of who we are in the world. You are a true gem – immensely intelligent, strong, passionate, and committed. I truly treasure your friendship, your respect, and your embracing of our differences; through you, I grow.

Thank you to both my parents for your years of support and for allowing me the freedom to make my own career decisions, follow my passion, and to love me even when I made a few big mistakes along the way. The life messages you have taught me have made me strong, resilient, and driven. I thank you for bringing music into my life – it is the best gift you could have ever given me. Dad, I know you would have loved to read this book, to have held it in your hands. You were always so proud of my achievements. Mum, you are my idol – you have taught me all I know about responding and adjusting to what life throws at me. You have shown me that being a woman is a gift not a problem, and that I can be empowered to create a world where my gifts and talents can be utilized and recognized.

To Nathan: You have witnessed firsthand my transition from a dynamic and caring clinician to a passionate academic and researcher. You more than anyone else in the world know how important this research has been to me. You not only support me but also encourage me to step outside my comfort zone, take a risk, stretch myself, and grow. You continue to hold true to your marriage vows of allowing me to become who I want to be, to fulfill my dreams and potentials. Thank you for giving me space to write this book, for taking care of our boys so I could travel and collect data, and for pouring me that glass of Pinot Gris when I needed to take a break. I am so fortunate to have you in my life. And to my boys Maximillian and Finnegan: you keep me grounded, remind me that life is about love, relationships, sharing experiences, connecting, and belonging. Your morning cuddles, cheeky 'I've been naughty' smiles, games of Monopoly, daily reading sessions, and weekend 'Hobbit' or 'Lord of the Rings' movie sessions are a source of meaning and vitality in my life. I love you boys.

Section I
Introduction

1

Introduction, Research Focus, and Approach

Early experiences of songwriting

I was first struck by the power of therapeutic songwriting in 1992 when I commenced working at a rehabilitation facility for young adults who had sustained traumatic brain injury. These young people were not only undergoing an intensive and exhausting rehabilitation program, but were also moving through a process of grief as they faced the reality of living with a permanent disability. At the time I (naïvely) believed that improvisation would assist these young people to explore their feelings and that they would, in their own time, draw on these experiences to process and resolve this grief. However I was grossly mistaken.

These young people who presented with complex cognitive impairments found improvisation too abstract and they were not motivated to engage in it. To them, they were creating noise, not music. My appreciation for therapeutic songwriting emerged as I began to introduce more song-based interventions into my practice. I first introduced simple song parody experiences and later incorporated the creation of completely original songs. To illustrate how powerful songwriting parody is within my work, I would like to share a short case example.

When I first met Fred, he was in his early 30s, had received a traumatic brain injury as a consequence of a motor vehicle accident, and was participating in an intensive rehabilitation program. The paralysis on one side of his body mainly affected his arm, and he could ambulate with the assistance of a walking stick. Fred demonstrated no difficulties with verbal communication, but he had cognitive difficulties that resulted in very poor initiation of conversation, idea generation, perseveration of ideas, and concrete thinking. He became fixated on hospital visits from his mother and often refused to attend therapy programs because of this fixation.

3

Fred attended music therapy twice a week, and over the course of six sessions we composed a song about his mother. Generating ideas about lyrical content demanded a collaborative approach, but he would only respond to direct questions and never initiated any interaction. I utilized specific techniques to stimulate Fred's creative expression of ideas. For example, the 'wh' questions – who, what, why, where, when, and how – were used to probe Fred for information that we later incorporated into the song (Baker, 2005). When we commenced therapy together, Fred was only able to contribute concrete ideas, such as describing his mother's appearance and the caregiving activities she performed. Over the course of creating the song, however, Fred began to contribute ideas that were focused on his feelings toward his mother rather than concrete visible characteristics. Fred was a big fan of Bob Marley and wanted his lyrics to be set to the tune of 'No Woman No Cry' (Figure 1.1). The song he created became a source of comfort for Fred. He would play this song when his mother was not there. It seemed to function as a transitional object during his many moments of separation from her, allowing him to feel close to her and safe.

I experienced many moments when songwriting played a significant role in the lives of people with acquired brain injury (ABI). It allowed some to express adversity, others to reminisce about a past life, while

CHORUS: My mum is a superstar
My mum is beautiful
She cleans my clothes
My mum cleans my clothes
VERSE 1: And my mum, she cooks good chicken
I love to eat her chicken
And my mum, she cooks good vegetables
I love to eat her vegetables
VERSE 2: And my mum, she loves her grandkids
She loves to feed them
And my mum, she wears good clothes
My mum dresses well
VERSE 3: And my mum, I love to hug her
No body can hurt my mum
And my mum, I will protect her
I love my mum
VERSE 4: And my mum, I want to thank her
For watching me grow up
And my mum, I wish I was with you
I miss being with you

Figure 1.1 'My Mum Is a Superstar' (song parody)

others used the medium to communicate with loved ones. Songwriting also served rehabilitative functions such as providing cognitive training to address poor abstract thinking, idea generation, concentration, and being able to organize and follow through on tasks. Over time, I became increasingly intrigued by the opportunities the intervention afforded and the immense motivation these songwriters exhibited when creating songs. At this point (with colleagues Jeanette Tamplin and Jeanette Kennelly), I began to analyze the songs people with brain injury had created to identify patterns and to better understand what these young people were communicating in their songs (Baker et al., 2005b, 2005c, 2005d). These early clinical and research experiences, some from more than 20 years ago, laid the foundations for this journey of discovery – a journey that is far from finished.

Rationale for researching songwriting practices

Over the past two decades, there has been increasing interest in and application of songwriting as a music therapy method. Following the publication of a book I edited with Tony Wigram, *Song Writing Methods, Techniques and Clinical Applications for Music Therapy Clinicians, Educators and Students* (Baker & Wigram, 2005), research and literature reporting the therapeutic value of songwriting across the lifespan was notably increasing. This book, together with an international survey (Baker et al., 2008, 2009), identified some of the specific steps, stages, strategies, techniques, and intentions that therapists draw on when engaging people – herein the songwriters – in a therapeutic songwriting process. However, many of these methods, particularly those reported in the survey, were not linked to specific therapeutic orientations and were not mapped out in a format that would assist many practitioners to apply these techniques in their practice. They were described only in reference to a specific clinical group and not related to therapists' contexts or theoretical perspectives.

The purpose of the book was to bridge the gap between the taxonomy of techniques described in the literature (Baker et al., 2009; Wigram, 2005) and recent developments in theory, research, and practice by synthesizing the findings of a series of studies undertaken over the past decade. In planning the structure of this book, I was faced with many options. Initially I considered mapping practices according to developmental age groupings, but after prolonged reflection these classifications seemed too broad. And focusing on broad clinical areas – for example, developmental disability, neurorehabilitation, mental health recovery, and so on – pathologizes the songwriters, an approach that is incongruent with contemporary thinking (e.g. Community Music Therapy, Stige, 2012). Further, dividing people into groups by developmental age or pathology discouraged discussion around theoretical frameworks. To really contribute to the music therapy discourse, there was a need to go beyond pathology and to identify patterns of songwriting practice as they related to practitioners' orientation.

Overview of the research process

In 2010, I was awarded an Australia Research Council research fellowship (Future Fellowship Scheme) which funded me for four years (2011–2015) to research and build the methods and models of songwriting across the lifespan. The series of studies involved a combination of expert interviews, lab-based studies, and clinically based studies which aimed to explore different facets of the songwriting approaches and experiences. The findings from these studies were then synthesized alongside pre-existing research, after which the salient features were identified and described in written form. The first and largest study involved in-depth interviews with 45 experienced clinicians and researchers from across the globe. Interviews were conducted either face-to-face or by Skype videoconferencing, lasting from 45 minutes to 3 hours in duration. The data were rich. In some cases I was also fortunate to observe songwriting in action, which aided in my understanding of the interview data. The interviews covered the following topics:

1. Purpose of therapeutic songwriting in clinical practice
2. Perceived strengths and limitations
3. Therapeutic orientation underpinning songwriting approaches
4. Methods of creating lyrics and music
5. Life of the song beyond the therapy setting
6. Roles of the songwriter, the therapist, and the music in the songwriting process
7. Factors impacting songwriting processes
8. Descriptions of unexpected breakthroughs and negative songwriting experiences

Clinicians and researchers were recruited from 11 countries: Australia, Canada, Denmark, Finland, Iceland, the Netherlands, Norway, Qatar, South Korea, the United Kingdom, and the United States. The 32 females and 13 males had between 4 and 35 years' clinical experience (Mean = 14, SD = 9). Analysis of the transcribed interviews followed the principles of grounded theory (Corbin & Strauss, 2008) to identify concepts and patterns in the data and build more abstract themes. The emerging data were continuously compared with the existing literature.

The second study (with Raymond MacDonald) involved working with 13 healthy university students and 13 retired Australians to better understand the meaningfulness of a songwriting experience and to increase our understanding of the differences between lyric writing, parody, and original songwriting. Each songwriter created three artifacts within a quasi-therapeutic context – song lyrics without music, song parody, and a song that contained original lyrics and music. We measured the nine dimensions of flow (Csikszentmihalyi, 2000) and the meaningfulness of the songwriting process and product, and later interviewed the songwriters about their experiences. The numerical data allowed us to establish predictive relationships between the meaningfulness of the songwriting experiences and perceived flow (Baker & MacDonald, 2013a), and the thematic analysis of interview data assisted us in building a theory about the features of therapeutic songwriting that lead to enhanced meaning (Baker & MacDonald, 2013b). We then developed a questionnaire (Meaningfulness of Songwriting Questionnaire, Baker et al., unpublished manuscript) that could measure the strength of the meaningfulness of a songwriting process and product, with the long-term plan of incorporating this into research to better understand why some people have better therapy outcomes than others.

The final study to date allowed me to return to my passion for using songwriting with people who have neurological injuries. In collaboration with Nikki Rickard, Jeanette Tamplin, and Raymond MacDonald, I designed a study that enabled us to examine the impact of a carefully designed songwriting protocol on the self-concept and wellbeing of people in the early stages of recovery from ABI or spinal cord injury (SCI). Five people with ABI and five with SCI received songwriting therapy, while five people with ABI and five with SCI were recruited as matched controls. Each songwriter created 3 songs (a song about their past, present, and imagined future) across 12 sessions. Measures were taken at pre-, mid- and post-session. We found that songwriting enabled people to explore who they were post-injury and begin to look to a new life after being discharged from hospital.

All the data that were collected and analyzed during this process were considered alongside existing research, and synthesized to construct the methods and models described in the book. But the process did not finish there. During each stage of building methods and models, and in creating the various maps and frameworks, I distributed drafts (sometimes multiple drafts) for comments and feedback from colleagues (some of whom were participants in the study). This final stage of the process allowed me to refine what I had created and ensure it was useful and relevant for practice (Stige et al., 2009).

Models and methods

When contemplating how I would develop and present the models and methods, I looked to Bruscia's (1987) seminal book *Improvisational Models of Music Therapy* for inspiration. I thought there was merit in describing and framing methods of practice according to the orientation of the practitioner, where my analysis could identify the ways in which song-writing practice aligned with the general features of each orientation. In constructing the models, Bruscia consulted various artifacts – including books, journals, audio recordings, and written notes – and also inter-viewed music therapists who used improvisation. What resulted was a collection of 25 improvisational models of music therapy. I was appreci-ative of the way that Bruscia provided clear definitive features of each of the models so the reader could compare and contrast them. But this was published more than 25 years ago, when music therapy was practiced within a more limited range of orientations – behavioral, humanistic, and predominantly psychoanalytical approaches. Present-day practice has expanded to include approaches grounded in anthropological, soci-ological, cultural, and feminist values (among others). I was faced with the question, 'Would it still be possible to construct models given the expansion of the discipline?' Further, many practitioners do not neces-sarily identify with one orientation but are eclectic. So how was I to make sense of all this and construct models of songwriting within a field so diverse and so eclectic?

My answer to this question came when I attended the Sear's lecture by Kenneth Bruscia in November 2011 at the American Music Therapy Association's National Conference. In his presentation, Bruscia outlined three 'main ways of thinking' about music therapy to describe the col-lection of orientations adopted in music therapy practice:

1. Outcomes-oriented: Medical, Behavioral, Educational, and Cognitive-behavioral;
2. Experience-oriented: Psychodynamic, Humanistic, Gestalt; and
3. Context-oriented: Cultural Psychology, Sociology, and Anthropology[1]

His lecture compared and contrasted these three primary orientation categories according to the roles of music, therapist, and client, the per-spectives on outcomes, treatment, efficacy, and evaluation, and how music is used and understood in the process. Perhaps most importantly, however, Bruscia stated that for practitioners to best serve their clients, they need to move away from 'one-way' thinking to more 'integral' thinking. Informed by Wilber's (2000, 2006) 'integral thinking', Bruscia proposed that practitioners should be flexible in their thinking and practice of music therapy to ensure they meet the needs of their clients. In other words, they should not feel disloyal moving between orientations if, in doing so, it meets the clients' needs and contexts. The orientation models of songwriting presented in this book are therefore grouped according to outcome, experience, and context-oriented thinking. From here, the practitioner can move between the broadly defined models to ensure he/she provides the most effective and appropriate songwriting experience for the songwriter.

Like Bruscia, my plan was to construct different models of therapeutic songwriting according to orientation. Typically, models are simplified representations of a phenomenon, with fundamental properties explicitly defined. These conceptual or mental representations may be of a system, a situation, or a process. All three are relevant in the context of therapeutic songwriting, with perhaps the strongest emphasis on process models, which are representations of the way a clinician would execute therapeutic songwriting in the clinical setting. But there is a dilemma here: songwriting is a music therapy *method*, one of many interventions or music-based experiences employed within a therapy program. For purposes of clarity, I have chosen specific uses for both the terms in this book. The term *model* has been used to describe the overarching features of the songwriting process. This includes descriptions of the theoretical framework underpinning the model, the salient features of the process including the role of the therapist, songwriter, music, and the aims of the songwriting process and product.

In contrast, the term *method* is used to describe a set of concrete steps, procedures, or therapeutic intentions employed to create a song. As will be described in Chapters 8–11, such methods include song parody, strategic songwriting, song collage, and mash-ups or improvised songs. These methods may be included within several models of songwriting, but it is the theoretical framework for understanding and guiding the process that differs according to the *model* being practiced (Chapters 12–14).

What you will find described in this book

This book is divided into four sections. Section I, 'Introduction', comprises of two chapters, including this one. The next chapter provides an introduction to songwriting as a method, defining it, presenting a brief history of its evolution as a therapeutic practice, its role as a health and wellbeing tool, the contexts and clinical and non-clinical populations where songwriting is employed, and the strengths and limitations of therapeutic songwriting. Chapter 2 also provides a context for how songwriting has developed into a formidable intervention over the past decade.

Section II, 'Factors Influencing the Songwriting Process', comprises five chapters that explore how different factors impact and shape the songwriting process and the song product. Chapter 3 outlines the environmental factors that influence intervention choices and methods. Organizational structures and organizational culture can dictate the length of treatment available and can therefore influence what methods of songwriting can be adopted. This chapter also discusses how the physical space and the degree of privacy in the therapeutic context can shape the way a songwriting process unfolds. These environmental factors play key roles in driving or limiting the therapeutic process and contribute to the clinician's decision-making.

Chapter 4 outlines the sociocultural factors that can positively or negatively impact a songwriting process. These include differences in religion, socioeconomic class, gender, and generation. I propose that songwriting may be more effective in cultures where music is an integral component of daily life when compared with other cultures where music is not practiced by women, or is reserved for purely religious or spiritual purposes. Challenges concerning language barriers between therapist and songwriter are identified – for example, how words may mean different things in different languages and do not always translate into meaningful lyrics. Similarly, the extent of sociocultural homogeneity within a songwriting group can support or constrain a songwriting process. At times monoculture bonds songwriting groups; at other times diversity in group membership stimulates deep reflective thinking and the creation of songs that encourage acceptance of different views and experiences.

The individual features of a songwriter play a significant role in shaping a songwriting process and product. These features are outlined in detail in Chapter 5. A person's physical state and physiological wellbeing will influence the degree of participation in the songwriting process. For example, those with low and inconsistent levels of arousal may create shorter songs or take several sessions to complete a song when compared with songwriters who have higher and more consistent arousal levels. A person's age and gender will impact the type of songwriting process that unfolds. I have identified that personality plays a role in how open a person is to sharing his story and creating songs.

Group characteristics – group composition, size, conflict and cohesion – are the subject matter of Chapter 6. This chapter outlines how groups of differing composition can lead to distinctive group songwriting experiences. In some circumstances group conflict within a songwriting process can lead to an impasse and halt a songwriting process, whereas in others conflict can be an opportunity for growth, for discovering a common experience but also acknowledging and respecting differences.

An important consideration in songwriting is the role that music plays above and beyond the creation of lyrics. Research has explored in detail how songs tell people's stories and are therefore a useful medium for people to make sense of their life narratives. Chapter 7 explores the role of music as a medium for conveying meaning and enhancing the emotional dimension of the lyrics. The chapter describes the capacity music affords to support identity building, an aspect that creating lyrics alone falls short of achieving.

Section III, 'Songwriting Methods', focuses on the varied methods employed by clinicians, irrespective of orientation. Chapter 8 provides an overview to orient the reader to the subsequent chapters. The methods are described in terms of whether they emphasize lyric creation, music creation, or a balanced attention to both. The extent to which the song creation approaches have a set of predetermined components are also mapped on the continuum. This helps the reader to understand how the different methods compare according to these two broad categorizations. The final section of this chapter describes the importance of the introductory phases of songwriting and how certain activities serve to prepare and prime the songwriter for in-depth songwriting experiences.

Chapter 9 explores the songwriting methods where the primary focus is on creating lyrics. Four methods – fill-in-the-blank (FITB), song parody, strategic songwriting, and rapping over pre-composed music – are described in detail. I illustrate examples of each method as described by my interviewees or from existing literature, highlighting how each method can play a pivotal role in the therapeutic process. Within this chapter, I also outline a rationale for choosing these approaches according to the types of songwriting experiences they afford.

Chapter 10 follows the same structure as Chapter 9, but instead focuses on songwriting methods where there is an emphasis placed on both lyric and music creation. Approaches described include rapping over original music, song collage, and four types of improvised songwriting. Chapter 11 mirrors the structures of Chapters 9 and 10, but describes the songwriting methods where the strongest emphasis is on music creation. More contemporary approaches – mash-ups, pastiche, and hodge podge – are described with case illustrations, as well as more traditional original songwriting methods.

Section IV, 'Songwriting Models', describe the various therapeutic and philosophical orientations that influence therapeutic songwriting practices. The first three chapters are structured according to whether the orientation is outcome-focused (Chapter 12: behavioral, cognitive-behavioral, neuroplasticity-oriented), experience-oriented (Chapter 13: psychodynamic, music-centered, humanistic), or context-oriented (Chapter 14: feminist, community music therapy, resource-oriented music therapy). Within each chapter, songwriting methods reflecting or epitomizing the orientation are described and named. Further, the chapters explore where the critical points occur in the songwriting process, the levels of depth achieved during songwriting, as well as the role of songwriting, music, the therapist, the songwriter, the artifact, and any other salient feature of songwriting within each of the orientations. Chapter 15 offers some final reflections, thoughts on songwriting within integral thinking, and presents an overview of the models.

2
Songwriting: A Coming of Age

Before delving into discussions on methods and models of songwriting, it is important to define what therapeutic songwriting is along with its boundaries, general features, and typical uses. This chapter also provides an historical account of the evolution of songwriting as a therapeutic practice by examining publishing trends and features of the literature available at the time of writing this book. It illustrates how songwriting has increased in status within the field – a coming of age. The final section of this chapter is devoted to describing the strengths and limitations of songwriting as identified by those interviewed in this study.

So what is therapeutic songwriting?

To answer this question, one must first answer the question: 'What is a song?' And any answer to this will depend on who is being asked; the term is culturally loaded. For example, a song in Australian indigenous communities might involve multiple participators, and is passed down in aural form from generation to generation. Such songs are not notated, are somewhat improvised within a predetermined song form, and may tell an oral history or be created as offerings to the spirits. Conversely, in Mexican cultures the 'corrido' song form describes oppression and the daily life of peasants. Songs created within Western cultures are described as poems or a set of words set to music (typically notated) and that are largely fixed in form (Oxford Dictionary, 2010). What is common amongst these descriptions, however, is that songs convey information – through lyrics and music, songs tell stories or express feelings.

In contemporary Western society, songs may communicate a diversity of themes. Over the past 70 years, the majority of songs of popular music genres have been focusing on relationships. At one end of the spectrum, songs may express or tell the story of longing, desire, passion, and happiness; songs about relationship loss, infidelity, rejection, oppression, or jealousy fall at the other end of the spectrum. Songs describing other relationships are also strongly represented in modern day repertoire, such as 'My Sister' (Juliana Hatfield) and 'Father and Son' (Cat Stevens).

Songs may communicate a social or a political critique, including experiences of homelessness ('Another Day in Paradise' by Phil Collins), rape ('Sex Type Thing' by Stone Temple Pilots), bullying ('Lunch Box' by Marilyn Manson), drugs ('Day Tripper' by The Beatles, 'The Drugs Don't Work' by The Verve), domestic violence (songs by Suzanne Vega), abortion ('Papa Don't Preach' by Madonna), and racism ('Killing in the Name' by Rage Against the Machine). Many of the issues described in these songs are relevant for the people attending music therapy programs across the globe.

This leads to the question: what is therapeutic songwriting? In 2005, therapeutic songwriting was defined as 'The process of creating, notating and/or recording lyrics and music by the client or clients and therapist within a therapeutic relationship to address psychosocial, emotional, cognitive and communication needs of the client' (Baker & Wigram, 2005, p. 16). This definition states that both lyrics and music are integral and that the process of song construction occurs within the songwriter–therapist relationship,[1] and the process is only therapeutic if it is directed toward meeting a songwriter's specific needs. Despite my prolonged engagement with data collected in this study and with the emergence of contemporary music therapy practices over the past 10 years, this definition remains relevant today.

Trends in songwriting publishing

A search of the literature revealed that prior to 1990 there were only two journal publications describing songwriting as an intervention within a therapeutic context (Ficken, 1976; Freed, 1987). Since then, however, there has been a steady increase in the published use of the method. Between 1990 and 1999 there were 14 studies, between 2000 and 2005 there were 23 studies, between 2006 and 2010 there were 17 studies, and between 2010 and 2014 the number rose to more than 50 studies. This sudden increase over the past five years suggests a growing recognition of songwriting's potential to affect personal growth and change. Most studies were conducted in Australia (40), the United States (31), Norway (9), Canada (7), and the United Kingdom (7). Authors from Israel (1), South Africa (3), Finland (2), Korea (2), the Netherlands (1), and Iceland (1) have also published studies that used songwriting as the main medium. The early studies (1990–1999) tended to be descriptions of case material (e.g. Aigen, 1991; Glassman, 1991; Hadley, 1996; Kennelly, 1999; Mayers, 1995) illustrating the process individual songwriters engaged in during their therapy programs. In the early 2000s, publications started to shift toward describing methods, and many authors described their specific songwriting approaches in the text edited by Baker and Wigram's (2005), *Songwriting: Methods, Techniques and Clinical Applications for Music Therapy Clinicians, Educators and Students.* In the early 2000s, there was an emergence of studies that examined the lyrics and themes of songs created during therapy programs, with the assumption that lyrics were central to understanding a songwriter's mental state and his progress toward recovery (e.g. Baker et al., 2005a, 2005b; McFerran et al., 2006). From 2010 to the present day, we see the shift to outcome studies (e.g. Grocke et al., 2014; Hong & Choi, 2011; Silverman, 2011a, 2011b, 2011c, 2012), and to my own studies that focused on understanding the factors and mechanisms of change that are active during songwriting (Baker, 2013a–2013f). These shifts from the case material to methods, to understanding the role of songwriting, and then to early effect, factor, and mechanisms studies suggest that extensive (but perhaps not yet exhaustive) work has taken place at the observation stage and the exploratory stage, and is now moving toward the explanatory stages of developing songwriting interventions and protocols. Certainly the cyclic process of observational, explorative, explanatory, and pragmatic studies has begun (Campbell et al., 2000), signifying that songwriting as an intervention is coming of age.

When examining the literature further, trends emerged in the ages and types of people engaged in songwriting practices (Table 2.1). There is a marked increase in the use of songwriting with adolescents during the last five years. There is also a noticeable increase over time in songwriting studies involving adults, although this increase is not as striking. Studies involving people with cancer have decreased in recent years, whereas there has been a surge in studies with people who have experienced trauma and grief, people who are marginalized or of refugee status, people with mental illness and/or with substance use disorder, and with male and female offenders.

Table 2.1   Types of people engaging in therapeutic songwriting

	1990–1999	2000–2005	2006–2010	2010–2014
Children	3	11	2	9
Adolescents	5	4	5	16
Adults	5	11	11	18
Older adults	1		1	4
SCI/ABI	2	3	1	
Cancer and other diseases	3	8	2	2
Trauma and abuse	3	3	3	6
Mental illness	4	4	4	8
Autism/developmental needs	1		1	3
Dementia				2
Palliative care		2	1	
Refugees and the marginalized		3	1	7
Substance Use Disorder		1	1	4
Bereaved			2	5
Offenders and people in prison				4
Caregivers				1

Strengths of songwriting

In my interviews with clinicians, I asked them to describe what they perceived as the strengths of songwriting. Several common themes emerged from the inductive analysis: (1) songwriting is connected to culture and society; (2) songwriting is versatile; (3) songwriting involves a therapeutic process; (4) songwriting combines language and music; (5) songwriting invites collaboration and a therapeutic relationship; (6) songwriting represents a therapeutic journey; (7) songwriting is a medium for emotional expression; (8) songwriting is a social activity; (9) songwriting can transform the songwriter's environment; and (10) songwriting creates artifacts.

Songwriting, culture, and society

Part of the appeal of songwriting as a medium for growth and change lies in its connections to culture and society. Songs are linked to growth phases – for parent–infant bonding, identity formation during adolescence, and in social settings and for relationship building in adulthood. Songs are connected with social and sporting events, family events such as births, deaths, and marriages, for leisure, and as sociopolitical statements. Songs have intrinsic value within society, and songs and songwriters (and those that perform their songs) are held in high regard by society. Even the creation of 'corny' or self-indulgent lyrics is regarded as acceptable.

Because of the status that songs hold in society, and the recognition that they are an appropriate medium for self-expression, people attending music therapy are often motivated and open to the idea of creating songs. Similarly, as society acknowledges the identity-forming potential of songwriting, those creating songs within therapeutic contexts have 'permission' to explore multiple and contrasting sides of their identities to discover their answer to the questions: 'Who am I?', 'What am I?', 'What am I thinking?', and 'What am I concerned about?'

Versatility of songwriting

One of the primary reasons why songwriting is an increasingly used method of music therapy stems from its versatility and potential for addressing a broad range of clinical and non-clinical goals. Through songwriting, songwriters have the possibility to explore and express their emotions, develop or redevelop a range of cognitive skills, address relationship issues, focus on coping strategies, construct a sense of self and identity, rehearse social skills, and engage in life review (Baker et al., 2008).

An important aim of the songwriting process is to create opportunities for songwriters to experience mastery, self-esteem, and self-confidence. As they create their own songs, they receive internal and external feedback about their capacity as a songwriter, and derive pride from completing an artistic work. Some songwriters gain confidence and feel empowered to have a voice; others may acquire insight into their self-worth. Catharsis may be experienced as songwriters project their emotions onto the lyrics and music, and this emotional release may reoccur when their songs are replayed either live or through a recording. The songwriting process enables internal feelings and emotions to be externalized and then processed at a cognitive level.

Songwriting experiences can be shaped to enhance language, speech, and conversational skills across a broad range of clinical areas such as neurorehabilitation, mental health, and aging, among others (Baker et al., 2008). When working with songwriters who may be unable to verbally communicate but can either write freehand or by using a communication aid, iPad, or other technological device, songwriting can focus on increasing their capacity to generate, develop, order, and self-monitor ideas. As they construct lyrics and make choices about the accompanying music, they have possibilities of practicing their handwriting, sentence construction, typing, and language skills. In some cases, pragmatic conversational skills such as providing specific and unambiguous information may be challenging. Some people may have difficulty maintaining a conversational topic or may offer a range of irrelevant information (Baker, 2005). They may be verbose, contributing excessive information, or conversely may benefit from increasing the amount of information they share. Songwriting demands that the songwriter be clear, precise, and succinct in what is communicated in the lyrics, and order the ideas in a logical and coherent manner. Songwriters need to be able to self-critique the content and the language expression used in order to create a powerful and impactful song.

For people who are being treated for life-threatening illnesses or are in palliative care, songwriting provides possibilities for life review and for creating legacies for those significant family and friends who will be left behind. The narrative potential of songwriting encourages people to 'tell their story' through the lyrics, which are then supported by an appropriate accompaniment. The process of telling one's story demands a level of reflection on that life. The resultant song may capture the essence of a person's life, a brief overview of key moments in his life, or a rich description of particular events or experiences in his life. Additionally, songs may be created to send messages of love, thanks, appreciation, or regret to important people in the songwriter's life. For example, Hilliard and Justice (2011) describe a case of a 62-year-old man, David, who was being treated for terminal cancer. David created eight songs. One song was dedicated to communicating with his fellow Church parishioners, and the other seven songs were each created with a specific family or friend in mind. In David's case, songwriting enabled him to communicate his appreciation of the special people in his life.

Songwriting is a medium for people to 'tell their story' and explore traumatic events in their lives. Through the narrative process, the songwriters put words to their experiences, and in doing so process the meaning and ramifications of their stories and their emotional responses to it. Through these emotional and cognitive processes, the songwriters may begin to accept the event or the consequences associated with the event.

Many people that clinicians work with present with impaired cognitive functioning. People with mental illness or with neurodisabilities are likely to display poor concentration, short- or long-term memory, organizational skills, self-monitoring, and problem-solving. Constructing a song engages these various cognitive skills, thereby providing opportunities to practice and improve on the songwriter's current abilities. Songwriting demands the songwriter concentrate and follow through on writing the song from start to finish, drawing on several executive functions. The creation process calls for a synthesizing of ideas, and ordering and reordering the ideas until a coherent story evolves. Problem-solving is rehearsed as the songwriter attempts to create music to match his story, resolve personal or interpersonal conflicts that might arise through the lyric creation process, or engage in more task-oriented activities such as refining the lyrics so a lyrical line has the correct number of syllables within it.

Songwriting is versatile because it can be implemented in a range of contexts – individual and group therapy, within the home, at bedside, in community centers, in hospital waiting rooms, and in residential units – and that they may occur in the absence of a formalized 'therapy' session. One clinician working with young marginalized people recounted in an interview how he sometimes recorded material on a video camera in places such as the car park or playground, which was later adapted or sampled and included in song creations.

Songwriting invites a therapeutic process

Songwriting presents many opportunities for people to engage in a therapeutic process. One of its virtues is that songs take time to create and therefore allow for prolonged engagement with issues. There are possibilities to process and reprocess issues across several sessions, which enables people to expand their awareness and understanding of the issues over time and to 'sit with' their feelings and experiences. The prolonged engagement creates opportunities to explore alternative paths of recovery and planned actions, and for these to be represented in the song lyrics.

Songwriting has the capacity to keep a songwriter focused in ways that clinicians perceived other music therapy methods could not achieve. The experience connects and holds the songwriter in the present and directs him to focus on poignant issues. Because the song becomes a description of a story, experience, or feeling, the process has a natural tendency to maintain the songwriter's focus on the specific topic and, by doing so, avoids a deliberate or non-deliberate shift to expressing other experiences. The song focuses on a single issue, and has an endpoint that the songwriter is working toward. This enables the therapist to redirect the songwriter when he digresses, and to challenge him (if appropriate) when resistance to explore the issue becomes evident.

Another strength of the songwriting process is its potential to be tailored to the songwriter's needs. Methods can be adapted to meet the songwriter's physical, cognitive, communicative, psychological, and social functioning levels. And it is flexible in that the songwriting experiences can be preplanned or may evolve organically.

Songwriting serves to give the songwriter a voice and to feel empowered; to tell his story. Society has condoned the use of songs as a form of freedom of speech, where people can describe what might be otherwise considered taboo. Lyrics may incorporate profanity and reference events that may be difficult or inappropriate to describe in face-to-face conversations. Songwriting allows for messages to be purposefully ambiguous, thereby protecting the songwriter from potential negative ramifications. Essentially, the songwriter has the freedom and control over the lyrical and musical material so that his voice is heard. This opportunity to 'speak out' is empowering for people who, for whatever reason, have been silenced.[2]

Creating a song can be regarded as an analogy for life itself. People are constantly creating their narratives. They explore different paths in life, respond to demands of completing work within given timeframes, and experience pressure to complete, perform, and excel. Creativity in life is now recognized as key to solving the problems of the world (Okuda et al., 1991). There are many circumstances in life in which people will encounter experiences that lead to feelings of joy, sadness, anger, frustration, and discomfort. And people do not operate in a vacuum but may be required to work in teams, take responsibility toward achieving team goals, resolve problems, and face interpersonal conflicts. Songwriting processes allow people to experience these aspects of life within the safe and structured context of a therapeutic environment and to grow from these experiences.

A facet of songwriting that might not be as apparent in other music therapy interventions, particularly improvisation, is the heavy emphasis on verbal output. While some would argue that the need to 'put' words onto feelings and experiences diminishes the potential for transformation, I suggest that for some people labeling their feelings in words brings to conscious awareness what might not have been conscious before. This process of verbally describing their inner experiences may alter the way they perceive their feelings and opens up the potential for transformation.

Unlike improvisation, songs typically have a form, a structure comprising of a beginning, a middle, and an endpoint. These structures provide a frame for the therapy process and product, and allow the songwriter to move outside his comfort zone but still feel safe within the given structures. All songs have an endpoint, regardless of whether the endpoint is resolved or unresolved. Motivation is maintained by the need to complete the song.

Combining language and music

Songwriting involves the combining of language and music to form an artistic creation. Both words and music have the potential to express emotion and convey meaning. It is the marriage of these two components that allows a person to harness the full potential of songwriting as a therapeutic agent. Here, music can be shaped to support or contradict the lyrical material (see Chapter 7). Songwriters may shape the music to match the emotions being communicated in the lyrics, thereby increasing the emotional impact of the song. In other circumstances, creating music that juxtaposes the lyrics can convey conflict, complexity, and ambiguity. Music can impact the meaning of the text, assisting the therapist and songwriter (and audience) to make sense of, increase the impact of, and shape the meaning of the lyrics. Music also creates the mood and atmosphere of the song while potentially signaling the context. For example, hip hop provides a rhythm to ground exploration and allow for conscious stream of thought. It also creates an atmosphere for the songwriter to transform himself into a character of his choice and explore his identity (Viega, 2013).

Songwriting in contemporary practice will often incorporate technology. By creating loops and manipulating sounds (including the vocal sounds), the therapist can support a songwriter to translate short phrases into powerful expressions. For example, single- to three-word lyrics can be sung and then manipulated using software programs such as GarageBand to increase or decrease their potency, or to transform their meaning.

Song creations represent a therapeutic journey

The autobiographical nature of songwriting experiences facilitates an examination of the self. Through the process of creating lyrics and music, the songwriter analyzes his own journey, reflecting upon the past and present, while considering the future. As lyrics begin to appear on paper, the songwriter can step outside himself and examine himself, his context, and his life journey from a new angle. The therapist contributes by challenging, commenting on, and probing the songwriter to consider alternative perspectives. At times, the songwriter may create songs in the third person or tell his story through a fictional character, as a form of defense. This may feel safer for the songwriter and the song may act as a container. The therapeutic journey is bolstered by the songwriter's 'sense of freedom' to create lyrics and music.

While the journey of creating is therapeutic, the song product provides audiences (including the music therapist) with insights into the songwriter's world. Songs may reveal issues not expressed outside of music therapy, thereby informing the therapist of the songwriter's present state or underlying concerns. The audience may gain insight and clarity into the songwriter's past or present life experiences as lyrics and music express pain, sorrow, confusion, or anger. Family members report a deepened understanding of the songwriter as a consequence of hearing the songs he has created, which in turn may flow through to improved songwriter–family interactions.

The social nature of songwriting

Therapeutic songwriting involves the collaboration of at least two people – a songwriter and the therapist – and therefore is innately a social activity. When working within a group context, the songwriting experience offers opportunities to engage in teamwork. For example, essential life skills such as negotiation, taking a role within a team, and taking responsibility for a part of a 'whole' process is rehearsed through the planning and creation of a group song. Further, group members need to manage the integration and synthesis of multiple stories into a single story – the song's lyrics.

Group songwriting experiences enable therapeutic group processes to emerge, such as trusting others, letting others in, and respecting others' experiences and perspectives. These can be experienced through brainstorming ideas, constructing lyrics, or creating music. Group experiences foster a sense of community and social support – a critical component for some clinical groups, such as those attending Alcoholics Anonymous or Narcotics Anonymous.

Transforming the environment

Many people attending music therapy programs may live in environments that are disturbing – and at times life-threatening. A number of clinicians interviewed were working in contexts where there were regular acts of violence, sounds of gunfire, and the constant noise of police sirens in the distance. Some of the songwriting approaches described in Chapter 11 allow for the possibility of incorporating these sounds into the song creations, to transform them into something artistic and beautiful – a recontextualization of the environmental sounds.

Songwriting creates artifacts

When music therapy participants improvise, they are 'making music' in the moment, with no intention of the creation to be made permanent in any way. In contrast, during most (but not all) songwriting experiences, the songwriter is crafting an artistic work that has more lasting permanency. This has advantages in many therapeutic contexts. For example, songs created can help to build, strengthen, or sustain relationships with others. If they are shared or performed before family and friends, there is a greater chance that there will be a shared understanding of the impact of the songwriter's context on his life (Baker, 2013c, 2013d). Similarly, shared listening experiences are opportunities for joint reminiscence between the songwriter and his family.

When song creations are recorded or performed to the wider community, songwriters are communicating their experiences of marginalization, disability, adversity, and trauma. Hearing these songs can transform the audience's perspectives and beliefs about people from these marginalized groups (Baker, 2013c) and may increase pro-social behavior (Greitemeyer, 2009). For example, women who had experienced childhood abuse had created songs, recorded an album, and created a video, which were publically released with the specific intention of raising awareness about childhood sexual abuse and its long-term effects (Day et al., 2009b).

The permanency of the artifact may assist the songwriter to experience a sense of accomplishment and self-esteem as he reflects on the tangible object, a product of his creativity and a synthesis of a process he has experienced (Aasgaard, 2002; Baker, 2013c; Grocke et al., 2009). The song provides concrete evidence that he can successfully complete tasks in life and serves as a reminder of his ability and capacity for achievement, irrespective of disability.

Song creations can also have additional benefits that extend beyond the therapy room. The songs provide clinical material for therapists to further understand, gain empathy for, and assess the lived experience for their songwriters. They can serve as a functional aid, a bridge between hospitalization and community living (Baker, 2013c). They can function as a coping tool when the songwriter is exposed to situations where his coping resources are challenged (transitional object). Evidence of this has been documented by researchers working with people with dementia (Ferguson, 2006), adolescents with brain injury (Lindberg, 1995), children with cancer (Aasgaard, 2002), and adults who have experienced childhood abuse (Rolvsjord, 2005).

Limitations and contraindications of songwriting

While the strengths of songwriting as a therapeutic medium are convincing, the clinician needs to be aware that there are a number of potential contraindications and limitations associated with the method.

Songwriting has negative influences on the songwriter

Songwriting processes can be narcissistic in nature, as they are primarily experiences of writing about the self. This may have negative connotations for those with certain pathologies. Even though clinicians strive to create a safe, therapeutic, and creative environment, songwriting is an unfamiliar process to most people (even for some types of musicians) who may find the very idea of creating a song intimidating. They may present with expectations that their song should 'sound as good' as their favorite artist's, and cannot conceive how this would be possible with the level of musical skills they possess.

Songwriters may be concerned about openly exploring their thoughts and feelings and representing these in lyrics. They may fear receiving criticism or revealing too much of themselves to others. Unlike improvisation, where the music created may be non-specific, it is more difficult to create ambiguity when lyrics are involved; their message is more recognizable. Similarly, singing and creating melodic lines may be too exposing for 'unwell' songwriters, as it can highlight their weaknesses or lack of resources.

The process of creating lyrics and music about the self can transport a songwriter back to powerful feelings and memories, and therefore should be viewed as potentially increasing their vulnerability. If these memories and feelings stimulate a movement through a therapeutic process, then this is a positive outcome. However, if the feelings are overwhelming or highlight the songwriter's weaknesses and lack of resources, then there is a risk that the songwriter's capacity for coping will be exceeded.

Songwriting demands time and energy

While some forms of therapeutic songwriting have been developed for time-limited contexts (see Chapter 9), many songwriting processes are time-consuming, sometimes needing several sessions to complete a song. The process of deciding on a song theme, brainstorming ideas, formulating lyrics, creating music, and then refining the song, is a time-consuming process that also demands sustained attention and concentration. Some songwriters may not have the prerequisite skills to sustain the required effort. Similarly, some songwriters, particularly children, lack or have yet to develop the capacity for delayed gratification (see Chapter 5), and need to create something within a short period of time. While this is possible with some forms of songwriting such as parody and FITB, there is a risk that these songs will be superficial in content.

Songwriting involves verbal expression

As songwriting draws on verbal and musical material, at times the involvement of language can be a hindrance in a therapeutic process. In some clinical contexts songwriters may have difficulty with verbalization or language, either because of a cognitive impairment (developmental delay) or due to a mental illness. Creating meaningful songs becomes more challenging when there is little verbal input from the songwriter. In such cases, it is not impossible to create meaningful songs, but careful thought into the strategies around creating lyrics should be considered before beginning a songwriting experience.

Distribution of artifacts presents risks

Earlier, I argued that the artifacts created can function to improve relationships with others and can bolster the therapeutic benefits for the songwriter in the long term. However, there are inherent risks associated with presenting a songwriter with a copy or a recording of his song. First, if the songwriter listens to the song while alone, there is a risk that he may perseverate on the emotion being expressed, and in doing so become emotionally stuck (Baker, 2013c). This is of particular concern when the songwriter listens to the song on his own, as there may be no one present to monitor his emotional state and support him should he become distressed. The clinician needs to weigh the potential for catharsis against the risk of retraumatization. For example, in Day et al.'s study (2009a) of women who had been abused as children, all of the women reported that they continued to experience negative emotions and anger toward the perpetrator when listening to their recordings of the song, even two or three years after participating in the songwriting program.

Related to this is the issue that the songwriters may not be ready to confront, integrate, or 'own' the expressed emotions contained in the song. Sometimes the expression of the emotions is so strong and intense that time is needed before revisiting the song. As one interviewee states:

> If you make a recording, it is a recording of the moment, but it's also a recording of a process. Sometimes a participant is not yet ready to accept that process at that moment. So if you make a recording, it might be that they say, 'Well that's not me. It's not true'. Then you have to go into discussion with, 'But this is you, look what you shared'. If they're very negative, sometimes it's too premature and the recording will not be accepted.

Sharing song creations poses potential risks to the songwriters' well-being, particularly when taken out of context and shared with others. There is a risk that family or audiences may misinterpret the song's meaning. The song therefore has the potential to disrupt relationships when the true meaning of the song and the importance it has for the songwriter are not acknowledged or understood by others. Audiences that have not been privy to what transpired during the song's creation process might not recognize the song's true 'worth', the significance of what it represents.

Section II
Factors Influencing the Songwriting Process

3
Environmental Factors

The impact of the therapeutic environment has not been an area of clinical practice that has been afforded a great deal of attention in music therapy literature. The environment can be understood from many levels. On one level, the environment is the surroundings and conditions in which a person (or organism) lives and operates. It is the forces, influences, and circumstances that lead to adaptation of a person or a community in order to survive and thrive. And it is also the sum of social and cultural conditions including customs, language, economic, and political practices that influence the life of an individual or community (Environment, 2011). It has been long recognized that the structure and culture of environments where music therapy is practiced have an impact on the interactions and behaviors (and therefore the health) of people operating within them (Jörgensen et al., 2009; Røssberg et al., 2006), such as the environmental impacts on therapy compliance and patient dropouts, and inpatient stay satisfaction (Jörgensen et al., 2009; Røssberg et al., 2006). The therapeutic climate[1] has been described as the perceived quality and form of relationships between staff and people participating in health-related services. Shechtman (1990) suggests that a good therapeutic climate is one where there is a sense of belonging, acknowledgment by others, freedom to express feelings, opportunities for self-disclosure, and open communication. Positive therapeutic environments are welcoming, create a feeling of safety, and all participants experience a sense of being at ease (Edvardsson et al., 2005). If there is evidence that the environment can positively or negatively impact health, wellbeing, and the effects of therapeutic interventions, one can assume that the environment is likely to impact therapeutic songwriting practices.

Analysis of interviews with music therapy clinicians revealed that there were four primary environmental influences: the influence of the physical space, the influence of organizational structures, the influence of organizational culture, and the extent to which songwriting was practiced within a private space. This chapter describes each of these in detail. It is important to note here, however, that the purpose of this chapter is to bring the potential influences into the reader's conscious awareness rather than present potential solutions or actions to reduce their negative or enhance their positive impacts. I assert that when aware of the environmental factors that impact the process, the clinician and researcher can consider what options and therapeutic choices are available to them. Regardless of whether the environmental forces are within or not within their power to influence, such awareness may shape their practice and inform decisions around the type of therapeutic songwriting interventions that would best suit the environmental conditions within which they are adopted.

Organizational structures

Organizational structures were found to be critical in shaping songwriting practices employed in different settings. The first of these structures shaping practice was the organization's treatment orientation. Many organizations were operating within specified orientations and expected all health practitioners – including the music therapist – to practice in ways that aligned with the organization's overarching orientation. For example, some mental health facilities employed cognitive-behavioral therapy (CBT) approaches, while in other settings recovery-oriented models formed the basis of the organization's approach to mental health. As will be outlined in detail in Chapters 12–14, orientation does determine how a clinician understands the role of songwriting, music, therapy, the therapist, and the songwriter, and therefore directly impacts songwriting practices. For example, a clinician practicing within a CBT-oriented organization may consider methods that use psychoeducational principles or cognitive reframing to create lyrics. In contrast, practicing in recovery-oriented orientations may call for person-centered approaches that promote autonomy and self-determination or address issues of social exclusion and discrimination. So while the group of people who may be creating songs within a therapeutic context may have similar diagnoses across the two settings, the songwriting approaches, therapy outcomes, and types of songs created are likely to be different. CBT approaches, which emphasize changing cognitive distortions, may adopt songwriting approaches that are predetermined, for example, groups creating theme-based songs on issues such as sobriety, coping, and stigma. Had the same group of songwriters been admitted to a mental health facility that adopted recovery-oriented models, songs on many other themes may have emerged organically from the session rather than predetermined by the clinician prior to commencement. I am not suggesting here that one songwriting approach is better than another, more that the approaches lead to qualitatively different outcomes and methods of implementation.

Challenges arise when the core beliefs of clinicians and their therapeutic orientations are in direct conflict with those of the organization. The clinician is faced with the choice to either be true to her beliefs about therapy, health, and songwriting practices, or to be true to the orientation of the organization. For example, one clinician interviewed described how her practice in a CBT-oriented facility limited her capacity to use deeper exploratory practices. Within the facility, the songwriters were short-stay inpatients that the clinician would only service once or twice, and within a group therapeutic context that had an open and transient group membership. She stated:

> We talk a lot in groups about action and the patients actually doing things and creating lists of coping skills, identifying lists of triggers and what's going to happen . . . I don't have the time to delve into the psychodynamic stuff, because I'm never going to see them again. They're in and out so quickly that we really want to get them as many skills as we possibly can within the limited timeframe. So I tend to be very cognitive-behavioral in that.

So while she wanted to go deep, the organizational structure of CBT prevented her from doing so. In another example, a clinician described how punitive methods were employed by staff to manage the children's behaviors. Their means of managing behavior was in direct conflict with her philosophy, which was grounded in principles of humanism. She opted for creating warm and nurturing spaces so that the children could create personally meaningful songs. The challenge for this clinician was that the children continually 'acted out' in her sessions, as they had habitual ways of interacting with other staff. She was continually confronted with what she considered approaches that exacerbated their disruptive behaviors.

The notion of voluntary versus involuntary attendance at therapy sessions sets up the therapeutic space for high engagement or disengagement in the songwriting process. In some contexts, mostly mental health institutions, inpatient admissions are dependent upon people signing an agreement to attend all therapies scheduled in their program. Refusal to do so could mean early discharge. This is particularly the case for drug and alcohol rehabilitation programs. In some cases, music therapists report that compulsory attendance exacerbates resistance to attend and to participate openly and authentically in the songwriting process; in contrast, voluntary attendance strengthens engagement with the process. By forcing people to participate in songwriting sessions, their defense mechanisms are heightened and they may actively resist participating, or may deliberately undermine the songwriting process by responding inauthentically, laughing inappropriately as other group members offer their ideas for lyrics and music, or trying to steer the songwriting session in a direction that directly avoids the very issues the songwriting process is designed to address. Conversely, those groups where attendance is voluntary may include people who are genuinely willing to participate because they are drawn to music-based therapies or because they believe the songwriting process may offer them some therapeutic benefit that might not be experienced in other therapy methods. Such willingness to attend the songwriting session may lead to high engagement in the songwriting process, and potentially increase their openness and the authenticity of their verbal and musical contributions.

The financial structures and constraints within an organization may impact the songwriting methods clinicians adopt within their practice. In some settings, clinicians may have a preference for including a co-facilitator (a second music therapist or other health professional such as a pastoral care worker, psychotherapist, or counselor). They perceive this second support person as integral, ensuring the songwriting process is smoothly implemented and that all songwriting participants' have an opportunity to have their voices heard. However, this adds considerable cost to the organization's budget and may be perceived by management as an unnecessary doubling up of staff. They might expect the additional health professional to lead a separate group independently, so those service users receive two rather than just one therapeutic group experience. The resultant consequence might be that the clinician is cautious to enter into very deep therapeutic discussions with the group members as she does not have the backup of a second support person.

The level of financial support provided to the music therapy department may impact the songwriting process. Access to sophisticated or high-quality recording equipment will influence the 'sound' of the songwriter's song. Within music-centered approaches, the inclusion of sampling, layering of sounds, and production effects (see Chapters 7 and 10) play a critical role in self-expression of feelings, identity, and context. Without access to music recording and production equipment, the songwriter is limited in what sounds he can achieve, which therefore limits maximum therapeutic impact.

Organizational systems influence the clinicians' choice of songwriting methods. The most frequently identified systemic influence was that of time. The duration of therapy sessions (30, 45, 60, 90 minutes or more) and the total program length (one or more sessions) is a critical factor in guiding decisions about the choice of songwriting methods. For example, shorter sessions or single-session programs might suggest that song parody approaches (Chapter 9) are indicated, whereas longer sessions and programs with multiple sessions allow for both lyric and music creation to be possible (Chapter 11) because then there is sufficient time available to craft a song. During shorter sessions, where there is only time available to create lyrics, the clinician might need to take the lyrics away and create the music independent of the songwriter – obviously a less than desirable scenario, according to the clinicians interviewed, but a factor they may have no control over. Longer programs may permit engagement in deeper therapeutic processes and allow the songwriter to take more time to reflect, construct, and refine lyrics and music, and record and produce a song product. In addition, longer programs enable the songwriter to process the meaning and significance of the songwriting process and product between therapy sessions. A number of clinicians suggested that songwriters need time to 'acquire insight, integrate the musical and lyrical content at a cognitive and emotional level, and experience transformation' (Baker, 2013b, p. 234).

> There's therapy going on when you are writing the song. But a lot of times the real transformational work is coming when you are talking about that song and what it all means . . . If you're fortunate enough that your client is still with you, that's when transformative stuff really takes place, when they can really analyze the song. (Baker, 2013b, p. 234)

Songwriting processes may be constrained by scheduling systems imposed by the organization. Fixed session lengths and scheduled times place pressure on the clinician and songwriter to finish a creative process within the allocated session time. Such inflexibility may bring moments of deep reflection and exploration to a sudden halt, so opportunities to fully process an issue may be interrupted and there is a risk that the songwriter may never enter this space again. Creativity in constructing lyrics and music may be brought to a premature end when a physiotherapist enters the room to take the songwriter to a 'scheduled' physiotherapy session, or the kitchen staff brings the songwriter's lunch to him at the allocated lunch period.

Scheduling songwriting sessions early in the day when concentration and arousal levels are at optimal functioning is preferable particularly for children or people who are at risk of over-arousal (people with severe neurological injuries or degeneration). However, this may not always be possible when working within a school system or pediatric ward. One interviewee recounted how she worked with children at an after-school program. These children had already attended school all day, so it was challenging to expect them to continue to concentrate and create songs when they may be fatigued.

Most frustrating for some clinicians was the engrained hierarchy of services evident in the organizations where they practiced and its subsequent negative impact on the songwriting process. It was common for medical practitioners, specialists, and at times nursing staff to unexpectedly interrupt songwriting programs to perform some procedure. Taking blood samples, checking urine bags, or administering medications midway through the songwriting process typically interrupted creativity or blocked unconscious streams of thought or, more seriously, coincided with meaningful and insightful moments, cathartic experiences, or moments of disclosure. It is also problematic when a group songwriting process is in session and a member of the songwriting group is temporarily removed from the group for some unexpected visit by a medical specialist who wishes to examine his patient.

Organizational culture

Since the early 1980s, it has been recognized that organizational culture impacts the quality and experience of a health, community, or educational facility. The ways staff behave and their approaches to interacting with the vulnerable people they care for are directly linked to the beliefs and values of the organization. Over time, a positive or negative culture of attitudes and care approaches pervades (Smircich, 1983). According to Duxbury et al. (2006), organizational culture comprises: (1) objects and artifacts which are the organizational rules, procedures, and observable behaviors of staff; (2) sociofacts, which are the espoused values of staff; and (3) mentifacts, which are the basic unconscious assumptions about appropriate behavior (p. 281). Management practice, ideology, and organizational constraints influence issues of power and control, as well as themes of democracy versus authoritarianism within treatment practices (Duxbury et al., 2006). Such influences may result in different levels of rigidity of routines and the degree of social distance that emerges between patients and staff (Duxbury et al., 2006).

It has been suggested that specific organizational cultures and therapeutic climates are most appropriate for some diagnostic groups of patients, while distinctly different cultures and climates are best suited to different diagnostic groups (Eklund & Hansson, 2001). For example, Friis (1986) suggests that people with acute psychosis respond more positively to high degrees of structure and organizational predictability. In contrast, people without mental illness typically respond most positively to cultures where spontaneity is embraced.

Music therapy clinicians' perspectives suggested that organizational culture does support or constrain their songwriting practices. In some contexts, staff do not understand or respect the potential for songwriting to contribute to a person's health and wellbeing. In such cases, staff have inappropriately organized for large numbers of unreferred patients to attend a group songwriting session, without consulting the music therapist. What resulted was large songwriting groups with an inappropriate mix of group membership (Chapter 6). As one clinician recounts, 'sometimes there are six- and seven-year-olds [attending alongside] 16-year-olds that are suicidal'.

The converse result emerges when staff on the ward have a deep understanding and strong respect for the role of songwriting in achieving important breakthroughs for the people they care for. This was especially evident when the staff members were either actively involved in the songwriting sessions as co-facilitators or were active musicians themselves. One interviewee stated:

> There were several staff engaging in music regularly, like playing guitars and enjoying singing. So I think many of my clients got a lot of encouragement from the staff when they came back with their song, and sometimes the staff were singing it with them and very interested and giving them feedback and asking them to sing this song for the other patients. So I think that was a good sense of support from the staff that doing music was valuable.

The physical space

The aesthetics of any environment affect how comfortable people feel when in that environment. An old, run-down, dark and dirty train station can stimulate a very different sense of comfort and safety in a traveler than a brightly lit, clean, and modern train station. The same principle applies to facilities where music therapy clinicians may practice. Mion (2009) found that hospitals perceived as enormous, unfriendly, and bewildering exacerbate patients' distress and can cause 'anxiety, anger, sleeplessness, depression and physiological reactions such as increased blood pressure and cortisol levels' (p. 268). The layout of patient rooms, the color schemes used, the furnishings, and the view from the room (e.g. a wall versus a garden) impact positively or negatively on people's moods and physiological states (Ulrich, 1984), and consequently impact health outcomes. For example, Ulrich (1984) found that people with rooms looking out at gardens recovered faster than those with views of brick walls.

The physical space is also a factor supporting or hindering the songwriting process. The aesthetics of the space contributed to the establishment of a therapeutic climate conducive to self-reflection and self-expression. Bright and spacious environments, with windows that enabled songwriters to connect visually to nature, were thought to assist in facilitating their connection with their inner and outer worlds. One clinician reported:

> I have a beautiful space to work in for my small groups. I work in this very serene and meditative room. It's just beautiful. It's a place that lends itself to self-reflection, which is important for writing their verses. The space lends itself well to using the songwriting concept as a means of making what's internal external, what's unconscious conscious.

At the same time, in some contexts the windows looking out onto beautiful gardens were at times distracting for songwriters. Background noise was also a distracting element of the environment where noise and echoes from outside activity in carpetless corridors interrupted lyric and music creation processes. Similarly, loud messages projected through announcement systems were intrusive and disturbed the flow of sessions. These disturbing environmental sounds also impacted on the song recording process.

While finding an appropriate location to allow creativity and therapeutic processes to flourish is desirable, it is not always an easy aspect of songwriting practice to achieve, and at times the clinician and songwriter have to be mindful of the sound level emanating from their songwriting location. Within the school environment, there may be another class such as mathematics or history being taught in an adjacent classroom, and there is therefore an expectation that the level of sound being produced during songwriting not exceed certain decibel levels so as to not distract other classes.

Wherever possible, having a designated space for creating songs will provide optimal conditions for creative exploratory experiences. For those who are inpatients in an otherwise sterile hospital environment, receiving songwriting sessions in a specific space designated for music therapy is perceived as a moment of escape from their usual reality. The music therapy space may include a different set of rules than those applicable to the usual ward, thereby offering a space to feel more relaxed and consequently creating a therapeutic climate conducive to songwriting processes.

Room size may impact the success of a songwriting process, particularly when working with young people. In some contexts, clinicians found it more challenging to manage children's behavior when creating songs within large treatment spaces. Smaller rooms are more effective in terms of managing children's behavior because there are fewer stimuli and therefore less distractions. Similarly, the set-up of the furniture and equipment impacts the therapeutic climate. Within a songwriting group, a circle of chairs creates important boundaries to signal when songwriters are in and out of the songwriting process. This set-up also locates the songwriters within close proximity to the clinician and each other, thereby increasing the intimacy of the songwriting experience. Finally, when the songwriting space is set up to resemble a recording studio, young people are naturally drawn into the songwriting process, as they focus more on the creation of the song than on thinking of the experience as 'therapy'.

The private space

Privacy is always a consideration for all therapeutic practices, and certainly the availability of a private space within which to create personally meaningful songs was identified as a core need. The presence of family may impede the open, authentic contributions of a songwriter. Clinicians have witnessed how the presence of over-protective parents, both of young children and adult children, limits the songwriters' full expression of thoughts or feelings. Children are more likely to close up or censor their expressions when parents are present, often afraid of causing their parents unnecessary anxiety, sadness, or distress should they reveal their true feelings, anxieties, and fears. One clinician conveyed that young children become more dependent and passive when parents are present:

When I'm implementing an insight-oriented songwriting process, I actually prefer if family members don't sit in on those sessions, because I find it's a bit of a hindrance. If someone is struggling, an eager mum will try and put words into someone's mouth. Or they don't want their child to look like a failure. Or else the child doesn't open up completely with someone else there. So I do try to do closed sessions most of the time.

Separating siblings increases the likelihood that they will freely express their individual journeys. This minimizes the possibilities that one sibling will dominate the session or that they will hold back their true feelings and expressions because they do not want to distress their brothers and sisters. Such private spaces are needed in some contexts, such as when working with children who have a deceased parent:

You have to play gatekeeper a little bit, because the child might be dominating or another child might be very subservient and a lot of times we will get multiple siblings from the same family. So even if they are close in age, we find a way administratively to separate them because often times, if you have an 11- and a 12-year-old sibling in the same group, often the older one will speak for the younger one . . . and they may express things when they are with each other that are quite different than when they are by themselves.

When people in hospital are very unwell, songwriting sessions may take place bedside. In many hospital contexts, these patients may share a room with one or more other patients, increasing the chances of privacy violation as unwelcome people enter the songwriting space. These patients may have various hospital staff enter the room as their medical needs are met or may have visitors. The space is no longer private. Even in the absence of additional staff or visitors in the room, the presence of one or more other patients may impact on the feeling of safety the therapist is trying to establish. The songwriters may be reluctant to openly share their innermost thoughts and feelings, or censor what is shared when there is a danger that others in the room may overhear the content of the song they are creating. This is even more pertinent when the songs they may be creating are expressions of their adversity, pain, or dislike of the hospital environment. One clinician stated:

If you want to have them talk about how bad their pain is or how scared they are, you don't want the physiotherapist or the nurse in there, because they [the songwriters] don't want them to know they're in so much pain, and they don't want to share their heart as well when everything is all stripped away.

Conclusion

The environmental factors described in this chapter stand to impact the various components of therapeutic songwriting: (1) the therapeutic relationship between songwriter/s and therapist, (2) the exploration of issues of personal significance, (3) the creation of lyrics and music, and (4) the resultant tangible record representing a synthesis of the therapeutic process, the songwriter/s story, or their expression of feelings. Based on the interviews with clinicians, I theorize that:

> Songwriting as a therapeutic process is most effective when the song-writers are located in an environment that is aesthetically pleasant and private, and where they feel relaxed and safe to express themselves openly. It should be distraction free; free from background noise or interruptions by staff, family or other participants. An effective songwriting process will be achieved when there is sufficient time (session and program duration) allocated to create the song and when the songwriting method chosen accommodates for the time available and the orientation of the organization. An organizational culture that values and understands music therapy as a discipline, and songwriting as a health promoting intervention creates an environment where songwriters will be motivated to participate and receive positive feedback when sharing their songs with others. (Baker, 2013b, p. 237)

4
Sociocultural Factors

This chapter outlines the sociocultural factors that play a part in how therapeutic songwriting practices are shaped. Several interpretations of the term 'sociocultural' have pervaded the literature, and I have no intention of surveying them here. For the purposes of this chapter, the term refers to the combination of both social and cultural factors that impact a songwriter–therapist relationship, a songwriter–songwriter relationship, and the various processes involved in creating lyrics and music that are shaped by social and cultural group membership.

Hays (2008) proposed that the term 'sociocultural' encompasses the diversity of all types of peoples – generational, extent of disability, religious and spiritual orientation, ethnicity and racial identity, socioeconomic status (SES), sexual orientation, indigenous heritage, national origin, and gender – and it is his perspective that is adopted in this chapter. Markus and Hamedani (2007) suggest that people do not live in a vacuum, and are in fact shaped by their social and cultural networks, communities, families, and every relationship that is part of their worlds. As people interact with others in their various networks, they go through a process of constructing values, beliefs, and traditions, and later enact these through their own behaviors and actions. These socioculturally shaped behaviors and beliefs determine people's roles within the family, their communication and affective styles, and spiritual and religious practices. Importantly, people's sociocultural identity is not fixed and unchanging. It is a dynamic process in constant states of flux and transformation as people 'appropriate, incorporate and contest values, beliefs, and practices of those people they encounter in their lives' (Markus & Hamedani, 2007 cited in Baker, 2013f, p. 124). This is further complicated by the fact that people often belong to more than one sociocultural group (bicultural) and therefore assume multiple identities and behavioral patterns that reflect their context at that particular moment in time (Nagayama Hall, 2001). For example, a second-generation young male of Greek origin living in Australia may have a particular set of behaviors when at home with his Greek family, which may differ considerably from his behavior when surrounded by peers who belong to a specific youth subculture.

East versus West

Living in a global era, many clinicians who use songwriting in their practices will encounter songwriters from diverse cultures. Typically, Western and Eastern cultures differ substantially with respect to their values and traditions. Laungani (2007) emphasizes that even within specific countries several cultural practices may be present. For clinicians practicing songwriting in facilities where they may create songs with diverse cultural groups, understanding how concepts of the Individualism (Western) versus Communalism (Eastern) continuum operate is imperative. According to Laungani (2007), Individualism respects that individuals are entitled to have control over their lives, to have responsibility for addressing their own problems, and to respect the need for the physical and psychological space of others. Conversely, in Eastern Communalism (Hindu and Islamic societies), family and community are at the center of all activity; so when one member of the family or community experiences difficulties, it affects the entire family and community. As will be outlined later in this chapter, this affects how therapeutic songwriting might be viewed as an individual or communal interest.

Another West–East difference that impacts the songwriting process is the perception of emotional expression. Within Western cultures, people have been socially conditioned to avoid expressing emotion and to function at a cognitive level. Tov and Diener (2007) understand this as a cultural belief that expressing strong emotions is a sign of weakness within a person. This contrasts with Eastern values that encourage emotional expression to allow people to experience catharsis. Within Eastern cultures, however, permission to express emotions is dependent upon the person's place within the family hierarchy. As Laungani (2007) states, people who are at the lower levels of the hierarchy are vigilant about 'who can say what to whom, how, and with what effect' (p. 141).

As emotions are socially and culturally determined, different emotions are more readily accepted in some cultures when compared with others. In Western cultures, pride is recognized as a desired emotion that encompasses autonomy and independence. In contrast, Eastern cultures celebrate sympathy and humility as socially acceptable emotions (Tov & Diener, 2007). When linking this with a therapeutic songwriting process, clinicians can therefore predict that accomplishment, pride, and autonomy are emotions that are culturally desirable and therefore relevant for Western songwriters to experience, but may be regarded as inappropriate for those in Eastern cultures. Similarly, some Indian communities discourage the expression of anger, viewing it as socially destructive. And unlike in Western cultures, in some Indian communities shame is regarded as a positive emotion when experienced by women because it reinforces their membership in a patriarchal society (Tov & Diener, 2007). Therefore, when songwriters express different emotions within their song creations, the clinician needs to consider carefully what these emotions mean within the songwriter's cultural community.

Culture is a determinant of perceptions and understanding of health, wellbeing, and treatment. People from Eastern cultures are more likely to seek out traditional remedies (Gurung, 2010), which may positively or negatively impact on their receptivity to songwriting. Indian traditional healers focus their healing practices on returning balance to the body-mind-soul state, while Chinese medicine focuses treatment on promoting flow through the body (Gurung, 2010). Consequently, Hays (2008) suggests that many 'Eurocentric' approaches to therapy may be inappropriate to use with people from non-European cultures. Examples of inappropriate behaviors relevant to songwriting practice may be the use of verbal skills such as paraphrasing, probing and asking questions, tone of voice, and non-verbal skills such as eye contact. In some cultures, the clinician may be perceived as a person of authority, and it is therefore inappropriate for the songwriter to make eye contact with the clinician.

Spiritual and religious beliefs

The role of spirituality and religion in health, treatment, death, and dying is well recognized. Religion as a formalized organization, whether Christianity, Judaism, Islam, Buddhism, or Hinduism, guides behavior (Robb, 2002) and instills hope, meaning, and purpose in individuals and families during challenging times (Koenig, 1998). Relevant to clinicians is the link between religious membership, social support, and internal locus of control, with those who have stronger religious practices typically coping better when facing crises (Koenig et al., 2001).

It is important to be cognizant, however, that the degree of religiosity differs between individuals within a religious community and therefore when creating songs with people of various religious backgrounds, clinicians need to be cautious when making assumptions about the potential responses their songwriters may offer.

As music has highly specialized roles in the rituals of some religions and cultures, clinicians intending to engage people in songwriting experiences (or any music therapy experiences) need to be clear about what musical practices are permissible. For example, Jones et al. (2004) reported that some Sudanese tribes only sing songs when seeking healing advice from the Gods/gods. In such contexts, the song is not the healing action but the conduit between the tribespeople and the Gods/gods they seek help from.

Socioeconomic status and gender

People's SES is now considered a predictor of health status with those from lower SES groups identified as being at risk of developing a variety of health concerns (Gurung, 2010). Their positions within a social system also dictate their mode of action and interaction with people within their own SES group and those within differing SES groups (Schooler, 2007). Those from lower SES groups tend to be less educated, have lower levels of home ownership, earn lower incomes (Schooler, 2007), have higher occurrences of mortality and morbidity, and are less likely to seek medical treatment because of escalating costs in countries where health is a pay-as-you-go system. The relationship between health status and SES 'is so regularly linear that it has been described as a gradient in which health status apparently improves with every increase of SES' (Schooler, 2007, p. 376).

Despite equity movements over the past 50-plus years, it is still apparent that people's gender determines their role in society and shapes their behaviors. These role expectations, and gendering of behaviors impact if, when, how, and what forms of treatment people seek, and gender is therefore another predictor of health outcomes, particularly for women (Gurung, 2010). An illustrative example comes from the United States, where African American women are forthcoming in sourcing advice and support from family and friends but are more reluctant to seek professional assistance when they are not coping with the various life challenges they are experiencing (McNair, 1996). Due to cultural expectations that African American women are stoic and strong, when these women do eventually seek professional assistance, they are more hesitant to self-disclose and more reluctant to admit any difficulties in coping. Therefore, in songwriting contexts, clinicians may need to alter their expectations about the willingness of the songwriters to reveal their stories and need to be gentler in their approaches to probing. When creating lyrics, probing by the therapist, such as asking, 'Can you tell me more about that?' might not always result in elaborations by the songwriter, but may result in avoidance behavior such as shutting down.

In the Korean culture (and indeed in many cultures), males are not socialized to express themselves and share their feelings with others. Therefore, they lack experience in and feel uncomfortable with identifying, connecting, and expressing emotions. However, women have experience with this, are comfortable expressing themselves, and therefore have less difficulty creating personally meaningful songs.

In some cultures and religions, such as Islam, gender also impacts the type of music engagement that is permissible for males and females. As one interviewee states: '[as] there are specific rules like women cannot sing in front of men, we work with these rules and record or perform only when women are present.' As a consequence, women often censor their contributions and choose not to share or sing the songs they create. Such gender differences must be particularly considered when planning for group songwriting experiences. In many cases, separating women and men for the purpose of a good therapeutic process may lead to more authentic expression and the experience of singing a self-composed song, even if only within the confines of a therapy session. One interviewee suggests that therapy situations become increasingly complex when some group members follow their cultural rules strictly, while others do not. The therapist is challenged to facilitate a therapeutically meaningful songwriting process that allows people to disclose at whatever level they feel is comfortable within their own cultural beliefs and customs.

Music's diverse roles in different sociocultural groups

Several clinicians and researchers have suggested that clinicians have an obligation to acquire in-depth knowledge and skills concerning the musical practices and repertoire of people from a wide range of cultures (e.g. Dileo & Magill, 2005; Stige, 2002), particularly its role in healing practices and in religious ceremonies for the deceased (Bradt, 1997).

The diverse roles of music in sociocultural groups were reflected in the interviews of clinicians who created songs in collaboration with people from differing cultural and religious backgrounds. In such contexts, the music therapist's knowledge of musical repertoire and skills in playing multicultural styles was important when facilitating the creation of original songs that reflected the songwriter's own cultural identity. One American music therapy clinician who now resides in an Arabic nation reported that studying Arabic music was essential in ensuring he could recreate Arabic style musical accompaniments for his songwriters' lyrics. He reported that he could not always assume he was recreating Arabic music accurately, so he continually 'checked in' with his songwriters to ensure he was 'achieving the right sound'. His research concluded that rhythm was the key component of the music, 'half flats' were common within lyrical melodies, and harmony was somewhat absent.

Several clinicians interviewed reported the complexity of creating songs with people from different sociocultural groups where music plays diverse roles. Songwriting was difficult – and indeed inappropriate – to use in some cultures such as the Amish community, where music is reserved for religious practices or for mother–infant bonding practices. One way to ensure appropriate use of songwriting as a therapeutic intervention with children of various cultures and religions is to check in with the parents and seek permission. Posing questions such as, 'Is this something that you would be comfortable with within your cultural beliefs?' is one approach to ensuring songwriting is appropriate to use. Music therapists suggest that there are diverse opinions within some cultures on what they will tolerate. Some families are comfortable with songwriting being incorporated into their treatment programs, while others are 'stricter with enforcing the norms of their own culture' and reject suggestions to incorporate songwriting (or any music therapy practice) into the child's treatment regime.

Songwriting as a form of expression is well recognized and accepted in some cultures, and in these contexts, such as in Latino cultures, the therapist may encounter little resistance from the songwriter. This may not be the case in other cultures. Clinicians working with immigrants from Nigeria, Sri Lanka, Uganda, and some parts of Asia found that the very notion of creating a personally meaningful song was an entirely new concept, and consequently the clinician needed to invest more time in assisting these immigrants to understand the potential for songs to express their stories (as opposed to the stories of people and events from their history that have been passed down via songs from generation to generation).

In some cultural contexts, musicians are respected and valued members of society. So when potential songwriters belonging to these cultures are invited to create songs, the idea of songwriting is very appealing and they may be more open to engaging in the therapeutic process. One clinician reported that the creation of an original song elevated the status of a Mexican man within his community because the community valued his artistic contributions. According to clinicians interviewed, when music is an integral component within the activities of those belonging to various subcultures (for example emo, goth, heavy metal, hip hop), songwriting as a form of therapy is experienced as more appealing than other forms of therapy. For example, many from the African American youth subculture feel connected to rap music. Rap tends to tell stories of issues that reflect their own experiences (Tyson et al., 2012). As such, they are often motivated to create their own rap lyrics and rap over precomposed or original music. Importantly, the authenticity and rawness of rap music gives these young people permission to 'drop their guard and open themselves up to the process' (interviewee).

A thought-provoking article by Aigen (2008) concerned the role of popular music in expressing, representing, and supporting spirituality. Aigen proposed that due to the decline of participation in traditional organized religion, people are using popular music as a spiritual practice; people derive meaning from songs. He argued that people's relationship to popular music (including their spiritual connection) is an important consideration in music therapy. When connecting Aigen's ideas to songwriting, I suggest that clinicians need to consider song creations as an expression of a songwriter's spirituality, not just expressions of their sociocultural background. During the songwriting process, the meaning that a preferred genre of music holds for a songwriter should be identified and discussed, and then highlighted as a potential vehicle for expressing spiritual beliefs and meaning.

Heterogeneity versus homogeneity

As will be described in great detail in Chapter 6, songwriting groups comprising a diverse cultural mix offer special opportunities to connect with others by acknowledging their shared diversity and at the same time being able to maintain personal and cultural individuality (Shapiro, 2005). In studies by Baker and Jones (2006), songwriting functioned like a cultural bridge between different African tribes of young Sudanese refugees. Through the creation of group songs, songwriting enabled group members to share, communicate, and reflect on differences in beliefs, traditions, and values. Here, heterogeneity offered possibilities for growth and transformation. But what is responsible for these shifts?

Several clinicians reported that cultural diversity enriched the songwriting process because the songwriters were able to share their unique stories through their own cultural lens. Songwriters benefited not only from the empowerment of sharing their own stories, but through hearing others' stories, and began to understand how people from different cultural backgrounds may have had traumatic experiences of similar significance even though due to differing circumstances and experiences.

It was noted, however, that when clinicians are facilitating songwriting experiences with people from the same geographical origin, it is important to be aware that a shared geography is not indicative of cultural homogeneity. While people may have the same birth place and share the same language, they may not share the same religion and ethnicity.

There are also advantages and disadvantages when culturally homogeneous groups create group songwriting experiences. Schwantes (2011) was the first to comment on this, following her work with groups of male Mexican farmworkers. By shaping her practice to incorporate Mexican principles of respect, dignity, family values, traditional male values, and religion into her songwriting practice, she was able to create therapeutically meaningful experiences for people who shared the same culture and history.

While one might consider that socioculturally homogeneous songwriting groups benefit from their shared values, beliefs, and ways of interacting, homogeneity can also challenge established hierarchies. A 'pack' mentality pervades prison inmate communities where the 'top dog' who sits at the top of the hierarchy has sufficient power to affect other inmates' willingness to partake in songwriting activities. If the 'top dog' has a positive view of the songwriting process and partakes of it enthusiastically, other inmates may be more open and inclined to also participate. However, within the prison culture, weakness of character (as defined by the prison inmates) is punished in various ways and stands to remind inmates of the hierarchy. Those inmates at the bottom may 'restrict contributions, censor content, or construct fictional stories of their experiences for inclusion in the song to avoid exposing themselves to those with more power' (Baker, 2013f, p. 133).

Heterogeneity and homogeneity also affects the group songwriting experiences of people with different SES. For example, the notion of voluntary versus compulsory attendance at songwriting groups impacts the level of participation and engagement in the process. Prison inmates from typically low SES backgrounds were offered songwriting as an optional therapy during their treatment for substance use disorder.

They perceived the attendance at music therapy as a 'temporary escape from the prison ward', and were therefore highly motivated to attend and engage in the songwriting process. In contrast, people from high SES backgrounds, also with substance use disorder and being treated within private hospitals funded by their families, were less motivated to attend because treatment was not always voluntary. This constricts the flow and ease of the songwriting process because the clinician is faced with resistance from one or more group members who are attending compulsorily rather than by choice.

Language barriers

According to the definition posed in Chapter 1, therapeutic songwriting involves the creation of lyrics and music within a therapeutic process; language (in the form of lyrics) is therefore an integral component. However, language creates barriers in songwriting when the therapist and the songwriters do not share the same language. This not only occurs between the therapist and songwriters of different ethnic origins, but also when communicating with young people from different subcultures. In some languages words may have multiple meanings, and in some languages there are multiple words for what can be described by just one word in other languages. For example, in Norway there are several nouns describing the different forms of snow, whereas in English we just use the word 'snow' and then add adjectives to describe how snow may have different qualities, such as small snowflakes, wet snow, powdered snow, and the like. Therefore, in creating songs with people where the therapist's and songwriters' first languages differ, there is a risk that the music therapist may misinterpret the songwriter's intentions and construct lyrics and music that are not an accurate representation of the songwriter's experiences. The risk has the potential to halt the therapeutic process and weaken the therapeutic relationship if the violation is serious.

Language barriers may be overcome when people are able to create lyrics using a language of their choice. As long as the therapist has a good enough understanding of the songwriters' stories and feelings, she can suggest appropriate musical accompaniment choices. There is no need to understand every word expressed in the lyrics, provided that the main message is clear. When people create lyrics in their own languages, they have a greater possibility to communicate their verbal messages accurately with the subtlety and richness we would aim for in all therapeutic song creations. Further, creating songs in the songwriters' native language reinforces their cultural identity and communicates that the therapist accepts and embraces it.

The language used by youth from different subcultures may impede the flow of the songwriting process as the clinician may be unsure of the meaning of the words and lyrics offered by the young songwriters. Some subcultures have slang words that may 'confuse' the clinician and may be an attempt to avoid authenticity and honest dialogue. For example, the word 'bodies' when used in song lyrics has two potential meanings depending upon the subculture with which the clinician is working. In one subculture, 'bodies' implies 'people I've killed', while in others it signals 'people I've had sex with'. Therefore, the clinician needs to be careful not to assume meaning from words or phrases offered by these young people.

Diversity and the therapeutic relationship

SES and ethnicity differences between the songwriters and the clinician lead to inappropriate preconceptions and inaccurate assumptions. Songwriters may assume that due to the differing sociocultural background of the clinician, she will be unable to recreate the genre of music that belongs to the songwriters' culture. Some Caucasian (white European) female clinicians have reported that songwriters believe that 'white middle class females' cannot rap. Such presumptions negatively affect the songwriters' commitment and investment in the songwriting process, impairing the development of the therapeutic relationship and ultimately the effectiveness of the songwriting experience. One clinician recounts:

> Some songwriting, recording, production process – I am sitting and talking to the youth. They are uncertain of the process and they can't invest yet. They don't know if I can do it, because ultimately I'm just a short woman. I walk into these places and people are like 'you're white and you're short.' I'm like 'just give me a chance, just give me a chance; I can sing; I don't sound like I'm white when I sing.'

Viega (in press a) discusses the need for the therapist to be aware of her own cultural messages that impact on how she views language, relationships, gender roles, the role of the caregiver, and her own cultural biases. In his work with a young person with SCI, Viega builds a successful therapeutic rapport through his demonstration of respect, knowledge, and deep admiration for the elements of Hip Hop Kulture and by presenting himself as a person who could offer music-making experiences that reflected the young person's (and his mother's) cultural values and preferences. Viega emphasized his engagement in reflexivity to identify his own values, biases, and judgments that may impact his therapy practice.

Conclusion

A number of sociological factors positively or negatively impact the songwriting process and its potential for affecting therapeutic change. Factors described in this chapter included: (1) cultural differences in health, healing, and the role of music, (2) spirituality and religion, (3) SES, (4) gender, (5) language, and (6) homogeneity and heterogeneity of songwriting groups. Based on the interviews with clinicians, I propose the following:

The success of a therapeutic songwriting process is dependent upon the clinician's knowledge of and skills in recreating the musical style of different cultural and ethnic groups. The absence of a shared language can impede songwriting, but when the clinician allows songwriters to create songs in their native languages, it reinforces their cultural identity and ensures that the song creations accurately, subtly, and sensitively

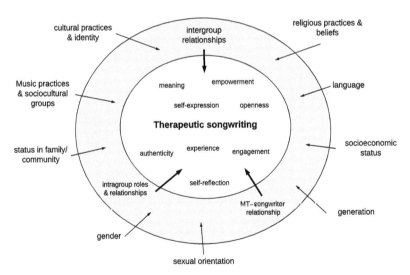

Figure 4.1 Forces that influence songwriting in the sociocultural field

Source: Baker, 2013f, p. 137. Adapted with permission from Taylor & Francis (www.tandfonline.com).

represent the thoughts and feelings of the songwriter. Perceptions of the therapist as a person of power may transpire in some cultures, which affects the degree of openness achieved within the songwriting process. Capacity to self-reflect and express via lyric creation processes may be limited when people's socially constructed gender norms are active. Sociocultural heterogeneity and homogeneity shapes the cohesiveness of groups and determines whether participation is voluntary, authentic, and with high levels of engagement. Culturally homogeneous groups may have active hierarchical systems, and therefore participation in a songwriting process is dependent on a person's position in that hierarchy and how participation is viewed by the person/people at the top of the hierarchy. Equally, cultural diversity opens up further opportunities to reflect on multiple perspectives, which offers opportunities to reframe people's view on issues being described within the song's lyrics. Clinicians should be wary of cultural divisions when rival groups cause tension that is counterproductive to the process. Figure 4.1 illustrates the different levels of influence of sociocultural factors on the songwriting experience. On the outer layer, various factors such as language, gender, and SES are listed as influences. These factors directly influence three types of relationships in the middle layer – intragroup relationships (the relationships between members within each songwriting group context), clinician–songwriter/s relationships (the relationships between the clinician and one or more songwriters), and intergroup relationships (relationships between songwriters and other groups outside of the songwriting context). These relationships then impact the songwriting experiences listed in the inner layer.

5
Individual Factors

My analyses suggested that songwriters' health status, presenting strengths, and limitations are important determinants of how effective the songwriting process is for them, and also guides clinicians' choices about what songwriting method to employ. Songwriters' physical, communicative, psychological, social, and emotional wellbeing determines their style and level of participation, and signals what songwriting strategies the clinician may need to adopt to accommodate any individual factors that may impede the process. This chapter outlines the various individual factors that support or constrain the songwriting process as identified by practitioners working across a range of developmental life stages and clinical conditions.

Physical and physiological wellbeing

One of the most basic requirements to voluntarily perform any activity in life, including songwriting, is to present with an appropriate state of arousal. Arousal may be described as a state of responsiveness to sensory stimulation and a readiness for action, and is the result of a physiological activation of the 'cerebral cortext by centres lower in the brain such as the reticular activating system' (Oxford Concise Medical Dictionary, 2010, n.p.). Fatigue, sleepiness, and drowsiness are physical manifestations of low arousal. If songwriters are not sufficiently aroused, they may be unable to focus on the therapist and/or the music, and are therefore unlikely to fully participate in the songwriting process. As creating songs demands active contributions from the songwriters in order to 'tell their story', generate ideas for song content, construct lyrics, and create music, maintaining adequate levels of arousal is vital.

Many congenital, neurodegenerative, or acquired brain dysfunctions affect arousal (Happe, 2003). Two-thirds of people with ABI report that low levels of arousal interrupt their everyday activities (Worthington & Melia, 2006), while two-thirds of people with multiple sclerosis rank fatigue as their third most debilitating symptom (Krupp, 2004). Fatigue in people with cerebral palsy is exacerbated by associated pain (Van der Slot et al., 2012) and the physical and mental weariness resulting from routine daily activities (Malone & Vogtle, 2010). Further, it was found that for people with SCI, multiple sclerosis, and muscular dystrophy, the affects of arousal and fatigue increase with age (Cook et al., 2011).

Although no universally accepted definition of fatigue exists, there is a general consensus that there are two distinctive forms: one asociated with performing cognitive tasks (central fatigue) and the other of physical or metabolic origin (peripheral fatigue) (Greenwald & Ripley, 2009). Central fatigue seems to dominate those with ABI and stroke, whereas those with SCI and multiple sclerosis may display either form or both forms.

When engaging songwriters at risk of fatigue, the sessions should be designed so that periods of optimal arousal are maximized. For example, in her work with adolescents with muscular dystrophy, one clinician reported that creating lyrics is more tiring than creating music, perhaps because of the emotional investment that is involved in sharing oneself in lyrics. To ensure the adolescent songwriters could complete the song before becoming too fatigued, the clinician focused her sessions on creating lyrics quickly and early in the session, allowing space for mental rest between lyric and music creation.

Low or fluctuating levels of arousal are not just a symptom of many clinical conditions but are also a by-product of pharmacological treatments, especially those used in the treatment of mental illness (Pahari et al., 2012). Anti-depressants can 'dull' the emotions and therefore impact people's ability to fully express themselves in the songs they create. In these cases, songs may be considered representations of 'medically modified' self-expressions. Further, some pharmacological interventions inhibit songwriters' creativity and their capacity to be actively involved. One clinician working with young people with mental illness states:

> Medication influences whether the client is able to be active or not active during songwriting, if the client is creative or not creative . . . You have to know what the client is taking so that you don't try, for example, to explore feelings while the medication works in the other direction. You don't need to try to do that because it's a waste of energy – or trying to get people to be more active while they're taking strong medication. They will not get into activity because the

medication is keeping them down . . . All the creative processes are under the influence of medication.

When creating songs with people who are agitated or in significant pain, pharmacological interventions have been purposefully prescribed to sedate them. Sedation leads to low arousal, difficulty in focusing, and at times, moving between sleep and wakefulness. Creating a song under such conditions can be problematic if the songwriter is unable to sustain sufficient arousal to contribute to the process. At times, it is hard for the clinician to determine whether the sedation is a side effect of the medication or a symptom associated with the condition. A clinician working within palliative care states:

> It's sometimes hard to tease out, especially in hospice, of what's the medication and what's their disease process? . . . There are times where we just can't go into songwriting because either the person's mental capacity isn't there because of the medication or because of the disease process. And I want to do songwriting, but sometimes they're either too tired, or getting a bit confused because of oxygen deprivation, and we can't kind of stay with it long enough to create a song.

When songwriters are fatigued and present with low levels of arousal, their emotional vulnerability increases and their capacity to cope with whatever emotions or cognitions arise during the songwriting process is challenged. Further, low arousal diminishes the capacity for insight, which in turn affects the depth of lyrical contributions and the potential for the experience to be transformative.

As songs involve the creation of lyrics and music, songwriters need to have sufficient communication skills and a capacity to respond to the clinicians' probing for information. Verbal communication may be impaired when working with people who have neurological damage sustained from injuries or neurodegenerative diseases. Dysarthria, dyspraxia, or aphasia results in poor articulation of words or difficulties in expressing language, and it may be necessary for the songwriters to repeat themselves multiple times before their statements have been understood by the therapist and written down. The need for repetition interrupts the flow of the creative and self-reflective processes and slows progress. This in turn increases the risk that the process will be experienced as tedious and terminated prematurely. Frustration or depression may result when songwriters are unable to convey words or phrases that represent what they are experiencing or feeling.

Physical impairments may impede opportunities to partake in the creation and performance of the musical accompaniment. Many people do enjoy performing their own songs, and doing so has been linked with a stronger sense of song ownership (Baker, 2013d). In her work with adolescents who have autism, one clinician described how her songwriters become frustrated when unable to break their perseverative behavior during the creation of the accompanying music. She states:

> They have some physical limitations because there are things that they want to do and their body wants to do but they can't. I see the frustration in them. They will start moving and smiling with the beat, so I'll put a drum in front of them, but they get stuck in that pattern and can't break out of it.

Cognitive factors

Anatomical and physiological understanding of the phenomenon of creativity – and specifically music creativity – is growing. As a consequence of an extensive array of technological diagnostic tools (e.g. functional magnetic resonance imaging, electroencephalogram) and lesion studies, research has identified how damage to various networks of the brain can affect the cognitive functioning that directly impacts people's capacity to participate in the songwriting processes.

Research has concluded that the temporal lobes are involved in idea generation, an aspect of songwriting integral to the creation of lyrics and music (Flaherty, 2005). An injured temporal lobe affects muse experiences and may result in pressured speech,[1] empty speech, limited insight, hypomania/mania, pressured artistic and musical expression, reduced associative thinking, and a tendency toward analogies. Any damage to temporal lobes caused by degeneration (e.g. frontotemporal dementia [Miller et al., 1998]) or brain injury will therefore partially impair the songwriters' abilities to generate ideas for song topics or musical styles (Baker & Tamplin, 2006), and they will appear apathetic. Conversely, songwriters may reuse previous topics (topic recycling and topic reintroduction), and are unable to initiate and develop conversations based on more than a couple of familiar topics (Adams, 2008). Nevertheless, in recent years reports of the use of therapeutic songwriting in neurorehabilitation suggest that clinicians perceive it as beneficial for clients with neurological impairments (e.g. Baker et al., 2005d; Hong & Choi, 2011; Tamplin, 2006). In an earlier publication about songwriting to address challenges with pragmatics, I described the use of 'wh' questions to assist people with brain injury to self-manage this challenge (Baker, 2005). Here, posing questions such as 'who, where, why, what, and how?' enabled songwriters to expand their ideas and develop strategies to improve their conversational skills.

Pressured speech (and pressured musical expression) or impulsive speech may result in a chaotic songwriting experience. Songwriters may present with excessive or irrelevant song material and may be unable to maintain the topic sufficiently for lyric and music creation. Discourse may be non-specific and ambiguous or unnecessarily verbose. They may have difficulty introducing or continuing with a topic, and they may frequently shift to unrelated topics (topic shift) or topics that are linked together (topic chain). When this occurs, clinicians need to provide clear and consistent feedback so that the songwriters' insight and awareness of their contributions are brought to the fore. Self-monitoring can never be mastered if songwriters are unaware of instances where topic shifts occur.

Creating a coherent and meaningful song is problematic when songwriters present with significant cognitive impairments that are associated with mental illness. Lyrics are challenging to create when songwriters present with flights of ideas, poverty of speech, or with tangential, incoherent, illogical speech, or concrete speech (Wiemer, 2014).[2] The clinician has the task to make sense of these fragments of ideas and help bring them together to construct a meaningful and coherent song. When songwriters present with severe psychotic symptoms, the clinicians interviewed suggested that single-session lyric-focused approaches might be the most appropriate, although this has yet to be shown in rigorous research. Similarly, the degree of mental wellbeing affects thinking and therefore impacts creativity. High levels of creativity have been attributed to states of mania (Flaherty, 2011), which might suggest such people have a predisposition to create songs. However, the deficits implicit in the disorder (e.g. lack of coherence and form) affect their ability to utilize this creativity in a meaningful or useful way (Grotstein, 1992).

People presenting with rigid thought processes may have difficulty considering alternative viewpoints, solutions, or situations. As songwriting may be directed toward a change in thinking, feeling, and behaving, a capacity to examine and create lyrics from different perspectives would be of benefit. Songwriters with rigid thinking may be anxious or fear taking creative risks and may have a strong need to control what may be perceived as an uncontrollable process (Ellis, 1987). According to one clinician's practice, the more 'well' people in prison are, the more creative, less rigid, and 'unblocked' their songwriting contributions are.

Deep within the left and right medial temporal lobes lies the amygdala, a structure involved in emotional processing. The amygdala processes and stores memories of emotional events and is also involved in process-ing current emotional responses. It is responsible for activating vivid memories of a traumatic event accompanied by bodily responses, as if one were reliving the experience. Mental health conditions such as pho-bias, post-traumatic stress disorder, anxiety, and depression are linked with abnormal functioning of the amygdala. Research has found that creativity is highly prevalent in people with bipolar disorders, and ana-tomically they tend to have larger left or bilateral amygdala when com-pared with the normal population (Flaherty, 2005; Haldane & Frangou, 2004). This is perhaps one of the reasons why songwriting is successful and regularly implemented within the area of psychiatry (e.g. Baker et al., 2012; Rolvsjord, 2005; Silverman, 2003).

Abnormalities in the amygdala also exist for those with autism (Baron-Cohen et al., 2000) and, with the exception of savants, negatively affect imaginative creativity to a greater degree than reality-based creativity[3] (Craig & Baron-Cohen, 1999). Research confirmed this point in one case study of an adolescent boy with Asperger's syndrome who participated in creating songs within a therapeutic context (Baker & Krout, 2009). Baker and Krout examined the creative process over three consecutive sessions and independently reviewed the two songs, noting the content and structure of the lyrics, the song structure, melody lines, and har-monic complexity. The second song created was slightly more creative than the first song, suggesting that songwriting is an intervention that may enhance creativity in people with autism. Overall, however, both songs were relatively unimaginative in lyrical content.[4] More extensive, rigorous, and longitudinal studies are needed to determine whether songwriting can play a role in increasing the creativity of people on the autism spectrum.

To create a song, the songwriter needs to successfully plan and fol-low through on several actions, such as brainstorming ideas, organiz-ing thoughts and feelings into a logical flow, identifying and removing less significant or irrelevant points, and so on. Because these executive functioning skills are impaired in many people with neurodisabilities, the therapist might need to support the songwriter in the planning and organizing of the songwriting process. Similarly, songwriters may experience songwriting as challenging when they have difficulties with abstract thinking or problem-solving or have impaired anterograde memory (common in dementia and brain injury). Songwriters may sub-sequently have difficulty recalling the creative activity undertaken in previous sessions; in these situations, clinicians will need to 'recap or refresh' what was discussed and created in previous sessions, as there is no guarantee that the songwriters will retain much (if any) memory of it. It is challenging for the songwriters to move forward in their processing of emotions and responses to significant events if they need to continuously revisit their feelings and responses to relevant issues.

When songwriting is too cognitively demanding to result in a transformative process, the clinician may opt to create songs at a supportive, activities-oriented level rather than creating songs reflecting in-depth self-explorations. Hong and Choi (2011) facilitated supportive song creation processes with people who had been diagnosed with dementia. In their study, the purpose of the songwriting was to stimulate the songwriters' thinking and reminiscence, rather than entering deep self-exploratory processes.

Developmental factors

A capacity to communicate using some form of language is integral to a creation process that involves lyrics and music. Communication could comprise spoken, written, or signed forms, or a combination of these. Developmental delays – whether congenital or consequential to early childhood trauma – affect language ability and therefore impact on the songwriting process. For example, children emotionally traumatized by abuse may have underdeveloped language (Sylvestre & Merette, 2010) and may be unable to sensitively express themselves in words; their thoughts and feelings may be inadequately expressed in lyrics and therefore more suited to the music-centered songwriting approaches that emphasize musical expression.

Emotional maturity and the capacity for emotional expression are acquired earlier in girls than in boys (Romer et al., 2011), and clinicians in some cultural contexts reported that girls have less difficulty with songwriting when compared with boys. The degree to which songwriters disclose their emotions will influence how the song creation process progresses. For those who share openly, the songwriting process flows. However, for those who are not so open to sharing thoughts, experiences, and feelings, flow may be inhibited, and the therapist may need to invest time to establish rapport and trust so that the songwriter feels more comfortable with disclosure and self-expression.

Levels of concentration differ according to developmental age (Thompson & Miranda, 2009). What can be achieved with older children may not be possible with younger children due to challenges in maintaining concentration. If the finished song product takes too long to complete, there is a risk that younger children will lose interest and motivation. To address this challenge, clinicians may draw on strategies to move the songwriting process forward at a rate that will maintain the young songwriters' engagement with the task.

Tolerance for delayed gratification (Lee et al., 2008) was also an individual factor noted by clinicians. Younger children typically have more difficulty with delayed gratification compared with older children and therefore need songs to be completed more quickly. It is critical that the clinician selects songwriting approaches that match tolerance levels and ensures that a song can be completed before songwriters begin to experience frustration.

Personality and psychological wellbeing

The personality and psychological wellbeing of the songwriter guides clinical decisions. People with perfectionist dispositions often set themselves excessively high performance standards, strive for flawlessness, and can be overly self-critical (Stoeber, 2006). However, perfectionism is also a source of the driving energy needed for achievement. Songwriters with perfectionist personalities may stall the songwriting process if they are not satisfied with the artifact they are creating. They may continually delete, re-create, modify, refine, or rearrange either the song lyrics or music, or both, until they reach a point of 'perfection'. These songwriters are focusing on perfecting the product rather than immersing themselves within a potentially transforming therapeutic experience. This preoccupation with creating that perfect song may result in songwriters offering phrases as lyrics that sound poetic or create a rhyme, rather than offering true authentic expressions of the self.

It was reported that some songwriters are uncomfortable (at least initially) with receiving attention from the therapist during the songwriting process. Songwriters may be accustomed to being medically cared for, to being asked questions about their pain and general physiological condition. However, during the songwriting process, there is this clinician guiding them through a more personal process, requesting their input at every possible moment, and asking them to open up and share their story. This unfamiliar attention can be unsettling. Time to adjust and feel comfortable with this more personal attention may be needed before the songwriter can become fully immersed in the songwriting process.

The 'pretend mode' characteristic of people with a personality disorder affects their capacity to engage fully in the songwriting process. Here, the songwriters believe that they are involved in the process, yet are unaware that they are acting a role (pretending) rather than living that role (Spitzer et al., 2006). Consequently, there is a degree of censorship of their lyrical contributions because it gives them a sense of feeling 'in charge'. In his work with people with personality disorders, one clinician states:

> A concept that's often mentioned in relation to this client population is pretend-mode. . . . You pretend that you are engaged with what is going on, you pretend that you take in the therapeutic interventions, but you're really not. You're really just pretending. It takes time for them to be able to recognize, and it actually can be quite difficult. Sometimes they don't realize it. But I think they sense it a lot, and I felt that it was important for them to have that kind of mastery of feeling or control because censorship was for them, in a sense, to feel in charge. They should only say what they wanted to say.

Another challenge for the clinician occurs when songwriters resist entering the songwriting process. When uncomfortable emotions are evoked, songwriters may begin to comment: 'This is stupid', 'This is dumb', or 'I don't know why we're doing this'. This is evidence of their resistence to engage in the verbal expression of feelings or experiences, a defense mechanism. Clinicians working in mental health contexts can accomodate this resistance by either rephrasing questions to be less confronting or exploring the same issues on a more general level rather than focusing the discussion on their specific contexts. One clinician states:

> Sometimes when I start asking a question, depending on the group, if it's too abstract, then I don't get any answers and I have to reword it. Conversely, if it is too personal for where people are at, then again, I might have to reword it or change it. If it puts somebody on the spot too much, then it doesn't work out as well, and I might have to generalize or make sure that I get a lot of different things from other people.

Creating songs always involves risk because it 'embraces the unknown' (Marade et al., 2007, p. 126). And while no song that is created is entirely novel, each song typically tells a story in an original way (Marade et al., 2007). Some people who have experienced emotional trauma, however, fear taking creative risks and resist opening themselves to the therapist or to other group members. Those who willingly engage flourish during the songwriting process, while those who refrain from offering musical or lyrical suggestions may regress. One clinician working with children who have experienced domestic abuse or neglect states:

> I have half of the children who are very excited to come and very open to write songs and who blossom within the session. But there are a third of children who are progressing, who are opening up just little by little during a session, and sometimes they do regress.

Songwriters with diagnoses of mental illness may over-intellectualize the issues being explored in the creation of songs. Intellectualization is a defense mechanism, which serves as avoidance to entering the emotional domain and therefore blocks unconscious conflict (Gabbard, 2010). When the clinician draws the attention to the songwriter's avoidance, the songwriter may strive to hold on to his sense of safety; the intellectualization serves its purpose when needed. One clinician who practices in an adult psychiatric hospital argues that songwriting can be effective in such contexts, as it can facilitate the connection between the theory (intellectualizing) and the emotional self. She states:

> Sometimes over-intellectualizing makes it a little bit more difficult to facilitate emotional presence and what is actually currently happening for them . . . But within that situation, I'll voice my thoughts and just say 'I feel like this isn't actually what you're experiencing at the moment', and that will take discussions in a different direction. But it sort of lets them become aware of those barriers that they're putting up for themselves and whether they need them up at the moment in time.

Songwriting might also enhance or awaken delusions of grandeur or narcissistic tendencies in people with mental illness and therefore be contraindicated. One interviewee stated:

> I know a therapist at a state forensic psychiatric facility who was working with a former presidential assassin in DC, who got called to a government court because his client was engaging in songwriting. The government felt this could be contraindicated given his narcissistic tendency that led this person to pathological and schizoid behavior.

Recurrent experiences of aspiring to achieve but failing to do so may lead to failure-avoidant patterns of behavior (Thompson, 2004) and dependence on the clinician for assistance in creating lyrics or music. In her work with young people who have been repeatedly excluded from schools due to behavioral issues, one clinician sensitively supports young people without them realizing she is influencing the process. This creates a perception that they have independently created their own song and serves to combat their sense of being a failure.

The rate of adjustment or acceptance to illness, injury, or imminent death varies between songwriters. Songwriters with permanent injuries (e.g. brain injury, spinal injury, and burns) will create lyrics that express feelings associated with their losses, including loss of function and independence; a change in physical appearance; loss of professional status, career, financial control, and security; as well as feelings of guilt, self-blame, and anger (Baker & Tamplin, 2006). The appraisal of each loss will influence the course of grief and adjustment. Typically, people move through five phases – the initial response to the event, activation of defense mechanisms, initial realization of the long-term implications of the injury resulting in an all-consuming 'crisis', retaliation resulting in resistance and efforts to maintain control, and reintegration (Olney & Kim, 2001). Similarly, people in palliative care or experiencing grief at the loss of a loved one also move through the phases of grief – accepting the reality of the loss, processing the pain of grief, adjusting to a world without the deceased, and finding an enduring connection with the deceased in the midst of embarking on a new life (Worden, 2008) – and this process is reflected in the song lyrics and music that they create as songwriters.

Process and progress on the creation of a song will depend upon where each songwriter is in their adjustment or grief process. Some songwriters may move faster through the process than anticipated by the clinician and may call for more frequent songwriting sessions to capitalize on their rapid progress. If clinicians leave too many days between sessions, songwriters may have moved on in their process and the content from the initial sessions may no longer be relevant, leaving the songwriter with an incomplete song. Other songwriters may need to stay in the therapeutic process for longer durations and may create songs over several sessions as they fully explore whatever issues are relevant to their phase in the grief process. Therefore, timing the commencement and completion of a song is important, and wherever possible these should align with the tempo of the songwriter's movement through the adjustment or grief process.

Challenges in creating a coherent song are experienced when songwriters' emotional issues and the intensity with which they are felt vary from session to session. Song content may continuously change to accommodate these fluctuations. In her work with people with SCI, one clinician illustrates the 'rollercoaster' of emotions which impact the songwriting process:

> They are on a rollercoaster. They'll be like 'yes, I can do this, I can' whatever, and they'll be sort of up there wanting to write, and then the next week they will have rolled down, and that can be an obstacle. It can be really tricky when they come back to a song they were writing that was kind of at this level – and then the next week they're feeling down in their boots, so that song just doesn't reso- nate for them at all anymore . . . And then the next week it might be different again.

Emotional wellbeing

The emotional wellbeing of songwriters impacts on how the song- writing process unfolds. Some participants experience 'burnout' from repeatedly telling their story. They may have a long history of attending various therapies with little or no change in their perceived wellbeing. As a result, these songwriters have become disillusioned or lack confi- dence that songwriting will have any potential benefit. They are not interested in retelling their stories yet again as experience tells them it does not lead to change. In such cases, songwriters may not be fully committed to the process. Without full investment, there is less chance the process will be effective, which serves to reinforce their views that there is little value in retelling their stories. To accommodate negative preconceptions about the potential of songwriting, drawing on a recon- structive approach, where the focus is on moving forward rather than looking back, may be of more benefit.

Self-esteem determines how confident and willing songwriters are to share their story with the clinician or other group members. This perception correlates with research in psychology, which has found a link between self-esteem, expressivity, and self-disclosure in individual contexts (Gaucher et al., 2012) and in group contexts (Goldstein et al., 1978). Songwriters with low self-esteem may believe that their feelings, thoughts, stories, or experiences are not valuable or interesting, and therefore not 'worthy' of being portrayed in a song. Songwriters who are supported and encouraged to recognize that they have valuable con- tributions to offer the song creation process are more likely to be more self-expressive in the songwriting context (Gaucher et al., 2012).

Extreme traumatization may result in people being emotionally closed and often choosing not to disclose the trauma to anyone. For example, women who have been victims of sexual abuse (Kearns et al., 2010), refugees (Bogner et al., 2010), and war veterans (Hoyt et al., 2010) tend to avoid all forms of disclosure. Sharing their story with others through song creations is therefore challenging for them, although research indicates that even revisiting painful emotions has long-term health benefits, and sharing should therefore be encouraged (e.g. Pennebaker, 1997). Avoidance to disclose may nonetheless impact the flow of the songwriting process, and songwriters may need intermittent 'breaks' from exploring the self. Clinicians may subtly offer to shift from lyric creation to the music creation process as a form of relief from the 'emotional work' of telling one's story (Baker, 2013e). When songwriters do not have the internal resources to manage overwhelming emotional responses evoked during songwriting, there is a risk that they may terminate the process or that the process will be interrupted, or they may emotionally withdraw and close.

For those songwriters in treatment for substance or alcohol misuse, a state of 'readiness for change'[5] will affect the direction of the songwriting process. Songwriters who are in the prepared state (high readiness) will be highly engaged in the process and will create lyrics that reflect a commitment to change. Conversely, those in the contemplation stage (low readiness) will be less engaged and create non-committal lyrics. Low readiness for change is considered a major obstacle in rehabilitating people with substance misuse issues (Laudet, 2003). Choice of words for lyrics may be indicative of remaining in the contemplative stage, with phrases such as 'I want to' (non-committal) emerging in the lyrics, rather than 'I will' (committing to change, high readiness for change). In her work with people with substance use disorder, one clinician relayed the events in a group treatment session:

> I divided the group in half pretty arbitrarily, but it ended up being [that] the half of the group that was really serious about their recovery ended up being in one group. The other half of the group were a group of young guys who really didn't want to be in treatment. The depth of their lyrics and their engagement with songwriting was very reflective of where they were in their process, either the contemplative or moving into preparation for action . . . One set of lyrics had incorporated some of the principles of Alcoholics Anonymous in it, while the other one was just really kind of goofy. It was almost like a satire of being in treatment.

Some songwriters have a fear of the songwriting process coming to a close and may therefore consciously or unconsciously use strategies to avoid stating that the song is finished. They may become fixated on refining the song, attempting to create the 'perfect' song that authentically represents their experiences, stories, and musical identity. This might be a sign that the participant has developed a dependence on the therapist–songwriter relationship and experiences anxiety about the songwriting process coming to an end. It can also be a coping mechanism, an avoidance of 'moving forward' and facing new challenges.

Relationship to music and musical skills

The final individual factor that affects the songwriting process concerns the songwriter's relationship to music, which interviewees assert affects motivation and degree of engagement. Clinicians reported that songwriters with a strong connection to a musical genre or artist are more likely to engage in the songwriting process. A clinician working with adults with mental illness indicated that very musically engaged and active members of the group will draw in others to the songwriting process: 'the group that reaches a tipping point where everybody else slides along with them'. Other group members subsequently become more connected and engaged with the songwriting process.

Songwriters who have had previous experience with the creative arts have a tendency to enter the creative space more easily. They tend to recognize the value of songwriting as a medium to explore the self and are thus easier to engage in the process. One clinician comments in relation to his work with young disadvantaged youth:

> I think the perfect candidate for me is someone who is already used to creative spaces, maybe writes poetry, has explored creating music in the past, so they already know how to establish a creative space for themselves.

Songwriters' willingness to participate in the songwriting experience may depend upon their perception of their songwriting skills or music performance skills. Some songwriters are preoccupied with how they sound as musicians, and this may impact their motivation to create songs. This is especially the case when their participation involves singing. People may feel vulnerable and disengage from the process if they are self-conscious of their singing voices. Voices are very personal instruments, revealing how we feel about what we say and sing (Uhlig & Baker, 2011).

6
Group Factors

Group songwriting is frequently adopted by clinicians working in mental health, rehabilitation, and special education contexts (Baker et al., 2009). In Grocke et al.'s (2009) study of group songwriting involving adults living with severe and enduring mental illness, group members reported that they experienced working as a team an enjoyable aspect of the songwriting process. Dalton and Krout's (2005) and Krout's (2011) studies with adolescents who were bereaved and Day et al.'s (2009a, 2009b) study of women who had experienced childhood abuse suggested that the group context offered a space for the adolescents and women to share their stories with others. The group allowed for common thoughts and feelings to be made conscious and then highlighted through the lyrics and music of the group song. In McFerran and Teggelove's (2011) work with adolescents affected by the Victorian bushfires, group songwriting fostered opportunities for people to experience being a part of something 'bigger than themselves', while group songwriting in Jones et al.'s (2004) study of young refugees bridged cultural divides between the different ethnic groups and galvanized them into a sense of belonging.

Despite group therapy processes being well recognized as catalysts for change, there were only fleeting descriptions of group processes in literature describing group songwriting programs. This chapter explores the issues of working within group songwriting contexts by identifying key factors that constrain or support the process: group composition, group size, group conflict, and group cohesion.

Group composition

The composition of the songwriting group greatly impacts the process. There are two potential group composition structures – homogeneous and heterogeneous. Homogeneous songwriting groups are those where the group members essentially have key characteristics that are the same or very similar, while heterogeneous groups have dissimilar characteristics. Characteristics for consideration include age range, gender, ethnicity, sexual orientation, SES, diagnosis, and stage of illness. Heterogeneous and homogeneous groups have potentials to support or impede songwriting processes.

In groups where there is a mix of songwriters who are at different stages of their treatment, illness, or their therapeutic journey, there are opportunities for the songwriters to collaboratively engage in dynamic discussions and stimulate insights. By including a mix of people at early and late stages of rehabilitation or grief work, songwriters are able to reflect on group members' experiences at different phases of their therapeutic journeys. As people in the early phases share their stories and suggest lyrics, songwriters in the later stages of their journey are made aware of, or at the very least reminded of, how far they have traveled and what they have achieved to date. Importantly, they are able to support those in the earlier phases by communicating that they have also experienced what the 'junior' members of the group are sharing presently. This provides the 'senior' members of the songwriting group with a 'sense of meaning and purpose' as they support and validate those who are early in their process (Baker, 2013a, p. 139). For those songwriters who are in the early phases of their journey, hearing the stories and lyric contributions of those in the latter phases can be comforting, inspiring, and instill much-needed hope that life can continue. As one clinician reported:

> The different places [in their journey] that they are all at, actually I think adds to the richness of the experience and can introduce tension and stir the pot a little bit . . . If everyone is on the same page all the time, it is not very dynamic.

For a group songwriting experience to be optimal, the group needs to comprise a sufficient critical mass of songwriters who are open to the process and are able to draw in other group members to engage in the songwriting journey. A small subgroup of active, motivated, and vocal group members can create an atmosphere where others feel more comfortable, willing, and motivated to partake in the group song creation. Other group members observe that this subgroup of members is not afraid to disclose, share their stories, offer lyrics, and essentially take risks. This gives them confidence and permission to also contribute ideas and stories for the group song. Without a critical mass of active contributors, there is 'a risk that the songwriting process stagnates, and becomes an unsatisfying and therapeutically contraindicated process' (Baker, 2013a, p. 139).

Including a mix of genders in songwriting groups creates opportunities for gender conflicts when working with young people. Perhaps most challenging is the diverse, almost polarized, musical preferences that are typically preferred by males and females (Colley, 2008). While tolerating and appreciating others' musical preferences is often an aim of group music therapy processes, it becomes problematic when the group needs to decide on a genre of music suitable to accompany the song lyrics. If multiple group members feel strongly about using their own individual music genre preferences, conflict may arise and bring the songwriting process to a standstill. As one clinician notes:

> With the kids, one of my struggles has been that there's been this boy and girl thing and some songs are boy songs and some songs are girl songs – I try to pick these generic things and they're not agreeing . . . So that holds them back. I like to let them do everything, but I find that I need to jump in and decide for them.

As outlined in Chapter 4, sociocultural homogeneity or heterogeneity may affect how a songwriting process unfolds. Cultural diversity has the potential to enrich group songwriting experiences, while in other contexts the clinician is unable to bridge the cultural divide. When working with refugees from Africa, one clinician explained that group members with the same language and place of origin were not able to relate to each other because of differences in ethnicity, religion, and political party preferences. Conversely, when groups are culturally homogeneous, at times songwriters attempt to maintain their place in the hierarchy of their community and may censor their contributions. Levels of authenticity and engagement are subsequently compromised (see the section 'Heterogeneity versus homogeneity' in Chapter 4).

Some songwriters are confident, outgoing, and talkative (and some what unaware of these characteristics) and consequentially dominate or monopolize the songwriting process. The clinician is then charged with the challenge of drawing out the voices of the more passive, submissive, introverted, and shy songwriters, so that their voices are equally represented in the song lyrics and music created. At times, clinicians experienced that the more dominant group members were able to steer the songwriting process and content in their chosen direction, to meet their own individual needs, rather than considering the 'whole' group's needs. Of greater concern is that when certain group members dominate the process, it gives the passive, submissive, shy, introverted songwriters permission to remain passive. One clinician suggests:

> You will always see the ones that are assertive and taking over the dynamics and the ones that are taking advantage of the fact that there's somebody already volunteering their thoughts. They can sit back and be more passive. So, in some ways, unless I'm willing to challenge those patterns, it can be a comfortable place for them to be. (Baker, 2013a, p. 140)

The songwriting process is partly shaped by the personalities and temperaments of group members. For example, some people verbally communicate a lot, and in these cases ideas for lyrics and music may flow easily. The clinician's task may be to contain the discussions to ensure that time and space is available for shaping the lyrics and music; that is, to ensure that the song is completed. In other situations, group members may communicate very little, and the clinician's efforts are focused on drawing out as much verbal contribution as possible while being sensitive and respectful if group members choose not to verbalize extensively. Some group members may actively provoke conflict with other group members. This conflict may become a focus for the group's discussions and may subsequently be represented in the lyrics or music created. In this sense, the conflict becomes a resource supporting the songwriting process. Dissonance in the group offers opportunities for therapeutic change, so long as the composition of the group (a charismatic leader, attraction to the personalities of other group members, sharing a common goal for therapeutic change) is sufficient to invite participation from individuals (Yalom & Leszcz, 2005).

If group conflict cannot be managed, and those seeking out conflict are unable to reflect on the need for conflict, then group conflict may impede the process. Similarly, if some group members are uncomfortable with conflict, then they may become passive when conflict emerges from other group members and there is a risk that they will not receive the full benefits from the process or have their voices represented authentically in the songs created.

Group size

Does size matter? When it comes to group songwriting, the answer is an emphatic yes. Group size shapes group interaction and group dynamics, and therefore affects the songwriting process and product. Small songwriting groups offer greater possibilities and potentials for individuals' voices to be represented within the song lyrics and for their musical identities to be present in the musical accompaniments created. However, the downside to small group sizes is that there are fewer songwriters contributing to the critical issues being discussed. There is a danger that discussions and lyric contributions are fewer and there are less people to bounce ideas off. In addition, songwriters may feel more visible in a small group and may therefore experience more pressure to contribute ideas and lyrics than they might in larger group contexts.

Larger groups may be more dynamic, as more people are contributing their own ideas and sharing stories when compared with small group songwriting contexts. There may be more lively debates on issues, more varied perspectives, a greater range of stories and experiences to consider, and more opportunities for reflection. What results are rich songwriting processes and songs that may represent a spectrum of experiences and feelings. However, in large groups, there are more opportunities to be invisible, to be passive, to limit contributions, and therefore not take risks and open up. Voices may be missing from the song, which limits feelings of song ownership and receiving the full benefits of a therapeutic songwriting experience.

Group conflict

As alluded to already, group conflict offers opportunities to hinder or enrich the songwriting process. Within mental health settings, group members may participate in the songwriting process with a conscious or unconscious agenda of their own. These agendas may not be agendas shared by other group members, and therefore are a source of tension that can negatively impact the songwriting process. What results are songs that are disjointed, lack a coherent message, and serve to reinforce chaos.

Another scenario that can shape the songwriting process is when a group member brings his own agenda to the session and subsequently influences others, and his agenda suddenly becomes their agenda too. This scenario has negative consequences when working with people who have personality disorders. Some people are already predisposed to having difficulty separating themselves from others (enmeshment), and therefore taking on others' agendas serves to reinforce rather than address this symptom. At the same time, there may be situations when the influence of a group member's agenda can lead the group to explore a certain issue in more depth. What results is a song with a single overall theme rather than disparate agendas.

In some contexts such as mental health or prison settings, group rules set at the beginning of a treatment session or program enable the group to function in a constructive and therapeutically meaningful way. When songwriters are able to follow group rules, songwriters feel safe, have clear expectations of how to perform in the group, and there are reduced risks of verbal or physical violence emerging. One clinician explained that when she begins her songwriting program with young children identified as at-risk, the first session involves the creation of a song that contains the group's rules. This process of creating lyrics about how to act and interact during songwriting inadvertently reinforces the rules, and there is a greater chance that the rules will be remembered because of music's mnemonic potentials. However, it was noted that children have more difficulty arriving at a consensus when compared with adults. It has been suggested that democratic systems such as voting work well in ensuring decisions are made in a fair and just way.

Group cohesion

Group cohesion is a factor that evidently supports the songwriting process. The level of intimacy, trust, and safety within the group affords opportunities for people to be open, to disclose, to trust in the group process, and to be authentic in their songwriting contributions (Day et al., 2009a; Johnsdøttir, 2011). This finding was not surprising, as these elements of group work are fundamental to group therapy more generally (Yalom & Leszcz, 2005). Some clinicians prefer to work with small groups with consistent group membership and where the group members know each other either because of experiences of being together in other therapeutic contexts or because they are living in the same community (hospital, prison, school, etc.). People are more likely to work constructively and collaboratively when they feel comfortable being together. Indeed being comfortable promotes honesty and authenticity in communicating what they are experiencing physically, mentally, emotionally, and spiritually. As one clinician reported, 'That's easier to do with people that you have some connection with, than with a group of strangers' (Baker, 2013a, p. 141).

Consistency of group composition impacts how cohesive a group is and therefore influences the course of therapeutic songwriting. Closed groups offer opportunities for group cohesion to develop as songwriters explore issues together over several sessions and increasingly become comfortable enough to go deeper into issues and share more of themselves with others. However, closed groups are not always possible in some contexts. In some inpatient hospitals there are continuous admissions and discharges occurring on a daily basis, so it is not usually possible to establish closed groups. As one clinician reports:

> It's so rare that I have everyone there and that they're there for the entire session. So the dynamics of the group are always changing depending on the personalities that are there, who's leaving when. (Baker, 2013a, p. 141)

In songwriting groups consisting of people with mental illness, Baker et al. (2007) and Dingle et al. (2008) reported that group membership changed from session to session. It was therefore important for cohesion and group processes to occur within single sessions rather than across several sessions. Dingle et al. (2008) found that songwriters within these open groups still had opportunities to feel connected with others, which reportedly countered their experiences of isolation.

Open versus closed groups has implications for how the clinician selects methods of songwriting. In closed group contexts where two or more sessions will be scheduled for the same group members, creating a single song across time will allow deep reflection on pertinent issues and engagement in a process that benefits from strong group cohesion. For open group contexts, it is more appropriate for the clinician to create songs within a single session so that group members can experience a shorter, less deep, but nonetheless a complete songwriting process. If songs are not completed within the single session, there is a risk that some members of the songwriting group may not be present at subsequent sessions. It may be difficult for them (and new members) to experience ownership of a song if they were unable to be part of the entire process.

7
Role of Music in Songwriting

When embarking on this program of research, I was intent on understanding the role of music in the songwriting process. In my years of research and following the research of others, there was notably a strong focus on the lyrics and what the lyrics meant in terms of diagnostic value or their role in gaining insight into the songwriter's therapeutic process. But lyrics are only part of the complete songwriting experience. What did the creation of music provide that was above and beyond just writing song lyrics? What did it add to the therapeutic experience and outcomes? And what would be missing if music creation were not a component of the process? What follows in this chapter is an overview of the main themes that emerged from the interviews I conducted (Baker, 2013e) and from the research where songs were created using three methods: lyrics only, song parody (lyric creation but to pre-existing music), and original songwriting where both lyrics and music were crafted (Baker & MacDonald, 2013a, 2013b).

Conveying meaning

One of the key aims of songwriting is to communicate the story and/or feelings of the songwriter to the self, the therapist, or to a familiar or unfamiliar audience. In songwriting, meaning is conveyed through the combination of lyrics and music. Lyrics clearly have a capacity to communicate, in a concrete way, the events that are core to the song. But music can also be key in conveying intended meaning.

Viega (in press a) suggests that in hip hop music the music created by the songwriter gives the text a storyline. Through the music production process, the songwriter offers the listener insight into his world. For example, when adolescents arrive in a foreign country as refugees, the lyrics to the song communicate the narrative but the music offers a window into how the songwriter has experienced his story. In line with this thinking, Viega offers a definition of songwriting as it applies to hip hop: 'the process of using the elements of hip hop culture to either spontaneously or deliberately create, mix, edit, layer, sample, loop and/or record lyrics and music by the clients and therapist within a therapeutic relationship' (Viega, in press a, n.p.).

As will be described in more detail in Chapter 13, lyrics created by songwriters in therapy may contain symbols and metaphors to express their feelings and experiences. In a study currently underway with people who have spinal cord or brain injury, several lyrics were intentionally or unintentionally ambiguous: 'Feels like I'm living in the middle of a storm', 'A fog has descended over my mind', 'At the end of the tunnel, a light starts to shine', 'As the days filter past and things fall in line', and 'Just like an 80s song, my life just rolls along'. In such cases, reading the lyrics alone does not provide sufficient information to make an interpretation or judgment about possible meanings. However, when the lyrics were superimposed over a musical structure specifically crafted to express the emotions, the music aided understanding of the story or events described in the song, the semiotic meaning of the lyrics, and importantly, the degree of significance or appraisal of the events or feelings which were portrayed in the songwriter's lyrics. As one interviewee described it:

> I see the benefit of a lyric analysis, but on its own you can't get the whole picture because the music and the sound created affects everything and can shape the lyric in a million different ways. There's a million different ways that a lyric can be interpreted and in fact there's a danger in saying, 'well, this lyric means this', when actually that's only part of it. The music may tell a different story.

Creating music to accompany lyrics also assists the songwriters to construct their own meaning. At times, their lyrics seem to have no meaning or the meaning is hidden, but when music is created their words are transformed, become seemingly relevant, and assume personal meaning (Baker, 2013e). One interviewee stated:

> A lot of times, people have something to say, and they don't think what they have to say really makes any sense or is worth anything. Once its slapped over the top of this musical structure and then all of a sudden, it's hugely validating for them because it makes perfect

sense, and not only is it that, even though it's painful or hard to hear or good to hear or whatever it is, it's more valuable now that it's on top of that musical structure than it ever was before. So, they can hear their value in it.

As outlined in Chapter 5, many songwriters present with language abilities that are inadequate to fully or sensitively express their feelings. This may be because they have not yet acquired sophisticated language skills or because there are some pathological reasons for their limitations in verbal expression. In these circumstances, the music they create to accompany their lyrics may provide the necessary information needed to convey the songwriters' messages. For example, the language skills of children who have experienced some form of trauma have not yet reached a developmental stage where they have words and sentences that can describe the extent of their emotional trauma. However, children do like to create songs, as is evident from the extensive literature on songwriting in various pediatric settings (e.g. Aasgaard, 2005; Abad, 2003; Baker & Jones, 2005; Baker et al., 2009; Burns et al., 2009; Robb et al., 2014). On her work with traumatized children, one interviewee reported:

> Sometimes their words are not very informative because the children don't have the language to express what they feel. But the quality of the music tells us what they feel about the emotions. Is it a very sad song, or a happy song, or what is it? Their words could be just sort of repeating the same words over and over again, just not meaning anything very special.

In many songs created as part of a therapeutic process, certain lyrics are likely to have more significance than others. Some lyrics may tell a story of events, while others within the same song may express how the songwriter feels about that story or event. In such circumstances, it is the lyrical expression of feelings or responses that carries the greatest weight. The music – particularly the shape of the melodic line and the accompanying harmonic progressions – can be purposefully crafted to highlight the key words or phrases and, as one interviewee shared, to bring these lyrics 'into sharper focus'. By creating musical contours, harmonic tensions and resolutions, and using pauses and sustained notes, the significant words can be brought to the fore.

In one example, a young woman with sickle cell disease shaped a melodic line that utilized a large ascending interval and a pause to signal

Figure 7.1   Example of use of melodic contour to signify importance of certain words

the relative importance of the words 'to me'. If the lyrics were read as a two-line poem with a steady beat, the words 'to me' would have a completely different meaning (Figure 7.1). The clinician working collaboratively with this young girl suggests that the melody (and harmony) create space for the 'listener to catch up and to really grab on it and then to be impacted'.

Music has long been regarded as a medium for the expression of the inner, emotional world of the person creating it. The same concept applies to the function of music within the songwriting process. Words are concrete and can describe the conscious thoughts and feelings of a songwriter. However, the music can tell a different story, expressing how the songwriter really feels about the issue described in the song, or can portray ambivalent, conflicted, or mixed feelings. In his songwriting practice with young disadvantaged adolescents, one interviewee stated:

> I think there is a benefit in hearing and talking about all the music and all of its complexities together with them [the adolescents]. So when they're choosing different sound effects, you can ask 'What is that sound effect like for this whole song?' . . . 'What does that bring to it, what aspect or color, what emotional quality does that bring, enhance?' So you have this lyric that's raw and tough and then you put this sound effect on it and that muffles it. And you ask them 'Well, what's that like?' It's tough but there's something covering it. There's something else underneath.

In Viega's (2013) research with young people from disadvantaged backgrounds, he suggested that the music exposes hidden emotions that are described in the lyrics created. The music the young people create expresses their internal struggles with life. For example, he reported that the softness of piano lines and acoustic guitars are 'enveloped by the pounding percussion and sharp synthesizers' (p. 257) and present contrasting emotions of pain and vulnerability to that described in the lyrics. In this example, these soft instruments allowed the young people to express their pain and vulnerability but without it moving to conscious awareness.

Enhancing emotional dimension of the lyrics

Music also plays a crucial role in enhancing the emotional dimensions of the lyrics. It is well recognized that music has the potential to create tension and resolution of the tension in the listener through the combination of certain musical elements (Meyer, 1956). The use of dynamic and tempo changes, rising and falling melodic contours, and unresolved and then resolving harmonic progressions build feelings of tension and expectations of a resolution (although some resolutions may not necessarily come). Spitzer (2013) proposed that the intensification of these features, particularly in songs where the human instrument of the voice is used, leads to a cathartic release. In essence, there is a gradual building from a low register to a highpoint in the song, which leads to a release of inner tension. Although Spitzer discussed this in relation to Schubert lieder, many modern day popular songs also follow this pattern where the verses build harmonic tension that is either intensified in the chorus or resolved in the chorus.

The potential for expressing climax and resolution can be incorporated into the songs created within a therapeutic context. One therapist who was working with at-risk children in the United States recounted her experience of facilitating the creation of a song titled 'In my Palace', which was a metaphor for having a home for these children. She described how she created a nurturing and calming melody for the chorus of the song that had a lulling quality. She helped create a melody that moved to a high pitch that represented the 'victory of being at home, having a home and some resolution' and used a chord that was out of key to create the tension which was later resolved.

For older adults in palliative care, one clinician recounted how a lady who was highly anxious used the music to connect more deeply with her emotions. The songwriter created this song titled 'Release Me', but was unable to sing the song herself because of her low energy and her inability to use her voice to express such intense emotions. She asked the clinician to sing the song to her and, as she did, the songwriter demanded the clinician yell (not sing) the lyrics 'release me'. The music crescendoed from singing to screaming, but in doing so, the music was able to support the release of the songwriter's emotions. The clinician reported:

> She made me literally yell 'release me' when we were recording it, really high-pitched, and she played the recording back and she said 'That's it, I can go now.' That was on a Monday, and I came back on Wednesday and she'd died. So she was able, on the Monday, to sit there with me in the music therapy room and guide me so that she could create a song that she wanted, and then she was dead on Wednesday . . . That was really profound.

Music can also add an emotional backing to the lyrics so that they are brought to life. The music gives the lyrics 'direction, substance, depth, and height' so that the lyrics can be experienced in a more enriching way.

Music plays a key role in expressing and holding the feelings of the songwriter so that they can be experienced fully expressed, illuminated, clarified, and resolved. Spitzer (2013) argued that songs could achieve this more easily than orchestral music because typically the song's effect, established in the initial moments of the song, is usually sustained throughout the whole song. This is evidenced in the repetition of motifs, melody lines, and repeated lyrics in sections such as the chorus – 'the characteristic figures are omnipresent' (Spitzer, 2013, p. 12). Within a therapeutic context, the repetition of lyrics and melodies serves to trigger the same emotions indefinitely (or until the song is complete), to hold the songwriter (and listener) in that emotion so it can be more deeply experienced. Given this, when using song parody as a method, it is important to select an appropriate song to rewrite the lyrics to. If the clinician wants to hold the songwriters so they can experience a certain emotion or feeling, then devoting time to finding the best song that already expresses those emotions or feeling states is advantageous. In her group work with adults who were undergoing therapy for drug or alcohol addiction, one clinician invested time in listening to songs when planning her song parody group sessions to ensure she selected appropriate songs:

> Before I use any song, I listen to it several different ways. I listen to it in an altered state with my eyes closed, my eyes open. I listen to it with the lyrics, when I'm feeling different ways and I note all the different emotional responses I have for it . . . I usually don't use

songs where the music does not support the emotional content of the lyrics. So the music is very important.

Identity building

There has been a rapid increase in the literature that supports the idea that songwriting used in therapeutic contexts can support identity building (Baker & MacDonald, 2013a, in press; Baker et al., 2005a; Tamplin et al., 2015). Extensive research by eminent scholars contributing to the edited text *Musical Identities* (MacDonald et al., 2002 [with a 2nd edition in production]) makes the case for the importance of music in facilitating exploration, expression, and development of their personal identities. Larson (1995) and DeNora (1999) indicated that music affords possibilities for people to experiment or test out different identities. From a therapeutic perspective, music is a resource that allows people to reclaim and reawaken a seemingly hidden self-identity, and serves to reaffirm a self-identity, to make sense of one's own identity, and to construct a new identity (Koelsch, 2013).

Given the above, it is not surprising that creating music within a songwriting process serves to reaffirm or construct identity. When the music created matches the musical identity of the songwriters, creating songs becomes a medium to connect or reconnect with their sociocultural identity. Assisting songwriters to integrate their own musical identities into their own music creations should take precedence over creating songs that have aesthetic beauty. After all, aesthetic beauty is subjective. Songwriters derive more meaning from the songwriting process and artifact when their musical identities are taken into consideration (Baker & MacDonald, 2013a). One clinician discussed the importance of creating a song that has cultural importance to adult songwriters with acute mental illness. He stated:

> Songwriting is creative and it's connecting to something that already has an intrinsic value to people . . . it's also significant because it's connecting them [the songwriters] to a particular artist or a particular style of music that has strong cultural implications, like rap music. So they're connecting to something that's culturally important to them too. So they may be a little bit more connected to their identity.

Here, the songwriters have deepened their sense of identity by adding a musical identity element to their overall sense of self.

As people construct or reconstruct identities during songwriting processes, songwriters are afforded opportunities to try on different identities or characters that they may want to emulate at that moment. This is particularly apparent for adolescents who are going through the individuation process and actively experimenting with different identities. Shaping the music to accompany lyrics allows people to create songs that express different identities. Manipulating vocal effects, adding environmental sounds, and layering and mixing the music offer people multiple ways to shape their sound and explore identity. For example, Viega (2013) found that the music created by youth with adverse childhood experiences, had 'apocalyptic soundscapes – sirens, missile blasts, pounding drums', which were the young people's way of presenting identities of being 'uncaring, unpredictable, tough, aggressive, and unconcerned with boundaries' (p. 91).

When songs created represent the songwriters' musical identities, the authenticity and meaningfulness of the song is strengthened (Baker & MacDonald, 2013b). One clinician who facilitates songwriting experiences with people in palliative care living in rural communities found that creating music that is stylistically similar to the music played in these farming communities is more meaningful for them and their families. She stated:

> What's important in hospice is that the music created is authentic to the person's style and voice . . . So, if I miss a chord or flub something, that's not as important as that I have to make it stylistically sound like *their* music . . . that it's style matches their voice, and that it would be meaningful for their family or to whomever it's left to.

Connecting with others

When music is created within a group songwriting experience, it has the potential to result in a powerful, shared experience, to allow the songwriters to be a part of something that is bigger (Ruud, 1997). In such cases, music might stimulate feelings of belonging (Baker & Ballantyne, 2013; Dingle et al., 2008; Jones et al., 2004; McFerran & Teggelove, 2011). The group performance of a song can create feelings of intimacy, mutual respect, and group cohesion. To obtain the full benefits of a songwriting process, it is therefore important to: (1) have sufficient time available to create the music, and (2) have time available to sing (or record) the song in its entirety. When creating songs with a group of people with complex mental health conditions, one clinician indicates that a critical component of the process is missing when there is insufficient time to create the music. She states:

If we run out of time and don't get to create the music, it's a strange feeling. Like it doesn't feel finished, because the process is always about that coming together and singing it. You've taken this time to write your story and share it with other people and hear their similar stories or different stories, and all respect each other's stories and then you come together on such an intimate thing as singing. That's where the finality happens . . . Without that, you've lost an intimacy of sharing and respecting and hearing each other.

Similarly, listening back to recordings of a group song facilitates deeper bonding and further therapeutic processing. In working with bereaved adolescents, one clinician stated:

I always offer them the chance to be in the music-making if we have the recording equipment and we have the time . . . We did that with a group of teenagers in a grief group where they all wrote a song together. They decided they wanted to use the rhythm instruments, so while I played the guitar they all just were shaking their instruments and singing along. So they really got a thrill out of hearing themselves sing those words on the recording and hearing them play the instruments. They bonded more because they were laughing together saying 'oh listen to you'.

As people sing and play their group songs, bonding also occurs as they physically feel the music of their song throughout their whole body. One interviewee shared:

I think being in that same musical space together – it brings you *in* entirely, it can be so much more than just reciting lyrics. It's that full-body experience. If someone's playing the drum kit, that's your whole body . . . what I love about drums is you're doing everything and you're sweating and your muscles hurt and it's so physical. I think it really brings them together and it can be loud.

Music, process, and outcomes

The musical creation component of songwriting bolsters the therapeutic process. First, it allows people to experience achievement and build their self-esteem. In Western society, songwriters are often held in high regard, often admired for their creative talents. When people create their own song within a therapeutic context, they derive a sense of achievement and self-worth, especially if other people hear the song and offer positive feedback about its value. Without the musical components of the song, the artifact would not hold as much prestige. One interviewee explained:

> The music gives the product [song] value . . . You know, talk is cheap but a song is worth a lot. So it's just words versus a piece of art. It's got that higher creative aesthetic that the society attributes to it.

Creating a song (as opposed to a poem) provided the motivation for people to engage and invest in the therapy process. Interviewees reported that people are more open and authentic in their contributions when the resultant outcome is the creation of a personally meaningful song.

Being in therapy and creating lyrics about personally difficult topics can be exhausting. As people explore their inner selves and describe their experiences, they may experience a range of complex and intense emotions such as anger, disappointment, guilt, and devastation. One of the benefits of creating music is that it can provide some time-out from these intense verbal discussions, and in doing so may allow people time to recover some emotional energy so that they can then continue with the lyric creation process.

As people recount their experiences and stories, share their feelings, and begin to construct song lyrics, people's defense mechanisms might be active and block thinking or feeling. Music has the potential to activate emotions, images, memories, and associations, and in doing so work to overcome unconscious blocks in the songwriting process and provide a concrete picture of the songwriters' internal world. One interviewee offered his perception of the role of music in his songwriting practice and explained how music can facilitate lyric creation:

> They're so focused on the lyrics, but it's the music that helps you get the lyrics. So they want to put the guitar down. I say, 'No, play it, sing it, something will happen. Patience, we always tend to get stuck. What is the next line going to be? You have to play it and play it and play it', and that's what I really like about songwriting. Because if you get stuck in the dialogue, you're able to play your way out of it. So I always play it and I sing it and I play it, and that always helps us to get unstuck, because you can hear it. But if you're just talking out the lyrics, it doesn't do any good. You need the music.

Creating music to accompany lyrics may deepen people's reflections on and understanding of the lyrics and their personal significance. Music may evoke emotions that lead the songwriter to think and feel differently about an issue, and consequently the focus of the song may move in a different direction, sections of the song may be deleted, or the song may be abandoned entirely, deemed no longer relevant. In essence, when music is superimposed over the lyrics, it creates new experiences for the songwriters and a new way of viewing their song, story, and the significance of these. Indeed the meaning of the words may change when music accompanies them.

Music genre

Some song forms provide natural structures to ground exploration. First, the framework of the blues genre is appropriate for 'complaining' or expressing sadness about a situation or context. A clinician co-creating songs with people in an adult psychiatric ward experienced that songwriters want to use the songwriting process as a medium to 'complain'. These complaints might be focused on aspects of the institution they are dissatisfied with, the noisy patient in the next room, or the expectations placed on them while they are inpatients. Typically, the blues form comprises a repeating progression of chords in an AA^{i}B framework – a call and response derived from African American music. Here, the A and A^i form a single lyric and melody and a repetition (often with slight variation) of it sung over the top of the blues progression (tonic, subdominant, and dominant). It is suitable for non-musicians because its form is familiar and the melody line is often spoken rather than sung, thereby minimizing anxiety about their musical capacity to perform the work. The use of the minor seventh interval, and a flattened third and fifth in the melody line, and the bent notes, minor second or sliding notes, allows for cadences and melodies to express tension and resolution in the emotional expression of the lyrics. The resolution of the third line presents opportunities for positive 'reframing' of the complaints (or other issues expressed by the participants).

Rap and hip hop genres are also suitable forms for exploration, again because an ability to read music and sing in tune is of less importance. In my own experience, songwriters are more comfortable reciting their lyrics using a driving (yet flexible) rhythm rather than singing them. Further, when working with a youth 'subculture', the deliberate avoidance of 'mainstream' music means these genres align with their expression of rejecting mainstream society.

Music technology

Recent recording technologies such as GarageBand allow songwriters to shape sounds through loops, samples, layering, distorting, adding reverb, and recording and mixing sounds from the musical instruments, the voices of the songwriters, and their environment. Shaping sounds in this way may ensure they create a sound that best expresses their story. Creating music in this way does not require the physical skill of playing a musical instrument, so it increases access to the music creation process in a way that may be inaccessible using traditional musical instruments. Songwriters may be more likely to participate in the process when they recognize that they can 'produce songs that sound like what they like on the radio'. One clinician interviewed described the story of a seven-year-old boy from the Dominican Republic who was undergoing weekly nursing procedures that were painful and involved injecting saline into a tissue expander under his scalp. Using electronic music technology, the sounds and the music he made took on symbolic meaning.

> He was very fearful of the nursing procedure. During music therapy, he was encouraged to explore and work through his anxiety concerning the tissue expander. As he described the procedure from his point of view, I periodically asked him to describe the feelings he felt with each step of the medical procedure. He struggled to find words beyond 'mal' (bad). When given options to choose from, he described himself feeling scared and nervous, and having pain with the expansion. He also reported he could hear the sound of the saline being injected into his expander.

During the following session, the music therapist brought a laptop and suggested the boy create a song that described the steps within the tissue expansion procedure as well as music to express his feelings and reactions toward those steps. Although he was initially reluctant, he soon engaged in the process, exploring and selecting sounds for his beating heart (fear). He also chose a loop to express how he felt sitting in the clinic room, waiting for the nurse to come. Next, he found the sound of footsteps and added it, saying it was the sound of the nurse approaching. After the footsteps sounds stopped, he added a siren to represent his fear of the needle and the procedure as the nurse prepares to inject him. At this point, he stopped all other loops and chose the sound of electricity to represent the needle insertion. Once that sound stopped, he chose a bass loop to express how his heart beat during the procedure and wanted the sound of water to show how he hears the saline entering the tissue expander. During this section, he added the sound of a police car siren to express his feelings of alarm and fear. This section ended with the removal of the needle, again represented by the electrical sound. The first theme returned with the initial bass loops. After these loops, he ended the song with the siren and an unsettled mysterious chord.

Once the song was finished, the music therapist and the boy listened to the song one time through. As he listened, he yawned and stated he was tired. Recognizing that composing this song required him to stay in his state of anxiety and fear and share these overwhelming feelings with the therapist, the music therapist ended the session early.

Microphones are another technological tool that can support the songwriting process. The microphone is symbolic; it allows for uninterrupted 'stage' time. It allows people to 'rap' and move into the flow. Even the way the microphone is held says something about the songwriter – holding it close to the mouth expresses the songwriter's vulnerability, whereas holding it away is more distant, less vulnerable. Similarly, adding reverb to the voice creates a feeling of space, making people feel freer in their vulnerability, whereas compressing the sounds makes them feel like they are in a hole (Viega, in press b). As one interviewee stated:

> Importantly, hearing your voice back in recordings is a meaningful experience; hearing yourself but it does not sound like yourself . . . it is a new version, enhanced with reverb, chorus, echo, etc. That is such a powerful metaphor for me in relation to therapy.

Many clinicians working with at-risk youth have recounted how young people just take a microphone and start to verbally share their inner worlds. A clinician working with young people at risk in the United States described a profound experience she has had with a group of children who used the microphones to share themselves with others. She explains:

> The children were talking into the mics, just talking, and a part of me was thinking, 'I can't believe that they're talking about this. I can't believe they're allowing themselves to share this much detail'.

In this instance, the microphone became a symbol of 'Now it's my time and I'm going to tell my story'. The microphone gave them the space to have uninterrupted stage time, to place them at the center of everyone's attention while they shared their stories. The microphone communicated the message: 'This is my story and can you handle it? Can you be with me in that?'

Section III
Songwriting Methods

8
Introducing Songwriting Methods

This chapter introduces the reader to the various songwriting methods that are utilized in the clinical practice of music therapists, irrespective of their therapeutic orientation. The descriptions are outlined in terms of their implementation procedures: a set of steps the clinicians follow until the song creation is complete. It does not describe how songwriting methods differ depending upon the orientation of the therapist. In this chapter, I first list the different methods and my rationale for assigning each to one of three separate categories: methods that emphasize lyric creation, methods that emphasize lyric and music creation, and methods that emphasize music creation. The chapter then describes the different ways songwriting can be introduced into a therapy program, focusing on techniques to prepare and prime the songwriter.

Categorizing songwriting methods

My research highlighted that there are currently ten methods of creating songs within a therapeutic context. My analysis indicated that it was the extent to which lyrical and musical components had been predetermined at the commencement of the songwriting process that were the most concrete and consistently endorsed distinguishing features. The initial iterations of the analysis focused on the degree to which approaches were structured and directive, with FITB located at the structured/directive end of a continuum and improvised song creations located at the polar opposite (unstructured/non-directive). However, this terminology gives the impression that improvised song creations were created through an unstructured or unplanned process,

Table 8.1 Predetermined song components for different songwriting approaches

	Lyrics	Song structure	Genre	Melody	Harmonic features	Tempo	Rhythmic features	Instrumentation
Fill-in-the-blank*	P	P	P	P	P	P	P	P
Song parody*	O	P	P	P	P	P	P	P
Integrative/strategic songwriting*	O	P	P	P	P	P	P	P
Rapping over pre-composed music/remixing* #	NP	O	P	O	P	O	P	O
Mash-up#	O	O	O	P	P	O	P	P
Pastiche and hodge podge#	NP	O	P	NP	NP	NP	NP	O
Original songwriting within known structures#	NP	P	O	NP	O	O	NP	O
Rapping over original music+	NP	O	P	NP	NP	NP	NP	NP
Song collage+	NP	NP	NP	NP	NP	NP	NP	NP
Improvised song creations+	NP	NP	NP	NP	NP	NP	NP	NP

Note: The * symbol signals songwriting methods where there is a stronger emphasis placed on lyric creation, the # indicates a stronger emphasis on music creation, and the + signals an emphasis on both lyrics and music creation.

which is misleading. As one interviewee pointed out, improvised song creations are:

> highly structured. I'm not 'winging' it or making stuff up. I'm working within constructs – but one of those constructs is the process, the creativity, the moment. My rhythms, harmonies, melodies, and lyrics are organized and structured – directed.

Through further engagement with the data and ongoing discussions with experts in therapeutic songwriting, it became clear that approaches differed in the musical components that were predetermined or not predetermined and where there were options to create, modify, manipulate, or extend pre-existing musical components. Predetermined components are indicative of the musical decisions that were made prior to commencing the songwriting process – this may have been decided by the therapist prior to commencing the session or in collaboration with the songwriter/s during the session. Table 8.1 details which of the song components were predetermined (P), not predetermined (NP), and optional (O).

Examining Table 8.1 closely, it becomes clear that there is a relationship between the degree of predetermined song elements and whether the emphasis is on lyric creation, music creation, or a balance of both. This relationship is represented pictorially in Figure 8.1. It is noticeable that the approaches at the *predetermined structure* end of the spectrum

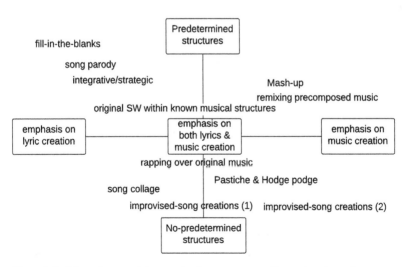

Figure 8.1 Map of songwriting methods across a two-dimensional continuum

emphasize lyric creation, those in the *middle* of the spectrum have a stronger emphasis on music creation, and those at the *no predetermined structure* end of the spectrum have a strong emphasis on both music and lyric creation.

Introducing songwriting

Precursors and strategies to introducing songwriting

Descriptions of songwriting methods vary in their level of detail and depth. Several book chapters (see contributions in Baker & Wigram, 2005) and numerous dissertations (e.g. Aasgaard, 2002; Hakomäki, 2013; Hammel-Gormley, 1995; Hatcher, 2004; O'Grady, 2009; Roberts, 2008; Thompson, 2011) have described songwriting protocols in considerable depth. Noticeably, however, authors have omitted detailed accounts of an important part of the process – the events that precede the initial phase of the songwriting process.

Recent research suggests that when healthy non-musicians (Baker & MacDonald, 2013b), young people who have experienced adverse childhood experiences (Viega, unpublished manuscript), or adults with severe mental illness (Grocke et al., 2014) engage in collaborative songwriting with a therapist, they initially experience anxiety as they move outside their comfort zone. One songwriter in Baker and MacDonald's study stated:

> Well I was dead scared when you came. I thought I was going to be an absolute disaster, I really did. I thought there is no way in the world that I'm [going to be] able to write a song or compose lyrics. I'm just wondering what this [is] all about. Will I do any good? Will I help? Or am I going to be a complete plop or what?

Therefore, creating an environment that minimizes anxiety about creating a song is essential for an effective therapeutic process, especially when dealing with vulnerable people. In this chapter I describe: (1) how clinicians introduce songwriting to their participants, (2) the specific strategies employed to lessen anxieties and facilitate a smoother transition to the songwriting process, and (3) what actually happens immediately before the therapist and songwriters launch into the creative activity.

Events preceding songwriting *within* sessions

A thorough review of the songwriting literature revealed that many clinicians engage songwriters in various music-based or non-music-based activities before introducing songwriting to the session. On the pediatric oncology ward, Aasgaard's (2002) songwriters 'scribbled texts' which became the foundation for song texts (Aasgaard, 2002). In his practice, the term 'therapy' is avoided and song creation activities are intentionally termed 'projects', perhaps in an effort to avoid inciting unnecessary apprehension in the songwriter. Labeling the intervention a 'project' also signals the constructive and positive engagement in a meaningful activity, in stark contrast to the 'treatment' paradigm. Aasgaard noticed that participants were disappointed when they discovered he was a therapist; presenting himself as an artist was much more appealing to the children he worked with. Discussing the case study of an adolescent in an oncology ward, Abad (2003) recounted that during one session the adolescent presented with a low mood. In her response to this, Abad intuitively improvised words and music to reflect the adolescent's feelings. Beginning with this action allowed Abad to connect with the adolescent, and in doing so opened an opportunity to introduce the idea of songwriting as an activity that might facilitate further expression and exploration of the songwriter's feelings. During individual sessions with adults in palliative care, Heath and Lings' (2012) songwriting interventions were preceded by song listening and the ensuing discussions or improvisations. These activities aimed to stimulate personal reflections or 'open' the songwriter on an emotional level.

Lead-in activities were evident in several studies implemented within a group context. In a study of participants with substance use disorder, Jones' (2005) treatment protocol commenced with a verbal 'check-in'. Here, participants were asked to choose phrases from a given list that resonated with their feelings. Sharing phrases with the group 'served to orient the group to one another, set parameters for sharing, create a focus on emotions, and familiarize the group with the style of the therapist/ researcher' (p. 100). Schwantes (2011) also engaged Mexican farmworkers in an initial check-in. Participants shared their feelings and, where relevant, the events or contexts that explained those feelings. Before continuing onto songwriting, her sessions also included instrumental instruction. Songs selected by the singing group preceded songwriting activities in Grocke et al.'s (2009) study of people with enduring mental illness. Songwriting was a significant component of Curtis' (1997) study of women who had been abused by male partners. Of the 90-minute sessions, 30 minutes were devoted to discussions about 'feminist analysis of power and gender-role socialization' (p. 308) through the analysis of lyrics of songs. Songwriting immediately followed the lyric analysis process. Movement to music as a strategy to build group cohesion was the first intervention included in a study of people with dementia (Silber & Hes, 1995).

Events preceding songwriting *across* multiple sessions

A substantial body of literature, and confirmed by many clinicians I interviewed, illustrates that songwriting is not typically introduced during the first session but after two or more sessions. Several other music-based and non-music-based activities are incorporated into the initial sessions. Song listening or singing with or without follow-up discussions contributed to the establishment of a relationship with adolescents with muscular dystrophy (Dwyer, 2007), adults with personality disorders (Rolvsjord, 2001), adults receiving palliative care (Clements-Cortes, 2009), and persons with dementia (Hong & Choi, 2011), particularly when the songs chosen were selected from the songwriters' music repertoire. Music education preceded songwriting in the music therapy program for a man with complex trauma (Hatcher, 2004). Guitar lessons served to establish rapport with the songwriter as well as teaching him to play guitar chords and common styles of music.

When working with a group of retirees, Baker and Ballantyne (2013) introduced songwriters to parody by creating and presenting an example of lyrics that they had prepared themselves set to a well-known song. This served to demonstrate how easily songs could be transformed into personally meaningful artifacts in the absence of any pre-existing musical talent.

Priming and preparation

My analysis of interviews indicated that clinicians utilize music-based or non-music-based activities for one of two reasons: (1) to emotionally and cognitively prime the songwriter for the therapeutic work involved in writing the song, or (2) to prepare the therapeutic space and equip them with skills to feel comfortable with creating a song. Priming strategies are designed to emotionally arouse a songwriter so that he is ready to engage and participate in the creation of a song. Purposefully selected music-based activities serve to increase a songwriter's awareness of his thoughts and feelings. Some clinicians begin with a verbal or musical check-in, which assists people to begin to look into themselves, become aware of their feeling states, and to articulate them.

Singing songs is often utilized to stimulate memories and arouse emotions, which may become the focus of the songwriting process. When songwriters choose their own songs to listen to or sing, they are (sometimes unconsciously) choosing songs that have previously evoked an emotional response within them or that activate important memories. The song may have been chosen because it represents or expresses part of their identity, or it may be associated with a person, an event, or a place that holds special meaning for them. In singing or listening to this song, these memories, meanings, or associations are heightened, thereby priming the songwriter for expressing these in his song creation. There is now strong evidence that music evokes autobiographical memories and that these are linked with emotions. For example, Janata et al. (2007) found that in a group of healthy young people (7–19 years of age), 30 per cent of the songs presented to them evoked autobiographical memories and that these were typically associated with strongly experienced positive emotions. Similarly, in people with brain injury (Baird & Samson, 2014) and in people with dementia (El Haj et al., 2013), music successfully stimulates autobiographical recall.

Therapists may also introduce songs to listen to or sing as an emotional or cognitive priming tool. In some circumstances, depending upon the clinician's orientation, the therapist will select a focus for the songwriting process prior to the session commencing and play or sing a song related to that theme. For example, if the songwriting session was focused on grief and loss, the song primer might be Everybody Hurts (REM); if the theme was home, it might be 'Take Me Home' (Phil Collins); drug themes are aroused in 'Drugs Don't Work' (The Verve), while feelings of loneliness might be stirred up in 'Sad Songs' (Elton John) and identity in songs like 'The Creep' (Radiohead). As the songwriters listen to or sing the therapist-chosen song, it arouses their own feelings on the subject matter, whether stimulated by the music, the lyrics, or both. They are then able to explore their own experiences during the song creation process.

Another useful priming technique is for the therapist to play and sing a song composed by another person she has worked with in therapy. Hearing what another person expresses offers opportunities to arouse similar feelings or possibilities to compare their own experiences with that of the other person. In addition, it illustrates what is possible to achieve within a music therapy process, thereby reducing potential anxiety around being able to successfully complete their self-composed songs. In each of these scenarios of listening to a pre-composed song, there may be an opportunity to deconstruct the meaning of the song's lyrics as a precursor to commencing creating their own lyrics. Through this deconstruction process, issues of relevance to the topic of their own song may come to the fore and may be incorporated into the lyrics and music that they create in their own songs.

Arousing unconscious thoughts, feelings, or memories are the primary reasons for introducing improvisation and Guided Imagery and Music into pre-songwriting activities. Both interventions are now well recognized for bringing hidden psychic material to the surface (e.g. Priestley, 1994). Once the material has surfaced, it is then transformed into concrete ideas through the songwriting process. Improvisation is a form of pre-verbal

communication that can convey unconscious inner experiences and emotions. Verbal reporting following improvisation is already an integral – and
in some opinions essential – feature of many psychodynamic approaches,
without which the unconscious may not move to conscious awareness
(John, 1992). John argues that while music bridges the unconscious and
conscious, thoughts and words are needed before the conscious level can
ever be achieved. Therefore, the improvisation and imagery experiences
stir up emotional experiences, and the songwriting process serves to explore
and process these experiences and bring them to conscious awareness.

Preparation strategies are also employed prior to commencing songwriting. These strategies are primarily aimed at ensuring that the songwriter feels comfortable and safe with the idea of creating a song and feels
inspired to do so. Inspiration to create a song can emerge by listening to
and discussing pre-composed songs (as described earlier) or a song created by a previous songwriter in therapy. As the expressive output of the
song is discussed, songwriters can feel inspired to express their own stories in song form. Another strategy that assists people to feel comfortable
or inspired to create songs is for the clinician to facilitate the co-creation
of a simple song on a safe topic. Gaining a sense of how simple it is to create, especially when supported by the therapist, demystifies the process.

Inspiration to create songs can emerge from discussions about the songwriter's own preferred music. Here, the therapist works to highlight how
the songwriter's favorite artists are merely expressing their stories through
lyrics and music. The therapist communicates that the songwriter can
achieve much the same outcome as his favorite artists – a creative product
that expresses his feelings or tells his story. But getting started with the
story is also an issue for some songwriters. To be inspired to create a song,
they have to identify a story to tell. Here, the therapist can facilitate some
preparation through use of strategies such as encouraging the songwriter
(when appropriate) to bring in and read out diary entries. This may facilitate a discussion on a topic, leading to the emergence of a theme and an
inspiration to create. Another approach is to 'interview' the songwriter,
using probing techniques (Egan, 2014) as a way of obtaining the details of
the songwriter's story. Once the therapist has written down some notes,
she can read some of the songwriter's story verbatim and respond with
encouraging comments such as: 'Hey, that sounds like a really good lyric
for a song; perhaps we could transform your story into a song'. Taking a
similar approach, the clinician might sing back some of the songwriter's
comments to illustrate how phrases can be easily transformed into lyrics.
Finally, and most relevant for palliative care work, engaging the songwriter in a discussion about legacies may inspire him to consider songwriting as one way to leave something to his loved ones.

9
Songwriting Methods that Emphasize Lyric Creation

This chapter describes the different songwriting methods where the primary emphasis is on creating lyrics. It begins with descriptions of the methods that are governed by high levels of predetermined components (Figure 8.1, upper left quadrant), and progresses gradually toward methods where the degree of predetermined musical and lyrical elements are lower (the lower left quadrant).[1]

Fill-in-the-blank

FITB, song parody, and strategic songwriting are approaches that involve the songwriter rewriting some or all of the lyrics to a pre-composed song. Here, all aspects of the musical framework have been pre-composed and the songwriter creates or co-creates new lyrics that are personally meaningful. FITB, sometimes referred to as the Cloze Procedure (Freed, 1987), is one of the first songwriting methods described in the literature (Schmidt, 1983), and has been reported to be used with children, adolescents, and adults with brain injuries (Baker et al., 2005a; Glassman, 1991; Robb, 1996), adolescents with depression (Goldstein, 1990), adults diagnosed with substance use disorder (Freed, 1987; Jones, 2005), and people with dementia (Hong & Choi, 2011).

In FITB, key words are 'blanked out' from the original lyrics. The therapist's role is to engage the songwriter/s in a therapeutic process that results in the identification of feelings and experiences, which are then translated into new key words and inserted into the spaces (Baker et al., 2005a; Baker & Tamplin, 2006). These approaches have typically been used in therapy programs for people with significant cognitive impairments or for people presenting with significant mental health challenges.

FITB is a useful approach when creating songs with people who have significant language or speech or cognitive impairments or who are easily fatigued, because it only entails the generation of small numbers of single words and not the more complex task of creating entire lyrical phrases (Baker et al., 2005a).

Figure 9.1 illustrates the key steps involved in the FITB songwriting process. After the initial introduction and warm-up, the therapist plays through the original song (either live or a recorded version) to familiarize the songwriter with the original song content, to give him[2] an opportunity to reflect on the issues and feelings expressed in the original song, and to prime him for engaging in the therapeutic process. The therapist may have selected the song prior to the commencement of the session or after an initial assessment of the songwriter's presentation.

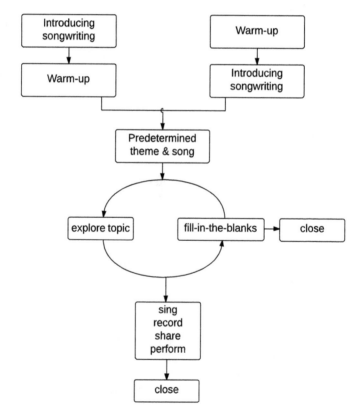

Figure 9.1   Steps involved in the FITB method

Alternatively, and depending upon clinical orientation, the therapist and songwriter may jointly decide to have certain lyrics of the song blanked out and replaced. The therapist then guides a therapeutic discussion with the songwriter, where the topic described in the song is explored in relation to the songwriter's own situation, and keywords in the original lyrics are replaced with lyrics that are personally meaningful for the songwriter. At this point the session may end, or the song is sung, performed, recorded, or shared.

Song parody

Song parody is similar to the FITB approach, but differs in that it invites songwriters to rewrite larger portions of the lyrics. Here, songwriters may: (1) rewrite all the words to a song; (2) rewrite the verses of the song, but retain the lyrics of the original chorus (Baker et al., 2005a; Robb, 1996); or (3) rewrite some lyrics, but retain others throughout the entire song. Rewriting extensive amounts of the lyrics empowers songwriters to tell their stories in more detail and to personalize the song to a greater extent than the FITB technique.

Within the available literature, song parody has been used with children and adolescents undergoing treatment for various forms of cancer (Abad, 2003; Brodsky, 1989; Ledger, 2001; Robb & Ebberts, 2003), children, adolescents, and adults with ABI (Baker et al., 2005a; Glassman, 1991), adolescents who have misused drugs (McFerran, 2011), adults with mental illness (Ficken, 1976; Silverman, 2009), university students and retirees (Baker & MacDonald, 2013b), older adults with dementia (Hong & Choi, 2011; Silber & Hes, 1995), and very frail older adults (Baker & Ballantyne, 2013).

Song parody offers opportunities for those participating in group therapy to create a meaningful group song. Each member of the group may create a verse that represents or expresses his own individual feelings or experiences. This gives each person the chance to have his voice expressed and heard. The chorus ties together the feelings and experiences that are shared amongst group members, and in doing so enhances the group experience and all the flow-on effects that emerge from that. Conversely, jointly rewritten verses and choruses may lead group members to identify with a 'common narrative', leading to feelings of group support and a sense of belongingness (Baker & Ballantyne, 2013).

Two vignettes in the literature serve to illustrate the differences between FITB and song parody. In both of these cases, the pre-composed song utilized was 'I Will Survive' (Perren & Fekaris, 1978).

In a demonstration of a will to survive, Ledger (2001) described her clinical work with a young adolescent girl, Chelsea, who was undergoing aggressive treatment for cancer. Chelsea drew on the expressions of strength embedded in the song to express her own will to survive. Her song exemplifies the FITB technique, as she only replaces a small number of single words (underlined below) with her own to express her intention to 'fight' and survive the disease. For example, she rewrites: 'As long as I know how to fight, I know I'll be alive' (the underlined words are the only new words in these two lyrics). When Chelsea retains the words 'oh now go, walk out the door, just turn around now, you're not welcome anymore', the 'you're' is referring to the disease, not an intimate partner as in the original song.

Ledger's example is contrasted with Glassman's (1991) in-depth case study of a young woman, Lori, who had received a traumatic brain injury. Lori engaged in a therapeutic process of exploring and accepting her current circumstances and discovering her new place in the world. Lori replaces whole phrases in the song with her own, while retaining those words or lyrics that resonated with her. With the words 'I Will Survive', Glassman asserts that Lori demonstrated an increased awareness of the self and a 'strong will to survive her ordeal' (p. 151). Lori writes 'Now you see me, somebody new / More optimistic, positive about what I can do'.

Derrington (2011) describes how song parodies may just emerge spontaneously from the singing of pre-composed music. Derrington accompanied John, a young adolescent boy who had been excluded from mainstream schools for anti-social behavior, while he sang along to his preferred music. Quite spontaneously, John began to improvise lyrics, replacing the original lyrics with his own in real time. Unlike other parodies described in the literature where lyrics were written down on paper through brainstorming and reflective processes, this parody was created in the moment as the thoughts, images, and feelings arose in John spontaneously.

The process of creating a song parody is similar to FITB, except that in song parody more time is needed within the session to shape the lyrics (Figure 9.2). Following the warm-up and introductions, the therapist will play through the original song again to prime the songwriter and to give him an opportunity to connect with the material expressed in its lyrics and music. The therapist may have selected a song to parody prior to the session with a predetermined theme to explore, or may do so after the commencement of the session. The therapist may or may not involve the songwriter in the song selection process. The songwriter's own experiences, feelings, reflections, and perspectives on the given theme are explored, or his own story is recreated, supported by the therapist. These stories and

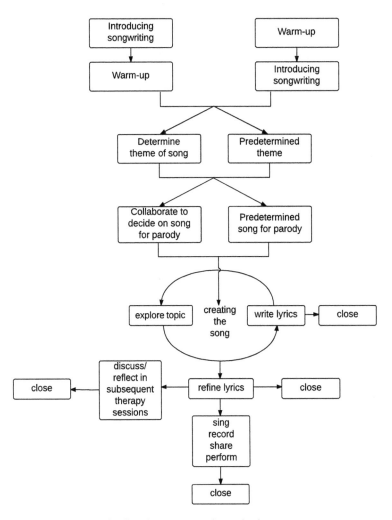

Figure 9.2   Steps involved in the song parody method

experiences are then transformed into song lyrics. The songwriting process may finish here, or may continue through a process of refinement where there are further opportunities for reflecting on the issues being expressed in the song. The song may have an extended life through a private or public performance, undertaking a recording of the song, or through the process of it being shared with others. The song may also be discussed and reflected upon in subsequent therapy sessions with the music therapist or with other therapists such as a psychotherapist or social worker.

Clinicians may choose this approach when:

1. The pre-existing song expresses an emotion, situation, issue, or story that resonates with that of the songwriter;
2. The songwriter's musical identity is strongly represented in the pre-existing song and it is therefore therapeutically important to reinforce this;
3. The songwriter's cognitive or communication skills are more suited to song parody than freely composed songs; or
4. The time available to create songs is limited.

Strategic songwriting

In strategic songwriting (Dalton & Krout, 2014; Krout, 2005), the therapist specifically composes songs for a therapeutic context or for a specific songwriter or group of songwriters. The pre-composed song contains lyrics that are likely to stimulate reflection on the subject, and the music will evoke an emotional response and prime the songwriters to be open to the therapist's targeted discussions. Using the same therapeutic approach as song parody, the songwriter or group of songwriters rewrite the verses to the song to either tell their stories or express their individual feelings. Strategic songwriting has been used with an adult man with developmental delay and autism (Fischer, 1991), children and adolescents who are bereaved (Dalton & Krout, 2006, 2014; Krout, 2005, 2011), and adults diagnosed with substance use disorder (Reitman, 2011).

Dalton and Krout (2014) created an integrative songwriting model (Figure 9.3) that utilizes the strategic songwriting approach across a seven-session program to guide the group participants through a grieving process (Dalton & Krout, 2005, 2006). Five song structures with a pre-composed chorus created by Dalton (2012) are used, with each song embodying a different progressive theme related to the grieving process (Dalton & Krout, 2014). Using the pre-composed songs as the basis for the groups provides a focus for each session, guiding the group participants through the process of describing what happened, sharing emotions related to loss, remembering significant memories, expressing attempts to move on, and then looking ahead to a new life while keeping the memory of the lost relative alive.

Reitman (2011) uses a similar approach with adults diagnosed with substance use disorder. In his work, the therapist composed blues songs targeting a specific therapeutic issue. Group participants worked together

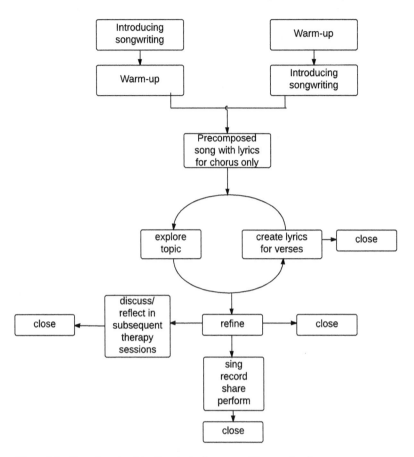

Figure 9.3 Steps involved in the strategic songwriting method

to complete the lyrics while simultaneously working through a process. For example, in protocol 1, 'Identifying the consequences of addiction', Reitman creates a three-verse blues song where the first verse identifies the consequences of addiction, the second verse identifies the behaviors that maintain the addiction, and the third verse identifies the behaviors that will assist in maintaining sobriety (Reitman, 2011).

Like other songwriting methods, the session begins with an introduction and a warm-up activity. The therapist then introduces the song she has composed for the songwriting session and explains that the chorus will remain the same (unless a songwriter has specific reasons for changing it). She explains that the verses in the song presented would be rewritten to fit the experiences and process of the songwriter (or songwriters, if in a group). The therapist then facilitates the exploration and lyric writing process. The session may end after the song has been composed, or the song may be refined, discussed, and reflected upon in subsequent sessions, and/or sung, recorded, performed, or shared with others.

Strategic reasons for selecting methods that emphasize lyric creation

There are several advantages in selecting methods that emphasize lyric creation, mainly because of the specific strengths that these methods present.

Therapist can control and manipulate the ratio of original words to new words

The first strength of lyric creation methods relates to the extent to which the therapist can control and manipulate the process to ensure that the songwriters experience success. Significant developmental delay, cognitive impairments, and speech and language delay can impact the ease with which songwriters can create a song (Baker, 2005; Baker et al., 2005a; Glassman, 1991; Hong & Choi, 2011; Robb, 1996; Silber & Hes, 1995). To ensure that the songwriting process is accessible to these people with significant impairments, the therapist can 'blank out' a finite number of words so that the songwriter focuses on addressing the target therapeutic issues without the need for extensive writing of lyrics or music creation. Alternatively, the therapist can control the ratio of original words and new lyrics to accommodate the developmental, cognitive, and speech and language challenges with which the songwriter presents. In variations to these approaches, the clinician identifies key words or statements offered by the songwriter and then incorporates or inserts these within the lyrics of the original song. This has been illustrated (Baker, 2005) through a vignette of two young men with severe traumatic brain injuries, who had been hospitalized for several years.

The song creation by Daniel and Craig illustrates the outcome of a collaboration I facilitated between these two men with traumatic brain injuries. Both men had sustained injuries resulting in severe physical disabilities. They were not able to stand even when being physically assisted by others, and were completely dependent on others for all aspects of their care. Although they were non-verbal, Daniel and Craig were able to communicate using alphabet boards – albeit slowly – and able to nod and shake their heads to answer questions. At the time

I brought these two men together, they had been sharing a hospital room for a number of months and yet had never attempted to communicate with each other. I wondered what it might be like to be either Daniel or Craig, sharing a private space (a bedroom) with another person for months on end and yet knowing virtually nothing about that person. I also wondered what they would experience on a weekend in the absence of the hustle and bustle of therapy staff and when contact with others was centered on showering and dressing. Concerned for the well-being of these two men, I initiated joint music therapy sessions and attempted to establish a meaningful co-patient relationship between them, with songwriting functioning as the bridge.

Given significant issues with short-term memory and fatigue, which are typical of people with such severe injuries, I began by offering suggestions – potential topics for the song and some suggested popular songs to parody – to give the collaboration some momentum. These were based on my knowledge of their leisure interests and musical preferences. From my suggestions, the Ford Falcon was selected as the song topic. Craig spelt out 'Sweet Child of Mine' on his alphabet board, so after some discussion we titled the song 'Sweet Ford of Mine' and planned to set the text to the well-known Guns n' Roses song.

The collaboration emerged as Craig and Daniel offered descriptions of an 'ideal' Ford Falcon. At times they disagreed, although I was able to accommodate all of their ideas rather than making 'forced' choices from the list they generated. I constructed the lyrics of the song using the same words offered by Craig and Daniel, always 'checking in' with them that they were happy with what I suggested. As neither of these males could vocalize or sing, I made a recording of the song for them, and it was played regularly for family and friends (Figure 9.4).

Functions as a primer and an ice-breaker or warm-up

When commencing a session where the clinician intends to introduce songwriting approaches that demand substantial musical and lyrical input from the songwriter, starting the session with an FITB or parody can focus the songwriters and prime them (Klauer & Musch, 2003) cognitively and emotionally for the issues to be addressed during the remainder of the session. The FITB or parody process may bring emotions, memories, and thoughts that were hidden in the unconscious or pre-conscious into conscious awareness. The songwriters may identify with the lyrics and/or be emotionally aroused by the music and then adapt the song to express their own needs and context. This process primes them for a deeper exploration through the creation of an original song.

"Oh Sweet Ford of Mine"

Verse 1:
The best car in the world is the Ford
Especially the XXGT and XM
Large and roomy, not too squashy
Covered in vinyl, hot and sticky

Chorus:
Oh Sweet Ford of Mine
Oh Sweet Ford of Mine

Verse 2:
As we went fast along the road
The powerful engine would roar
Because of the single or double bumper carbie
We'd go so fast we'd break the law

Verse 3:
They're good value if they're fast and have a nice interior
And are good value if they haven't clocked up much mileage
If they haven't got much rust they could last forever
The Ford Falcon I definitely our DREAM car!!!!

Figure 9.4   Example of song parody
Source: Baker, 2005, p. 156. Reprinted with permission from Jessica Kingsley Publishers.

Demystifies the songwriting process

Because the very thought of creating a song can be anxiety-provoking for those who view themselves as non-musicians (Baker & MacDonald, 2013b), demystifying the often perceived notion that songwriting is only for the talented may be needed. FITB, parody, and strategic songwriting can function as preparation for original songwriting by illustrating that, with the support of a therapist, anyone can create a song that has personal meaning (even if it isn't a hit!). The safety and predictability of the predetermined song structure and the minimal effort required to replace a finite number of words or lyrics removes some of the trepidation associated with engaging in an unknown activity. Songwriters become comfortable with songwriting as a method by experiencing the self-exploration process and the subsequent transformation of their thoughts, feelings, experiences, and stories into meaningful lyrics.

Builds songwriting skills

Songwriting calls for creative action, opening the self to a therapeutic process, using metaphor, sharing the self with others, being courageous, telling one's own story, and making music. Even experienced songwriters argue that songwriting is a craft that one learns, rather than being 'born' with the talent and ability (Zollo, 1997). Songwriters in therapeutic contexts rarely present with previously acquired songwriting skills. FITB and parody present opportunities to be introduced to and to practice these lyric creation skills, thereby building songwriting skills.

Suitable for developing rapport early on in therapeutic relationship

Therapeutic relationships are integral for ensuring that effective therapeutic processes emerge. Depending upon a person's age, previous experiences of relationships, gender, diagnosis, personality, and cognitive abilities, the therapist may need to invest significant amounts of time to establish sufficiently strong therapeutic relationships. FITB and parody approaches can function to build rapport between the songwriters and the therapist. Beginning with a parody that might be about some light or nonsense topic, such as the hospital food, may be a starting point for some. For those songwriters who are feeling safe and comfortable within the therapeutic space, the parody approach permits varying degrees of disclosure with the songwriters actively controlling and limiting the amount and depth of what is shared. At the same time, they can still create a song that holds strong meaning. As rapport and trust develop, the songwriter can engage in more personally challenging songwriting experiences where trust and safety are integral to the success of the process.

Suitable for brief therapy models

In some therapeutic contexts, environmental factors – such as the organization's therapeutic orientation, program timetabling, budgetary constraints, maximum length of stay allowed to the patient (Baker, 2013b), whether group attendance is open[3] (Silverman, 2009), or whether the group of songwriters is coming together for a single session (Baker et al., 2012; Krout, 2011) – result in the need to implement brief therapy models (one to three sessions). Similarly, because of the unpredictable medical status of some people – such as those undergoing life-saving surgery, people in palliative care, or people with acute mental illness – the clinician needs to approach each songwriting session as if it were the songwriter's one and only session. One of the strengths of FITB, parody, and strategic songwriting methods is the suitability for brief therapy models because the approach inherently removes the need to create music – it is 'time-saving'. Further, strategically selected songs dictate the theme of the song parody and therefore the theme for the therapeutic process. FITB and parody remove the time-consuming activities such as music creation and identification of a relevant theme, freeing up time to dialogue and unpack the therapeutic issues of concern for the songwriter.

Clinicians recommended that the songs selected for FITB, song parody, and strategic songwriting be chosen because they musically or lyrically express a feeling or context relevant or related to that experienced by the songwriters. As the songwriters listen to the original version of the song, they may be emotionally aroused by the song, or identify how their own situation, experiences, or feelings align or misalign with that of the original songwriter. Such opportunities enable the therapy process to address the core issues or commence the cognitive restructuring quickly, thereby accommodating for time pressures.

Songwriters need to experience success

Achieving a satisfying creative product is a challenge for many songwriters, and yet many therapeutic songwriting goals focus on developing mastery, self-confidence, and self-esteem (Baker et al., 2008). FITB, parody, and strategic songwriting enable songwriters to feel a sense of achievement and success as they shape a pre-existing song into a personally meaningful creation. In some contexts, feelings of success are needed for continued motivation to participate in therapy or participate in life more generally, and feelings of success are linked with long-term subjective wellbeing and a sense of flourishing (Seligman, 2011).

Deeper therapeutic songwriting approaches are contraindicated

When working with vulnerable songwriters, timing when to introduce more creative songwriting approaches depends upon the songwriters' emotional and psychological state. At early stages in the therapeutic process, songwriters may not be emotionally or psychologically ready for the full expressive capabilities of freer songwriting forms. FITB, parody, and strategic songwriting can be the preferred approach when a deeper therapeutic process is contraindicated. These approaches allow the therapist to keep the songwriter's processing at a surface level. For example, exploring issues about past abuse experiences may be too confronting to explore through original song creation processes, and doing so may lead to unintentional distress. Even though an experienced music therapist has the skills to manage this if it were to occur, sometimes avoidance may be the best option at that particular moment. Selecting song parody guides the songwriter to focus on a specific theme as embedded in the pre-composed song presented to him.

Some songwriters have poor concentration or poor delayed gratification

As FITB, parody, and strategic songwriting can be implemented in a single session, these approaches maintain the interests of those with poor attention and concentration (Baker et al., 2005a) and those who may have low tolerance for delayed gratification. Children (particularly those with attention-hyperactivity disorder) may not have yet acquired this important life skill, and parody may therefore be a quick and easy way for them to have gratification in the form of a completed song. Similarly, people with substance use disorder or other addictions may have difficulty rejecting immediate rewards in favor of later, better rewards. Song parody may be a useful method to employ in the early stages of treatment because the therapist can influence the duration needed to complete the song. By choosing simpler songs with fewer lyrics, the song parody may be completed faster than with songs that are longer, have several verses, and other such components. The clinician can therefore modify the duration of the delayed gratification through her choice of songs to be used in the song parody and the degree of lyrical material to be reworked.

Songwriters present with cognitive challenges

The structure of FITB, parody, and strategic songwriting may be preferable for people with severe developmental delays, neurodegenerative diseases such as dementia, or with brain injuries where cognitive challenges impact on an effective and satisfying songwriting process. Cognitive challenges include poor planning, problem-solving skills, working memory, active regulating functions, and metacognitive processes (Cicerone et al., 2006). Some songwriters have difficulties in initiating or generating ideas or thoughts for inclusion into a song. They may also present with an inability to expand and organize simple ideas (Baker et al., 2005a), and their information processing speeds may have been severely compromised (Sloan & Ponsford, 2012). These songwriting approaches allow for these cognitive difficulties because they provide a framework through which songwriters can structure and organize their thoughts. As they only need to create lyrics ranging from single words to a complete lyrical rewrite, the song parody method provides a story framework within which they can rewrite and shape the song's original lyrics to better represent or express their own feelings and experiences. The therapist can assist by breaking the task down into components and by eliminating non-vital steps (in this case, the creation of the music itself).

Suitable for songwriters who need grounding

Many songwriters who have a diagnosis of severe mental illness have difficulty focusing their attention and need grounding because they are preoccupied and consumed by their overwhelming emotional internal state. Grounding is a therapeutic strategy that aims to assist a person to detach from these emotions by having them focus outwardly on the present and develop a detachment from the internal world. According to Baker et al. (2007), the songwriting experience may focus on the present and help the songwriter become better able to tolerate negative emotions. FITB and parody provide opportunities for mental grounding by encouraging songwriters to focus on the here and now.

Pre-composed songs can be familiar and 'speak to' the songwriters

Clinicians I interviewed reported that songwriters select specific songs for use in parody because they already feel connected in some way to the lyrics or the song. In these cases, it is the clinician's role to assist the songwriters to determine which of the original lyrics express feelings that differ from their own. The clinician must then guide the songwriters to replace the irrelevant or unsuitable original words with their own. In such circumstances, it is not a matter of brainstorming new ideas but of refining or subtly adapting the original lyrics to align with the songwriter's own experiences.

Using pre-composed familiar songs leads to increased group engagement

When facilitating group songwriting experiences, clinicians may be challenged to arrive at an original song composed by a group within the given timeframes because each group member may have different ideas about how the music and lyrical structure should be shaped. This may lead to some dominant members of the group having a stronger voice, and other members may disengage from the process as a consequence (Baker, 2013a). Predetermining the musical structure places the emphasis on the lyric creation and the dialogical therapy process rather than on the music creation process, and this can lead to increased group engagement. At the same time, the therapist may find that the group has difficulty arriving at a decision as to what song they will create a parody on. Again, some less dominant members of the group may be silenced and feel disempowered. In such cases, the music therapist can actually preselect an appropriate song for parody that is relevant for the theme she wishes to explore with the group. Baker & Tamplin (2006, pp. 204–210) and Silverman (2009, pp. 56–58) offer examples of a range of songs that could be used as a starting point.

Reinforces or re-examines the songwriter's identity

Exploring identity is a common outcome derived from the therapeutic songwriting process (Baker et al., 2008; Baker & MacDonald, 2013a, 2013b, in press). Rewriting the words of one's favorite songs encourages the songwriter to look at the issues through the eyes of the original songwriter, while simultaneously reflecting and (re)examining the self by using music that is associated with individual and sociocultural identity. Further, using the songwriter's own musical preferences for song parody minimizes interference of the music therapist's musical contributions, which are influenced by her own musical identity.

Strategic songwriting removes influence of a pre-existing relationship with a song

There is a risk that when a pre-composed song is used in parody methods, the songwriter's expressions and subsequent lyrical ideas will be influenced by the original songwriter's message. Further, the songwriter may have a negative or positive association with the original song, which again may influence the process (see elaborations later in this chapter). Strategic songwriting methods control the potential influence of pre-existing relationships with a song, because the songs are created specifically for use in a therapeutic setting and the songwriters will therefore have no prior relationship with these therapist-composed songs.

Limitations and contraindications

There are a number of limitations and contraindications associated with FITB, song parody, and strategic songwriting.

Familiarity with original lyrics influences the songwriter's ideas and expression

When rewriting lyrics of pre-composed songs, there is a risk that the son writer will be influenced by the content of the original song. The songwriter may become confused between his own experience in the here and now and that of the original songwriter, particularly if he strongly identifies with the message of the original song. Positive associations may limit full cathartic expression of really painful experiences, while negative associations may color his view of what is positive about his context and current situation. In summary, while this 'identification' with the content is one of the strengths of parody, it can also be a limitation when the songwriter becomes overly influenced by the original content.

The song product is never completely authentic or owned by the songwriter

In FITB, parody, and strategic songwriting, the song's musical structure is pre-composed, and a significant proportion of the original lyrics often remain unchanged. While the songwriters 'own' the personal expression communicated in the lyrics, they may never experience that the songs are fully theirs. Such a lack of strong ownership reduces the potential to receive maximum benefit from the songwriting experience; however, this compromise is unavoidable and an inarguable limitation of these methods.

Songwriters may not want to have their favorite songs altered

Many people have strong attachments to music and sometimes even strong attachments to certain recordings of the same song. For example, I have a strong attachment to Gloria Gaynor's song 'I Will Survive' but do not enjoy Shirley Bassey's or Cake's version of the same song. While the very notion of changing the lyrics to one's favorite songs may be appealing to some people and motivate them to attend and engage in a therapeutic process, it may be offensive for others. The latter recognize that their favorite songs are perfect the way they are, and this perfection should not be violated in any way by changing some or all aspects of the song. To avoid this context, the clinician may choose to parody songs that are outside of the songwriters' strongest musical preferences.

Limited ability to facilitate a deep therapeutic process

Some clinicians suggest that when songwriters merely change some words of an original song, as is the case with FITB, or when only occasional lyrics are replaced during a song parody process, the possibilities for in-depth therapeutic processes are limited or discouraged. A songwriter who has a limited number of words he can change may become so fixated on finding the right word to replace the original word that the therapeutic process of exploring an issue becomes secondary to the process. Conversely, it can be therapeutically beneficial to invest time in identifying the right word or phrase to accurately and sensitively describe their experiences. For example, when songwriters are looking to make personal changes in their lives, there can be deep discussions around the choice of words. Compare 'I should . . .' with 'I want to . . .' and with 'I will . . .'. The choice to include *'should'*, *'want'*, or *'will'* can stimulate deep reflections on the strength of people's motivation and readiness to change.

Some group members may disagree with or dislike the songs used for group parody writing

Given the diverse sociocultural groups, ages, and musical tastes of people who may form a therapeutic songwriting group, arriving at a consensus with respect to a song to rewrite may be challenging and has the potential to divide the group and lead to resistance during the songwriting process (Baker, 2013a, 2013f). Therefore, there is a real risk that a song parody process can be ineffective and potentially detrimental to the development of group cohesion. Clinicians need to be aware of the diverse musical tastes of the group and pre-warn them that it may not be possible to accommodate everybody's musical preferences. Indeed in such contexts some clinicians argue that the therapist should pre-select a song for a group parody experience rather than engage the group members in an empowering (but potentially disempowering) experience of choosing their own song on which to create a parody.

Using preferred music during FITB or parody may change people's relationships to that song long-term

The very process of changing the lyrics to a pre-composed song is likely to change people's relationship with that song forever. Every time they hear the original recording of the song, they will be transported back to the therapeutic experience of creating it. This poses significant challenges. First, it may be a song that represented a feeling, experience, or journey that the person has now put behind them. There was never an intention for the song to have ongoing meaning; it was merely a representation of a moment in time (Baker, 2013c). Similarly, the original song may remind them of the therapeutic process, which may have been painful (Day et al., 2009a). A study by Gleadhill (2014) found that when song parodies were composed in bereavement workshops for parents who had lost a child to cancer, the process changed their relationships with that original song long-term; it connected them to their deceased child. Some parents experienced distress when hearing the original song played in places such as supermarkets. Re-experiencing music that holds special meaning for these parents, in such a public space and without warning or preparation, took some parents by surprise and caused distress. Therefore, parody does pose some risks in some contexts.

Rapping over pre-composed music/remixing

Rapping over pre-composed music and remixing is a process whereby songwriters create lyrics to accompany a pre-composed rap song or pre-composed rap beats, samples, and melodies (Viega, 2013). Here, the emphasis is still on lyric creation, although the songwriter and therapist may add additional musical tracks and/or remix musical components to enhance the emotional expression and musical aesthetic of the song product. According to Navas (2009), to remix is to take 'samples from pre-existing materials and combine them into new forms according to personal taste' (p. 159). There are two distinct methods of creating rap songs to pre-existing music: rapping over pre-composed rap beats in synchronous time (or ST) and rapping over pre-composed rap beats in asynchronous time (or AST).

Rapping over pre-composed rap beats/samples/melodies in synchronous time

Here, the songwriters spontaneously constructs lyrics while the music is sounding in real time (Derrington, 2005; MacDonald & Viega, 2012). This approach, often referred to as free-style rapping, is grounded in both the music-centered approach and analytical orientations whereby the subconscious is allowed to flow as a stream of consciousness or a flow of thoughts, expressions, and memories. Such flow is a feature of creating rap music per se (Adams, 2008). This process of rapping over the top of music enables the rapper to process and voice internal struggles (Viega, 2013, p. 239) by tapping into the emotions in an immediate way (Derrington, 2005).

Working with young Sudanese refugees, Jones et al. (2004) found that free rapping over a techno beat provided a medium for the youth to express their tribal backgrounds and come to an appreciation of the diversity of cultures within the specialist English-language school they attended. The group took turns rapping into the microphone while other group members supported them by playing the techno beat on instruments (mostly djembes). Therapist-composed choruses provided additional structure and gave the songs 'themes' for the young people to work with. As many of these young people had witnessed abhorrent atrocities such as war and genocide, rapping allowed them to express their feelings in the here and now, without necessarily keeping a permanent record of the song. These young, mostly African-born songwriters were permitted to rap in English or their first language, or a mixture of these (as is quite common now in music created by professional songwriters from non-English speaking backgrounds). These young people were able to gradually integrate their emerging command of the English language into their rap material.

Viega (2013) reports on a range of approaches to creating rap songs with adolescent youth who were living in unstable socioeconomic neighborhoods of Philadelphia. Sometimes the young rappers would create improvised raps over pre-composed instrumental music. The user-friendly software GarageBand was used to create drum tracks via the electronic sampler. From here, rappers would record free-style rap in a single 'take'. Later – and integral to Viega's approach – there would be a production phase, where the musical elements were mixed, altered, and effects added to shape the young songwriters' 'sound'. What resulted was the creation of songs that were aesthetically pleasing to the songwriters and authentic expressions of their experiences and identity. Importantly, when using semi-professional studio equipment, the therapist can assist the songwriter to create a song that resembles the style and sound of songs that he might already have listened to (Whitehead-Pleaux & Spall, 2014).

The process of creating rap songs in synchronous time (Figure 9.5) begins with the introductory and warm-up phases. From here, a theme may be selected as the focus for the rap song and, usually in a collaborative process between the therapist and songwriter, a rap beat or pre-existing rap track is selected. The songwriter then proceeds to rap freely and spontaneously over the top of the rap backing track. If this has been recorded, then the recording may be mixed in the studio to ensure that the resulting 'sound' reflects the songwriter's intention. The process may be complete at this point or (1) continue to be discussed and reflected on in subsequent therapy sessions, (2) shared with others, or (3) performed in public or private forums.

Rapping over pre-composed rap beats/samples/melodies in asynchronous time

In this approach, the songwriters create lyrics before rapping them over the pre-composed music. Songwriters approach songmaking by creating and refining lyrics to authentically express their specific issues of concern. Drafts of the rap lyrics may be modified, added to, or lyrics deleted before the songwriter arrives at a final script. Such a refining process enables the therapist to facilitate a discussion and leads the songwriter through a valuable and meaningful therapeutic process. In her work with young people trying to abstain from drug use, McFerran's (2011)

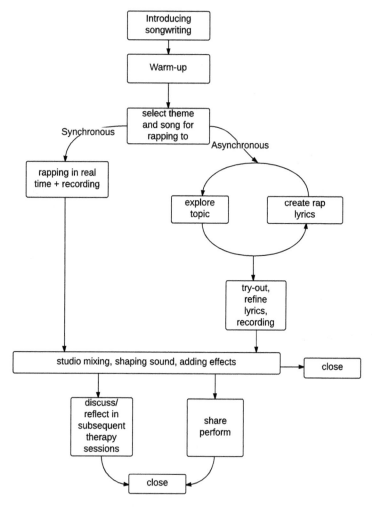

Figure 9.5   Steps involved in rapping over pre-composed music

therapy group members collaboratively created lyrics that were later rapped over a beat based on German Electronica.

Some of the young songwriters who worked collaboratively with Viega (2013) pre-composed lyrics outside of music therapy sessions. Viega subsequently assisted these young people to select pre-composed loops from GarageBand and added melodic lines that matched the lyrics.

Again, part of the features of Viega's approach was to employ production, arranging, editing, and mixing techniques so that the young people could add effects to the instruments and their own voice recordings
to create the desired effects. As the songwriters were using pre-existing
material, mixing with effects such as delay, reverb, distortion, and echo
offered the young rappers the possibility to refine their rap songs to
ensure authentic expression and to enhance ownership of the song creations. This is evident in one of his descriptions of a song creation process
with a young male songwriter:

> The songwriter came to the session with the completed lyrics for this
> song in poetry form. He chose the drum pattern and sound effects
> using pre-composed loops in GarageBand; the songwriter also impro-
> vised on a synthesizer in order to enhance the atmospheric production
> of the piece. I provided the lead and rhythm guitar with the song-
> writer's approval of the harmonic structure. The vocals were recorded
> piecemeal to help with his vocal phrasing. In addition, he added lay-
> ered vocals to increase the tension of the lyrical content. (p. 114)

Original music can also serve as an instrumental backing to songwriters
rapping their stories. The lyrics of 'Lost' by three young rappers (Viega,
2013) were rapped over the instrumental music of 'Drop the World' by
Eminem. Viega suggests that the lyrics and music created expressed a
fantasy of achieving power while acknowledging that with power there
is a 'price of self-destruction and violence towards others' (p. 80).

The use of rapping over pre-composed music is less evident in the
songwriting literature when compared with other songwriting methods,
although its presence is rapidly increasing. Recent references to rapping over pre-composed music include its use with children and adolescents who are living in unstable and low socioeconomic neighborhoods
(MacDonald & Viega, 2012; Viega, 2013) or families (Kowski, 2003),
adolescents who have misused drugs (McFerran, 2011), and adults with
cancer (O'Brien, 2012).

The process of creating rap songs in asynchronous time (Figure 9.5)
begins with the introductory and warm-up phases, and the selection
of a theme or story to guide the rap lyric writing process. A rap track
will be selected and played to emotionally and cognitively prime the
songwriter. Then the songwriter creates the rap through a circular process of a verbal exploration of the topic with the therapist or through
private reflection and lyric writing. The rap track is then played while

the songwriter tries out, refines, and then records his lyrics over the top of the rapping track. Studio mixing aims to create a rap song that reflects the songwriter's emotional expression and identity. The therapy process associated with that song may be completed at this point or may continue through ongoing discussion of the meaning of the rap song, its performance, or the wider sharing of the recorded copy of the song.

Strategic reasons for selecting rapping over pre-composed music

There are a number of contexts where rapping over pre-composed music would drive the therapy process for a songwriter or group of songwriters.

Facilitates 'flow' experiences

When songwriters rap synchronously over a pre-composed rap beat, they can get into the groove of the music (Sylvan, 2002) and experience a sense of flow. Indeed the speeds with which 'rappers' create freestyle rap lyrics are rapid, demanding that a stream of conscious thoughts be quickly generated. And all of this is executed with a lyrical rhythmic drive and rhyme. Clinicians I interviewed about their songwriting practices often described cases where transformative experiences happened during the flow of rapping. For example, a young 14-year-old girl, excluded from all mainstream schools for conduct issues, disclosed incidents of rape and abuse while rapping synchronously to a pre-composed rap beat. The microphone, perhaps symbolic of giving her permission to have a voice, was almost an extension of her and a vehicle for allowing the flow of her thoughts and feelings to be brought from her inner world to the outer world. Strong flow experiences during therapeutic songwriting were noted by Baker and MacDonald (2013a, 2013b) and were direct predictors of the meaningfulness of the songwriting experience.

Rap songs express issues relevant to marginalized youth

While many rap songs express anti-social themes such as violence, drug use, racism, and misogyny, many rap songs also make strong statements about oppression (social, economic, and racial), humanistic values (perseverance, love, friendship, and loyalty), and empowerment, or they may be critiques of behaviors such as social complacency, parental neglect, violence, and drug abuse (Tyson et al., 2012). Irrespective of whether the themes are positive or negative in content, they 'speak' to socioeconomically marginalized youth because they are socially and culturally connected to the songs. Therefore, there is a general recognition and acceptance that rap is an appropriate medium for expressing the challenging issues they face, enabling them to tell their authentic story.

Rapping doesn't demand strong singing skills

Apart from a sung hook, the majority of rap lyrics are 'rapped' – spoken with a driving rhythm. In rap the pitch content is secondary to rhythmic content (Adams, 2008), so that songwriters can perform their own songs even in the absence of good singing abilities. Performing one's own song and using one's own voice to communicate connects people more deeply to their experiences (Baker, 2013d), so practitioners inevitably aim to have their songwriters perform as much of their own songs as they are able to. Rap therefore lends itself well to being performed by those who create it, without being dependent on musical abilities. Being asked to sing, especially in a solo capacity, is exposing, placing the person in a position where others can judge him, which may ultimately cause intense anxiety (Baker, 2013d). For some young people, anxiety associated with self-perception of vocal skills is minimized through rapping rather than singing lyrics.

Rapping does not require good 'singing' skills, but this does not mean that a rap artist is not as talented as a singer. As one interviewee argued, rap is a craft and demands great skill.

New music is created when newly composed lyrics
are rapped over pre-existing loops

One of the features of rapping over pre-existing loops is that songwriters create personally meaningful and original songs. To some extent, music is not original; it has been borrowed, rearranged, reorchestrated, and reinvented. Pre-existing rap music or loops can be remixed and additional musical material added to offer the songwriters more ownership of the songs.

Rap permits breaking the rules

In the rapping of lyrics, many of the musical rules of contemporary songs (e.g. country and western, mainstream pop) are violated. As the rappers incorporate multiple syncopations and play with meter and metrical subdivisions of the beat, they 'break the form' (Sylvan, 2002). When working with young songwriters who may also be entering an individuation process, such rule breaking and experimenting with form through rapping with various rhythms poses opportunities for experiencing rule-breaking behavior in a non-harmful way. Similarly, the vocal style – an angry melodic yell or an aggressive vocal timbre and use of explicit language – is permissible within the context of a rap song, but not so in some other musical styles such as mainstream pop, and not in many other non-musical contexts. By welcoming such rule-breaking behavior within the appropriate context of music, rapport may be built between therapist and songwriters, thereby fostering acceptance and creating the conditions needed for an effective therapeutic process.

Rap music focuses on truth-telling

Rap music is a suitable genre for therapeutic songwriting because of its truth-telling features. Rappers value 'keepin' it real' and authenticity (Sylvan, 2002). Songs about personal experiences, descriptions of societal values, or stories of people within their community may be explicit, sometimes disturbing, accurate, and confronting. There is no sugarcoating. Fans of rap music recognize the truth-telling elements of the songs and can therefore relate and respond to invitations by therapists to create an authentic expression or story of their own.

Limitations and contraindications

Creating rhymes that communicate a songwriter's story is challenging

Creating (rhyming) lyrics that express one's story and that are embedded in a strong driving rhythm is a skill that comes naturally to very few. Even creating rap lyrics on a non-personal topic may be challenging if the songwriters have not had opportunities to express their feelings or stories verbally. The resulting song should be meaningful and authentic to the songwriter in terms of its content as well as in meeting their expectations of how a rap song should sound. Combining two challenging tasks – creating rhyming lyrics and sharing one's story – may be too demanding for some, and there is a risk that they will feel overwhelmed.

Songwriters avoid a therapeutic process when focusing on creating rhyming lyrics

By investing their attention in the creation of 'rhyming' lyrics, songwriters may consciously or unconsciously avoid focusing on the self and resist engaging in a therapeutic process. As Lightstone (2012) suggests, 'the opportunity to engage in wordplay can provide a convenient cover for them to continue avoiding themselves and their issues or otherwise manifest therapeutic resistance' (p. 49). The real risk here is that the resulting song creation may not have come from a transformative therapeutic process. At the same time, as is explicated in the different songwriting models, who determines what a transformative therapeutic process is? For some, the self-expression of musical identity – being a rapper – may be the aim of the therapeutic experience.

10
Songwriting Methods that Emphasize Lyric and Music Creation

This chapter describes songwriting methods that emphasize both lyric and music creation. Songwriting methods are influenced by improvisatory styles of creating music where music and lyrics are built from the ground up. Their origins are grounded in music-centered music therapy, although there are exceptions to these as is described below. The approaches covered in the sections comprise rapping or singing over original music, song collage, and improvised music creations.

Rapping or singing over original music

Rapping or singing over original music refers to, as the term suggests, song creations where the rap music is created and the lyrics are either rapped or sung over the top. Songs can be rapped or sung over original music in synchronous time (otherwise known as free-style rap) or asynchronous time. Synchronous methods of creating rap have been used in programs with adolescents from at-risk or traumatized communities (Fouche & Torrace, 2011; Lightstone, 2012; Viega, 2013) and adolescents with behavioral problems (Uhlig, 2011). Asynchronous methods of creating rap were reported to be effective and meaningful in the work with children with cancer (Aasgaard, 2002), adults with cancer (O'Brien, 2012), adolescents who were refugees (McFerran, 2011), and at-risk youth from low socioeconomic communities (MacDonald & Viega, 2012; Viega, 2013).

While the process of creating rap lyrics and music in synchronous and asynchronous time is often somewhat organic, the two approaches can be distinctly mapped out (Figure 10.1). Following the introductory

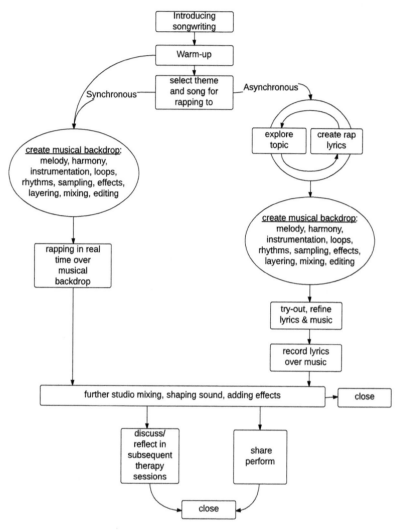

Figure 10.1 Steps involved in rapping over original music

and warm-up phases, the songwriter commences the *synchronous* creative process in one of two ways:

1. The songwriter may engage in a dialogue with the clinician to identify a pertinent theme or story to rap about and then begin to create the rap music that expresses the feelings associated with that story or theme (or purposefully juxtaposes it).

2. The songwriter may skip the discussion about the theme or story and begin creating and shaping a musical backdrop for the rap song, an approach that allows for a theme or story to emerge as the songwriter immerses himself in the creative process and moves into 'flow'.

During the music creation stage, melody, harmony, and rhythms are created and combined to form loops and the overall musical backdrop of the song.[1] The songwriter, supported practically and emotionally by the clinician, engages in studio editing and production to add sampling, effects, and layering to shape the sound. This process is important in helping a songwriter to create a sound that: (1) expresses his musical and sociocultural identity, and (2) expresses the feelings or reflects the story to be told in the lyrics.

Once the rap backing track has been created, the songwriter is then ready to rap in real time over his musical creation. Creating the music offers the songwriter space to ponder and process past, present, or future issues, arousing his emotions, and priming him for free-style rap (free association; see Chapter 13). While the free-style rapping is being created, the performance is recorded. The songwriter then has the opportunity to continue to edit, add effects, and shape the sound until he is satisfied with the product. The songwriting process may end at that point, or may continue if the song is brought to subsequent sessions for further reflection or if the song is performed or shared with a wider audience.

The process differs slightly with the *asynchronous* approach to rap creation. Following the initial phases of introducing songwriting, warming-up, and deciding on a focus for the rap, the asynchronous process moves to a phase of exploring the boundaries, dimensions, and events that underscore the story, while providing opportunities to engage in therapeutic dialogue with the therapist, either about the songwriting process itself (e.g. in music-centered approaches; see Chapter 13) or on the personal issues and the songwriter's response to them that are being explored (according to other experience-oriented methods; see Chapter 13). The therapist also supports the songwriter in creating rap lyrics inspired by or reflecting the issues or story discussed in an iterative process of writing, reflecting, and exploring until the songwriter has arrived at a set of lyrics he is happy with. Rap music is then created using the techniques described earlier. Once the backing track has been created, the songwriter 'tries out' rapping the lyrics over the top of the backing track. A process of refinement where lyrics and music are adjusted may occur at this point so that the final version of the rap meets the songwriter's needs and level of satisfaction. The final version is then recorded and edited until an aesthetically pleasing product (from the songwriter's perspective) has been achieved. In some cases, the song will be brought to future therapy sessions for further reflection and/or shared with a wider audience.

Viega (2013) and Whitehead-Pleaux and Spall (2014) provide examples of how studio techniques can increase the experience for people when creating asynchronously composed songs. Viega describes the process of composing a song titled 'Reek Mugga', which was created within a single therapy session. In this creative process, the songwriter improvised raps over the music he created during the session. Viega's role was to ensure that the songwriter maintained 'flow' by providing technical assistance in the recording, production, and editing of the song. Elements of pastiche (see later in this chapter) are also evident because the songwriter's vocal delivery emulates his favorite artist, Roscoe Dash. Viega suggests that this was driven by a desire to 'escape the confines of his daily life by taking on the role of his favorite rapper who has access to power and influence over others' (p. 99). At the same time, the music – rhythm and melodic/harmonic textures – 'contain' the songwriter.

One clinician I interviewed described working with a young boy identified as at-risk. The songwriter used his songwriting experiences to experiment with different ways of being, different identities. The therapist quotes:

> There's one kid who had a real raw talent for rapping, but everything he rapped about was this improvised, very nasty, adolescent potty humor and sex humor . . . There was one day when I put Auto-Tune on his voice where all of a sudden this sensitive lover character came out. Then he started channeling 'R Kelly' (an American rhythm & blues artist) and 'Drake' (an in-between artist of rap and rhythm & blues). He began to experiment with this kind of character . . . to be more authentic with his expression. It was a really interesting dynamic and his songs are quite unique. I think I did six to seven sessions with him and there's this general progression of the improvisations moving from this very adolescent thing. Now it never reaches a sense of depth – they're just exploring these characters in such a juvenile way. But there was a definite shift.

Sadnovik (2014) rightly indicates that recording processes can be either process-oriented or product-oriented. In process-oriented recording, the quality of the song product is not the focus of the session, but may be an invaluable component of the process as the songwriter communicates his story. For example, recording and then replaying the song provides possibilities to reflect and view the expressions from alternative perspectives. Conversely, in product-oriented songwriting, the therapist and songwriter work collaboratively toward transforming the creative expressions into an aesthetic work of art. The process is art-driven and the aesthetics of the final product is critical. When these songs are played back to the songwriter, the focus is on assisting with self-awareness and self-esteem as the songwriter is able to hear himself as an artist.

Strategic reasons for rapping over original music

Five of the advantages of creating rap lyrics over pre-existing music (outlined on pages 120–122 in the previous chapter) apply when considering incorporating rapping over original music into therapeutic practice. To avoid repetition, these are just listed here for reference:

1. Rapping facilitates 'flow' experiences;
2. Rap songs express issues relevant to marginalized youth;
3. Rapping doesn't demand strong singing skills;
4. Rap permits breaking the rules;
5. Rap music focuses on truth-telling.

In addition to these, I have added three additional reasons for selecting rapping over original music.

Creating the original music increases authenticity and truth-telling

When original music is created either in-the-moment (synchronous) or gradually composed for the specific purpose of rapping over the top (asynchronous), there is an enhanced authenticity to the song creation process. It truly comes from within the songwriters; it connects them with their musical identity and contributes to ensuring that the music adequately expresses the songwriters' thoughts, feelings, and stories.

Creating original music increases ownership

As highlighted earlier, one of the challenges associated with parody and FITB is that the songwriters will not feel complete ownership of the songs because they include pre-existing material that they have 'borrowed' from another artist. By creating lyrics and music, full ownership of the song can be claimed. This leads to enhanced self-esteem as the songwriters come to realize that they can create works of art – something they can truly say 'they created' (Baker, 2013c).

Creating original music increases participation

Young people are more likely to be engaged and invested in the process if they are creating music, particularly in a group context where there is an opportunity to engage in music that is highly groove-oriented (Lightstone, 2012). Aigen (2002) suggests that the rhythms of groove-based music invite participation. Lightstone reflects on his work with street youth and suggests that using a drum machine as a basis for improvised songs allows the familiar musical framework and timbres to liberate his songwriters, because 'the comfort and familiarity it provides allows the participants to engage in rhythmically intense, life-affirming, and expressive musicing that invites movement' (Lightstone, 2012, p. 48).

Limitations and contraindications

Staying in flow, rhythm, and rhyming can be demanding

Because of the 'flow' of rap and because spontaneous singing/rapping may reach the core of the self, the songwriter may find it challenging to keep in the flow and rhythm of rap music. Commercially available rap music tends to feature lyrics that rhyme. Indeed these popular artists would have spent time shaping and refining the rap lyrics before recording them in the studio. In the therapeutic context, particularly those informed by music-centered or psychodynamic approaches, the rapping occurs in-the-moment, and may later be refined. It might be quite challenging for a young person to spontaneously create rhyme or stay in rhythm. What results might be authentic and meaningful, but perhaps loses the groove of the rap. If the product is unappealing and does not meet the songwriters' aesthetic expectations, there may be some negative ramifications (Baker, 2013c).

Song collage

Song collage is a technique whereby the songwriters use lyrics from a range of pre-existing songs and arrange them to form the lyrics of a new song (Baker et al., 2005a; Tamplin, 2006). During the process, the songwriters peruse songbooks, CD covers, or listen to songs and draw inspiration from the lyrics that are contained within these songs. Some of the lyrics may 'speak to' the songwriters, or they may find metaphors that relate to their own feelings, story, or context. Words or phrases are then selected and arranged to create a coherent story or expression. In the process of lyric creation, the songwriters may use original words or phrases or may rephrase or reword the ideas presented in the original songs for inclusion into their own songs. Schmidt (1983) presented a variation of this songwriting approach within a group therapeutic context. Her group members would each select one meaningful lyric from pre-existing songs, and then these were combined to create a group song.

Tamplin (2006) provides compelling cases for the use of song collage methods in her work with people who have sustained brain injuries.

One of the songs created epitomizes the song collage technique, because the lyrics can be traced back to the original lyrics of 15 popular songs. The song her young male songwriter created is detailed below (Table 10.1). Almost every lyric has been directly drawn from the original songs.

His song expressed his fears, sense of confusion, and grief related to his accident, and its subsequent impact on his identity. The songwriting process lasted four weeks, which gives a sense of how challenging this

Table 10.1 Lyrics created by the songwriter and their origin

Lyrics created in music therapy	Original songs
V. 1: Try to see it my way My life is changing every day My identity, has it been taken? I'm not half the man I used to be	The Beatles, 'We Can Work It Out' The Cranberries, 'Dreams' The Cranberries, 'Empty' The Beatles, 'Yesterday'
V. 2: All my plans fell through my hands These days turned out nothing I planned It's been a long hard year And people, they don't understand	The Cranberries, 'Empty' Powderfinger, 'These Days' Line came from the songwriter The Strokes, 'Last Nite'
Chorus: There's no one here to blame And nothing stays the same I'd like to dream my troubles all away There are many things that I would like to say . . . But I don't know how	The Proclaimers, 'No One Left to Blame' Luke Sital-Singh, 'Nothing Stays the Same' Wilco & Billy Bragg, 'California Stars' Oasis, 'Wonderwall'
Bridge: I'm sad but I'm laughing I'm brave but I'm chicken shit I'm weak, but I'm strong I try, but it's tearing me apart Chorus:	Alanis Morissette, 'Hand In My Pocket' Songwriter's own words but inspired by lyrics of Alanis Morissette The Cranberries, 'Linger'
V. 3: I open up and see The person falling here is me Never needed anyone's help before But now I need you so much more	The Cranberries, 'Dreams' The Cranberries, 'Dreams' The Beatles, 'Help' The Beatles, 'Help'
V. 4: Memories seep from my veins And nothing is the same The damage has been done My independence, it has gone	Sarah McLauchlan, 'Angel' Songwriter's own lyric Powderfinger, 'The Day You Come' Inspired by The Beatles' 'Help': 'my independence seems to vanish in the haze'

Source: Tamplin, 2006, p. 185. Adapted with permission from Taylor & Francis (www.tandfonline.com).

process was cognitively for this songwriter. While the lyrics were almost entirely borrowed from other well-known songs, Tamplin reports that the songwriter felt deeply connected with the song and experienced a sense of ownership toward it. 'He played the recording to family, friends and hospital staff and proudly displayed the lyrics on the wall in his room' (Tamplin, 2006, p. 185).

The process of creating the songs begins in similar ways to previously described methods, with an introduction to songwriting and optional warm-up (Figure 10.2). The therapist then guides the songwriter through

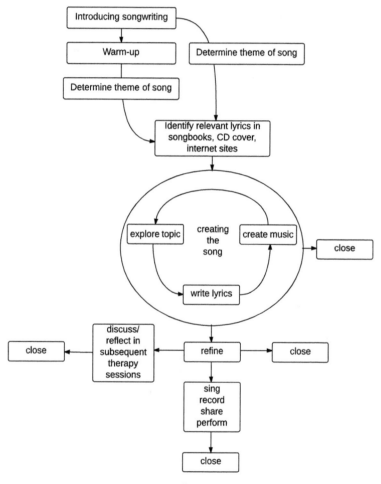

Figure 10.2 Steps involved in song collage method

a reflective process to arrive at a focus or theme for the song. The song-writing process then shifts to perusal of songbooks, CD covers, internet sites, and any other material of interest, to identify words, phrases, or lyrics that resonate with the songwriter. It is an iterative process in which the therapist supports the songwriter in fully exploring the topic, writing lyrics, and creating music, but when needed, returning to the songbooks, CDs, and other sources for further inspiration. The therapy process may end once the song has been created or may be extended through refining, discussing, sharing, performing, or recording the song.

Strategic reasons for selecting song collage

Tamplin (2006) outlined three predominant reasons for selecting song collage as a method.

Difficulty articulating feelings or fear of emotional expression based on cultural or gender factors

Cultural and gender factors (see Chapter 4) suggest that some songwriters are not comfortable with or experienced in sharing their thoughts and feelings. Engaging in a therapeutic process and creating lyrics for a song may be too challenging for some. In these contexts, providing the songwriters with opportunities to identify with pre-existing thoughts and feelings as expressed by other songwriters may compensate for their lack of experience or discomfort in sharing.

Cognitive difficulties including poor initiation and idea generation

Creating original lyrics can be challenging for some songwriters. This is particularly the case for those who have poor ability to initiate, generate, or develop ideas after an ABI or degenerative neurological condition. Providing these people with a pool of lyrics to review, reflect on, and then select for inclusion into the song can minimize anxiety about not being able to think of ideas and facilitate a deeper therapeutic process. Song collage offers them greater possibilities to produce something that is creative and aesthetically beautiful, which is at the same time personally meaningful and expressive.

Suitable for brief therapy models

The availability of time may be a factor guiding the choice to use song collage. If time is limited and the therapist believes creating a song will be important for the songwriter, song collage can move the songwriting process along a lot faster than if the songwriter needed to generate all the ideas himself.

Songwriters experience success

I have identified an additional strategic reason for selecting song collage – song collage provides possibilities to experience success. Creating interesting and expressive lyrics may be important for songwriters, but such creativity may not be a skill acquired by those with little experience or those who are compromised by cognitive impairments. By drawing on an existing corpus of song material, songwriters can incorporate previously used metaphors into their song creations and identify expressive ways of wording what they may be feeling or experiencing. As an outcome, the lyrics are expressive, present illustrative metaphors and imagery, and lead to the creation of a song product that the songwriter can feel proud of.

Limitations and contraindications

Lyrics from existing songs may influence songwriters'
ideas and expression

One of the strengths of selecting existing lyrics from a given collection of songs is that it may influence the thinking and process of the songwriters, allowing them to move through a therapeutic process more easily and resulting in the rapid creation of a song. However, the lyrics they are exposed to and identify for inclusion in their own songs may not be accurate expressions of their own feelings. Further, there is the potential to overly identify with material presented in existing songs, which may result in becoming confused between their own experiences and those expressed by the original songwriters.

The song product is never completely authentic or
owned by the songwriter

Although the therapist and songwriters co-create original music, the song's lyrics are mostly or completely borrowed from existing songs, and so there is a risk that the songwriters may not feel that they own the songs. In Tamplin's example in Table 10.1, for instance, only four of the 25 lyrics were not borrowed directly from other songs. There is a risk that the songwriter may recognize this and not consider the lyrics his own. At the same time, and as Csikszentmihalyi (1997) suggests, all ideas and creations are never completely new, but contain ideas drawn from previous artists.

Improvised song creations

Improvised song creation is the term given to songs that are created *in-the-moment* rather than by allocating time for a brainstorming process and constructing lyrics in a more formalized, planned, or organized way. At the same time, this does not suggest that the songwriting approach is unorganized or unplanned; it is more that the content is created in-the-moment rather than gradually built, shaped, refined, and edited over time. The in-the-moment song creation experience aligns with psychodynamic approaches to music therapy more generally (Chapter 13). Several researchers and clinicians describe improvisational songwriting methods in their work with children and adolescents with ABI (Robb, 1996) and those who display emotional or behavioral difficulties (Aigen, 1991; Derrington, 2005; Kowski, 2003; Oldfield & Franke, 2005; Tyler, 2003), who have been sexually abused (Henderson, 1991), or who are bereaved (Roberts, 2006).

There are four methods of songwriting evident in the literature and described by clinicians in my interviews.

Once-upon-a-time

Oldfield and Franke (2005) described the 'once-upon-a-time' method of creating songs, which they use in their work with children with severe emotional and behavioral difficulties. Their approach enables children to share their inner selves with the therapist through improvised storytelling. The therapist uses her therapeutic skills to facilitate the child's story-telling by beginning with the statement, 'Once upon a time . . .' and leaving space for the child to complete the statement (Figure 10.3). There is a continual dialogical exchange whereby the therapist prompts the story-telling experience through additional probing statements and questions (Figure 10.4).

During the improvised story-telling, the therapist and the songwriter create musical effects to match the story. For example, Oldfield and Franke (2005) would support a running action with ascending chromatic scales on the piano, or the child may narrate an attack by monsters with clashing cymbals. The therapist may repeat verbal phrases in the story (with accompanying music) to offer space for the child to think and reflect or to emphasize an important event in the story. From a psychoanalytical frame of thinking, Oldfield and Franke indicate that it is sometimes what is *not* said, is disconnected or unimaginative, that can be more important than the story as told by the child.

Therapist: 'Let's make up a story . . . once upon a time there was a . . .'
Child: '. . . a fish'
Therapist: '. . . where did the fish live?'
Child: '. . . in a dark deep lake'

Figure 10.3 Example of the once-upon-a-time method

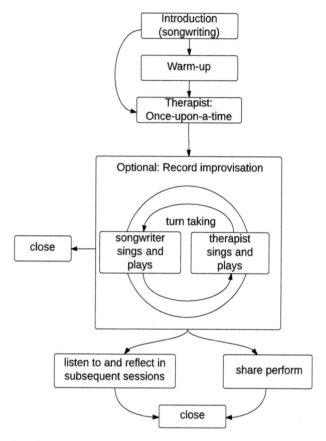

Figure 10.4   Steps involved in once-upon-a-time method

Improvised lyrics over therapist's musical accompaniment

An alternative method to improvised songwriting occurs when the therapist plays music while the songwriter spontaneously sings over the top. While this music may traditionally be played on an instrument capable of creating harmonic frameworks (such as the piano or guitar), it may also be possible to create a musical accompaniment using rhythmic instruments such as djembes, drums, and marimbas (Figure 10.5). From the perspective of those clinicians practicing according to psychodynamic or psychoanalytical orientations, this form of improvised songwriting serves to assist songwriters to access their emotions and thoughts in an immediate way (Derrington, 2005). One clinician

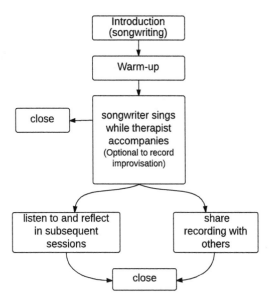

Figure 10.5 Steps involved in improvised lyrics over therapist's music

describes a breakthrough moment in her work with an at-risk male adolescent. Up until this pivotal session, the adolescent had been jamming with the therapist. During this session, he had asked the therapist to play some 'sad' music on the piano, and the therapist obliged. The adolescent then took the microphone and improvised in a ballad style about feeling alone and that nobody cared about him. This was the first time he had outwardly expressed his thoughts and feelings. Such a direct communication of his inner self had not been evident in his other music therapy interactions.

Instrumental/vocal improvisational songwriting

Instrumental/vocal improvisational songwriting (Robb, 1996) is a third form of improvised songwriting whereby the songwriter first creates and records an instrumental improvisation and later creates vocal expressions to form a song. In many senses this is akin to rapping over original music, since it draws on the same concept of creating the music first. For this method, however, the approach relies more on spontaneous improvisation in the creation of the music rather than shaping a rap backing track through processes of layering and mixing loops and so on. Robb (1996) suggests that this technique is best suited to those potential songwriters who enjoy and feel comfortable singing in front of the therapist. To facilitate this process, the therapist engages the songwriter in an improvisation using percussion instruments. Once an improvisational process is underway, the therapist encourages a vocal improvisational interplay between the songwriter and the therapist, perhaps beginning with vocalizing and moving through to singing words as the songwriter becomes increasingly comfortable with the process (Figure 10.6). Each time the songwriter sings a phrase, the therapist has an opportunity to respond with her own lyrics. Robb (1996) describes this interaction as 'conversational singing' (p. 35).

Lyrical narration/instrumental songwriting

Lyrical narration/instrumental songwriting (LNIS) is yet another alternative form of improvisation-based songwriting. In direct contrast to

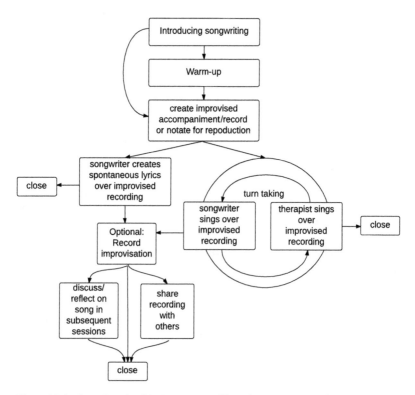

Figure 10.6   Steps involved in instrumental/vocal improvisational songwriting

the previous method, LNIS begins with a narration (lyrics) before creating an improvisation based on the story or feeling expressed in the narration (Figure 10.7). LNIS is closely aligned with the 'once-upon-a-time' approach described by Oldfield and Franke, although unlike the once-upon-a-time method the LNIS does not happen synchronously. The process is very asynchronous, with the lyric created first and the instrumental backing track re-created later. In her work with adolescents with ABI, Robb begins by allowing the songwriter to narrate an experience of the circumstances around the time of acquiring the injury. The therapist then engages in an interactive discussion about the music that would be best suited for this adolescent's story. Robb indicates that this form of improvisational songwriting reflects Priestley's Analytical Music Therapy model by offering a space for the songwriter to explore the inner self and facilitate growth.

Strategic reasons for choosing improvised songs

My research has identified five primary reasons clinicians would select improvised songwriting in their work.

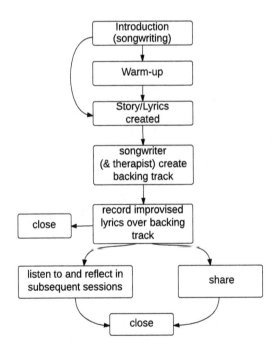

Figure 10.7 Steps involved in lyrical narration/instrumental songwriting

*Improvised songs create a musical space for exploring
and expressing the self*

At times, a songwriter needs to be present in a musical space that allows him to explore and express the self. Through holding techniques, the therapist can create a safe space for the songwriter to verbalize and create lyrics spontaneously. Some songwriters need this holding space to feel safe enough to look inward and bring painful emotions and memories to conscious awareness. It is only through the improvised songwriting approaches that these songwriters can bring these feelings to the surface and put words to them.

*Improvised, play-based songwriting appeals to younger children
because of its interactive nature*

Children are naturally drawn to interactive play-based approaches (Winnicott, 1999), and therefore improvised song creations that involve turn-taking are particularly well-suited for young children (Roberts, 2006). Improvised songs can be regarded as a form of play-based therapy because the interactions are spontaneous, free, and 'playful'. Such improvised songs are useful because of their potential for stimulating symbolic play. There are more opportunities for this form of therapeutic interaction than in other songwriting approaches.

*Improvised songwriting provides opportunities for therapists
to mirror and reflect a songwriter's contributions*

As this form of songwriting is spontaneous, the therapist has an opportunity to mirror and reflect the songwriter's contributions in real time. Such mirroring can take the form of lyrics where the therapist repeats, develops, or extends the lyrical contributions of the songwriter (Kowski, 2003) or musically reflects the emotions being expressed in the songwriter's lyrics (Tyler, 2003). Within a psychodynamic framework, mirroring can assist to increase a songwriter's awareness of the self while also allowing the therapist to contain and hold the songwriter (Tyler, 2003).

Improvised music can unblock songwriters' moments of being stuck

At times, songwriters can become stuck in their therapeutic process either because of defense mechanisms such as resistance or because they have difficulty using verbal dialogue as a direct path to reflecting on the self (Kowski, 2003). In such cases, writing lyrics before the music may be ineffectual in meeting the therapeutic aims. Because music conjures up emotions, images, memories, and associations, it can stimulate lyric creation by overcoming blocks in the process (Baker, 2013e). Improvised songs that contain improvised music have the effect of stimulating emotional responses that deepen reflections on the issues they would like to express in their lyrics. The music stirs the songwriters, thereby assisting them to move forward in the therapeutic process.

Involves collaborative music-making experiences
with songwriter and therapist

Some forms of songwriting involve the songwriter creating (with the support of the therapist) all or most of the lyric and music material. These methods focus the creative efforts on the songwriter's contributions with therapeutic strategies that are designed to ensure that the songwriter experiences ownership of the song. For some songwriters with low self-esteem and who have experienced dysfunctional early childhood relationships, the intense focus of the therapist may be too overwhelming for the songwriter. They are unfamiliar with experiencing 'unconditional positive regard' (Rogers, 1961). While many psychodynamic-informed music therapists might contest this view, improvised songwriting can be structured to be more of a shared collaborative process than other methods of songwriting, because it involves playing and creating the song together in synchrony or in an interactive turn-taking process. This creation of a shared songwriting experience may minimize the songwriter's feelings of being at the center of the therapist's attention.

Limitations and contraindications

There are three considerations that clinicians should be aware of when intending to incorporate improvised song creations.

Improvised songs may not lead to aesthetically
appealing song products

It is notable that with all the researchers and clinicians I have interviewed and in the available published literature on improvised songwriting, the songwriters tended to be children and, in some cases, adolescents. A primary reason for this is that the song product is not one that would be appealing to adolescents and adults. Adults would more typically prefer a product that contains a recognized song structure, whatever the genre. The songwriters may therefore have difficulty relating to improvised song creations. At the same time, as improvisation is at the heart of many music therapy practices for people with mental illness (e.g. Erkkilä et al., 2008), many clinicians may disagree with this statement.

Improvised songwriting might be too abstract for some songwriters

Based on my own experience and on the comments of many clinicians I have engaged with over the years, many adolescent and adult songwriters find improvised songwriting too abstract. They are unable to relate to this 'foreign' style of music and experience anxiety in not having a predetermined structure to work with. Lack of predictability is unsettling for many, although it does offer growth opportunities if they are able to experience anxiety at an acceptable level.

11
Songwriting Methods that Emphasize Music Creation

Mash-ups, pastiches, hodge podge, and original songwriting within known musical structures all emphasize a strong musical creation process. This does not suggest that lyrics are unimportant but that the music creation process takes on a more prominent role. These approaches are classified as moderately predetermined because they retain or draw on pre-existing musical structures, sounds, and genres at the outset of the process but at the same time these can be adapted so that the compositions are still significantly different from the original source of the music.

Mash-ups, pastiche, and hodge podge

A mash-up is a compositional approach whereby the recordings of two or more pre-recorded songs are blended together to form a new work. Available inexpensive music recording technology and iPad apps enable the songwriters to overlay the vocal track of one or more artists over the music of another artist. Illustrative examples of this in the commercial music domain are:

1. 'Stayin' Alive in the Wall': a mash-up of 'Stayin' Alive' (Bee Gees) and 'Another Brick in the Wall' (Pink Floyd)
2. 'Boulevard of Broken Songs': a mash-up of 'Boulevard of Broken Dreams' (Green Day), 'Wonderwall' (Oasis), and 'Writing to Reach You' (Travis)
3. 'Come Closer Together': a mash-up of 'Come Together' (The Beatles) and 'Closer' (Nine Inch Nails)
4. 'Smells Stronger': a mash-up of 'Smells Like Teen Spirit' (Nirvana) and 'Harder, Better, Faster, Stronger' (Daft Punk)

Within the clinical setting, the music therapist can assist the songwriter to select and blend pre-existing music to create something original and potentially meaningful on a personal level. While software tools such as Cubase, Wavelab, and Cool Edit Pro can mix songs together, more advanced tools such as Acid Pro and Ableton Live enable the songwriters to easily synchronize samples of different tempos (known as beat mapping). The resultant therapeutic song creations may also include the songwriter's own contributions, such as singing new or pre-existing melodies, adding rap lyrics, or by adding instrumental tracks, samples, or effects to the song.

A young boy with SCI created a mash-up combining the music to the Super Mario Brothers computer game with music from his video clips. The removal of his halo traction[1] caused him to lose his sight and therefore lose the ability to watch his favorite YouTube clips. Through sampling and combining his favorite YouTube videos in a mash-up, the young boy remained able to connect with his musical and cultural identity (Viega, 2013, personal communication).

As illustrated in Figure 11.1, mash-up approaches begin with the therapist and the songwriter listening to songs that are relevant and/or appealing. Relevance might relate to the songs being reflective of the songwriter's own musical identity, or the song might contain messages, stories, feelings, or 'sounds' that have meaning for the songwriter. The therapist then assists the songwriter to combine and layer aspects of the song to create a new song. One song might provide the basic structure for the song creation, while another song might contain a musical riff that is sampled and overlaid in selected places. Lyrics from songs or environmental sounds may be sampled, manipulated, or combined and then superimposed over the other tracks. The process becomes iterative as the songwriter continues to listen to his creation and searches other songs in an effort to identify other segments of music to include. Through this process, the therapist assists the songwriter to discover his identity or to explore the issue being expressed in the song. There is an optional step whereby the songwriter can add his own lyrics or music. Throughout the whole process, the songwriter listens to, reflects on, adds to, and refines his song. As with other methods, there is an option to share the song with others or to bring it into future therapy sessions for continued therapeutic discussion.

Another therapeutic song creation approach is known as pastiche. When creating a pastiche, the songwriter imitates or borrows motifs,

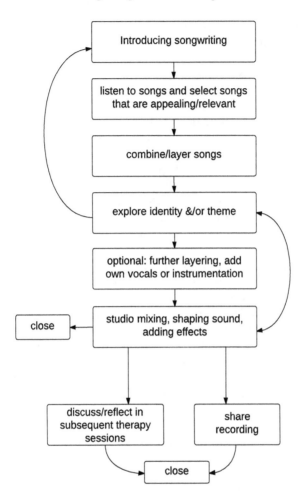

Figure 11.1 Steps involved in mash-up songwriting methods

techniques, or forms from one or more sources. There are two approaches to pastiche: imitation and hodge podge. Imitations, sometimes termed style parodies, are, as the name suggests, songs where the songwriter has imitated a style of music that can unequivocally be attributed to a certain artist. Here, a style parody is not merely playing in a certain genre such as reggae, but imitating a specific artist within the genre, such as Bob Marley. The style would incorporate the distinctive features of artists, including specific vocal style, a guitar riff, instrumental 'sound', and so on. In the commercial domain, Weird Al has several examples of this, to name just a few:

1. 'Why Does This Always Happen to Me' – an imitation of Ben Folds' style.
2. 'Skipper Dan'– an imitation of Weezer's style.
3. 'Velvet Elvis' – an imitation of The Police's style.
4. 'Twister' – an imitation of the Beastie Boys' style.

Hodge podge is another form of pastiche whereby seemingly incongruent motifs, styles, forms, and other components are combined. A recognized example of hodge podge is Queen's 'Bohemian Rhapsody', where several distinctive musical styles are combined.

From a clinical perspective, pastiche and hodge podge can be utilized when songwriters would benefit from expressing multiple (sometimes incongruent) identities. These methods can be a means of exploring different aspects of the songwriter's identity or 'trying out' different identities (Baker & MacDonald, in press). Roberts (2006) recounts her experience of working with 'Jason', a 10-year-old boy living with his grandmother while she received palliative care at home. Jason used pastiche approaches combining his favorite artists Eminem and Michael Jackson to express his stress and frustration at his home situation. Jason identified loops from Michael Jackson's 'Bad' to create a song that was similar to the original. Jason then added his own lyrics and melody to the song.

Original songwriting within known structures

The most frequently documented approach to songwriting is inarguably original songwriting within known structures. Here, lyrics and music are created from the ground up, but guided by pre-existing musical structures. The extent to which musical elements are borrowed and combined may vary from song creation to song creation. At the broadest level, overall forms may be drawn upon to create an original song. Most notably, we have the ABABACBA form, where A are verses, B is the chorus, and C is a bridge. Typically, the verses would either tell the songwriter's story from beginning to end via the song's verses. The lyrics and music contained in the chorus repeat at least once (sometimes with a slight variation), and the purpose is to carry the main message or theme of the song. The chorus tends to engender more emotional intensity than the verses. It is the connecter between fact and feeling, between the story and its perceived impact on the songwriter. Finally, some songs contain a bridge (sometimes referred to as a middle eight). Typically located after the second verse and chorus, it is musically distinctive from the chorus and verses, contains dramatic melodic and harmonic changes, and is emotionally charged. Its musical and lyrical purpose is to reflect on the subject matter and prepare the listener for a climax, create a climax, or introduce a solution or alternative perspective to the thematic material.

Numerous examples of original songwriting within known structures are present in the music therapy literature. It has been utilized in the work of adolescents, particularly those with Asperger's syndrome (Baker & Krout, 2009) and personality disorders (Rolvsjord, 2001). Original songwriting has benefited women who have experienced abuse, either in their childhood years (Day, 2005) or as adults (Curtis, 1997; Lee, 2007). In work with adults who have various forms of mental illness, original songwriting has been successfully employed in individual and group therapeutic contexts (Cordobés, 1997; Grocke et al., 2009, 2014; Perilli, 1991; Thompson, 2009). Hatcher (2004) employed original songwriting with a man presenting with a complex trauma, while Hilliard and Justice (2011) used original songwriting with an adult man receiving palliative care.

There are two ways to approach the original songwriting process (Figure 11.2). The first is for the therapist to have a predetermined theme that she considers would be useful for the songwriter or group of songwriters to write about. The second approach is where the therapist and songwriters use a component of the session to decide what the song should be about. Sometimes discovering the song's focus can be a significant part of the therapy process itself – to discover what needs to be addressed. Once a focus has been decided, the therapist facilitates a process of exploration, creating lyrics and music. This might be as structured as exploring and brainstorming, writing lyrics, and then writing music, or the process may be iterative – brainstorming, writing lyrics, writing music, more brainstorming, and so on. Following the completion of the song, it may be recorded, shared, or performed, or it may be used in subsequent therapy sessions to extend its therapeutic benefits.

From a clinical perspective, these known structures can assist the clinician to guide the songwriters through a process of identifying and expressing: (1) their stories, (2) the most significant or prominent emotional response to their stories, and (3) factors or situations that may impact on resolution and enhanced wellbeing. Despite imposing a preexisting structure, this approach still permits originality and flexibility through the creation of both lyrics and music.

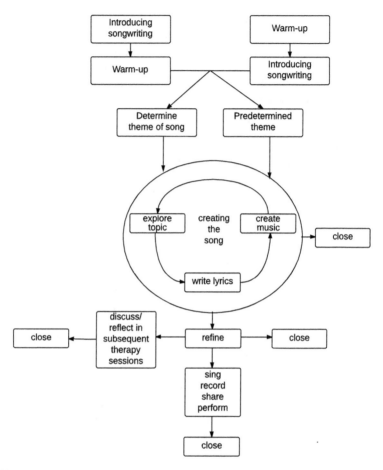

Figure 11.2   Steps involved in original songwriting

An illustrative clinical example of the way song structures can guide a process involved a young songwriter with a severe chronic illness, whose songwriting process was facilitated by the extraordinary music therapist Kimberly Khare from the United States. The song expresses the songwriter's story of coming to terms with her chronic illness using an AABABACA form. The verses musically move her story along, communicating her struggles to find her place in the world. The chorus presents a self-affirmation of her worth and uses a repeated melody with an upward motion to communicate her strength. The climax is reached in her bridge when a change in harmony creates a slight tension and strong resolution to intensify her feeling of 'shining' (Figure 11.3).

Miracle

Verse 2: I let tears do what they do and I just cried
It hurt so much inside, I felt the need to hide
So I let go of the pain, and I let go of the lies
Even though it was so hard, I now realize

Verse 3: There were so many things I could not understand
So many times I just needed a helping hand
But I know I can overcome anything
I have the courage to face what lies ahead of me

Figure 11.3 Example of an original song, 'Miracle'

Source: Permission to reproduce song given by Kimberly Khare.

The blues is a song structure that lends itself well to original song-writing (e.g. Silverman, 2013). It has been used with aggressive and depressed adolescent boys (Goldstein, 1990; Rickson & Watkins, 2003; Uhlig, 2011), adult acute psychiatric patients (Silverman, 2011a, 2011b, 2012, 2013), adults in detox (Silverman, 2011c), and people in palliative care (Dileo & Magill, 2005). Blues lyrics typically offer complaining statements, which make the form ideal for use in therapy. People in hospital sometimes need a medium through which they can complain. Dileo and Magill (2005) outline the structure of 12-bar blues music (Table 11.1).

A lovely example of a blues song was recorded on a CD titled 'Rehab Rhythm and Blues: Songs from the Royal Talbot Rehabilitation Centre' (n.d.). The CD has recordings of 16 songs created by people with ABI or SCI, including a number of songs composed in the rhythm and blues style. A song titled 'Spinal Blues' by Jim Blake (Figure 11.4) illustrates the opportunities to 'complain' about his life.

Dileo and Magill (2005) discussed several forms of original songwriting structures, including Latino forms of the 'son' and 'rumba' from Cuba, which they indicate are highly interactive and improvisatory. Such forms that are simple, repetitive, and improvisatory provide a 'holding function' (p. 240) and allow the songwriters to insert improvised statements into the song structure. Like the blues, the repetitive nature of the songs' structures provides time to deeply reflect on the songwriters' single key statements. Schwantes (2011) used songwriting with Mexican farmworkers living in the United States and studied its effect on the farmworkers' mental wellbeing. One song was written by a group of farmworkers who had lost two friends in a car accident. Drawing on culturally sensitive therapeutic approaches, Schwantes facilitated the creation of a 'corrido', a popular narrative song of Spanish origin.

Table 11.1 Structure of the Blues

Chord type	No. of bars	Lyrics
I	3 bars	First statement of song idea
I^7	1 bar	Usually without lyrics
IV	2 bars	Repetition of song idea
I	2 bars	Usually without lyrics
V^7	1 bar	New idea or expansion of original song idea
IV	1 bar	Continuation of above, possible resolution of issue
I	2 bars	Usually without lyrics

Source: Dileo & Magill, 2005, p. 241. Reprinted with permission from Jessica Kingsley Publishers.

Chanting provides an alternative approach to creating songs with significant meaning (Curtis, 1997; Dileo & Magill, 2005). The songwriters select word or phrases that are significant and meaningful for them. These words are then transformed into a chant, which Dileo and Magill suggest can then entrain and regulate breathing. Songwriters are lulled into relaxing as the repetitive patterns and drones are repeated multiple times. Dileo and Magill (2005) describe the case of Ana, a woman with ovarian cancer. In her sessions with Ana, the clinician played an Eastern Indian chant containing words offered by Ana (Figure 11.5). Ana was soothed through the clinician's repetition of Ana's own meaningful lyrics.

"Spinal blues"

Do you ever get angry when you're in your chair
You look out the window with a vacant stare
Well alright, don't get uptight
It's a long_____, long long way to go

Did you get your online lover and call her in
She saw your state so she pulled the pin
Well alright, another lonely night
Sitting in the dark, hoping for a little light

Have you travelled over mountains just to try and find
Some friendly people of the kindred kind
Well alright, aint it a pleasing sight
It aint, such a long long way to go

Do you ever get lonely when you're by yourself
Lying in your bed and you cry for help
Well alright, I do it every night
Hanging on your hoist, swinging in your sling tonight

Figure 11.4   Example of a blues song creation
Source: CD 'Rehab Rhythm and Blues' Songs from the Royal Talbot Rehabilitation Centre (n.d.). Permission to transcribe and print song 'Spinal Blues' given by Jeanette Tamplin.

"Ana's chant"

There is peace flowing through me (repeated three times)
Oh spirit around and within me

There is love flowing through me (repeated three times)
Oh spirit around and within me

Figure 11.5   Example of a chant song form
Source: Dileo & Magill, 2005, p. 250. Reprinted with permission from Jessica Kingsley Publishers.

Strategic reasons for selecting original songwriting approaches

Using song structures demystifies the songwriting process

Society values songwriters as artists with special talent, capable of creating songs that are aesthetically enjoyable and that stir listeners' emotions. It is for this reason that the thought of creating an original song is somewhat daunting to people attending therapy. Original songwriting within known structures can contribute to demystifying the songwriting process. The therapist can assist the songwriters to understand that many song structures conform to a formula, such as ABABACA, which allows a story to have a beginning, middle, end, and key message. Similarly, most harmonic progressions within popular songs are not original – all songs reuse harmonic progressions in some way. Therefore, illustrating that songs are based on simple harmonic progressions (e.g. tonic, subdominant, dominant) can also help the songwriters to understand that they can successfully create an original song. By demystifying the process in this way, the songwriter is more likely to approach the process with lower anxiety.

Allows deep engagement with and experiencing flow within the therapeutic process

Creating an original song from the ground up demands investment of time and deep engagement in the therapeutic process. In FITB and parody techniques, the songwriters are, at least to some extent, influenced by the lyrics and music of the song to which they are rewriting the words. In original songwriting, they are not influenced by other songwriters' experiences, but are encouraged to reflect and explore on their own. Creating a song takes time, and by providing space (through prolonged periods of time), the songwriter is able to sit with and work through his feelings, memories, and experiences. The process of telling his story and then shaping this within a song structure directs the songwriter to identify the issues that are most pertinent. The creation of the original music extends this process further as the songwriter shapes a sound that matches or expresses the ambiguity or conflict of his stories.

People experience significantly stronger flow when creating original songs when compared with parody techniques (Baker & MacDonald, 2013a). In a study of retirees and university students, Baker and MacDonald (2013b) found that when creating original songs within a quasi-therapeutic context, songwriters experienced several of the flow dimensions (Csikszentmihalyi, 1990): 'achievement without effort', 'a balance between challenge and ability', 'changed perception of time', 'increased energy', and a 'feeling of being in the zone'.

Health and wellbeing are mediated by frequent flow experiences (Asakawa, 2010).

Allows for creative, meaningful, artistic artifacts to be crafted

To flourish in life is to be creative and to create meaning (Seligman, 2011). Original songwriting promotes greater creativity than FITB and parody techniques because it involves creating both lyrics and music. It allows for people to insert their own 'take' on a story. The music created can reflect their personal identity or their creativity process. The songwriters experience strong ownership of and pride in their songs because they are artifacts that conform to the typical formula of a popular song, and are at the same time authentic expressions of their inner selves (Baker & MacDonald, 2013a, 2013b). Songwriters are often surprised by their creativity (Grocke et al., 2009) and the impact it has had on their mood (Baker & MacDonald, 2013b).

Original songwriting also opens up opportunities for people to experience honing a craft over time. The inherent benefits of working on a craft in songwriting has psychological benefits, the most rewarding being increased agency, which is of primary importance for adolescents (Aigen, 2005a).

Structure guides the songwriter to stay focused on communicating a story

As previously mentioned, songs tell people's stories. The verses structure the story, ensuring that there is a beginning, middle, and end. Within a therapeutic process, one of the goals of the therapist may be to facilitate the retelling or revising of a story (see Chapter 13). Thus, the overarching structure of popular song forms guides the songwriters to share their story and provides them with a clear structure and focus for ordering their ideas.

Flexibility allows for original melody lines and harmonic frameworks to express climax, conflict, and/or resolutions

Because original songwriting involves the creation of original music, this method provides for the songwriter to shape a melody and/or harmonic framework so that the listener experiences the emotional intentions of his lyrics. Parody and FITB approaches do not allow for this possibility, as the musical accompaniment is essentially fixed. An example of an original song's capacity to express the emotional intent of the songwriter was illustrated with the song 'Miracle' (Figure 11.3, p. 147). In the chorus of the song, the second three lines were pitched higher than the first three lines, and contained upward melodic movements.

This served to bring the chorus to a climax, reinforcing the feeling that the songwriter experiences herself as 'a miracle'.

Removes possibility of being influenced by pre-existing songs

As outlined earlier, one of the main contraindications of FIBT and parody is that there may be pre-existing relationships with a pre-composed song. A pre-existing song may stimulate a songwriter's associations with a feeling, an event, or a person. Alternatively, the pre-composed song that might be presented as an option for parody may be among the songwriter's favorite songs. Creating an original song removes any links to a pre-existing song and eliminates its potential influence on what the songwriter may be experiencing or feeling. In original songwriting, the lyrics and music are entirely internally driven.

Eliminates the possibility of changing people's relationship with a pre-existing song

In some circumstances, using a pre-existing song to parody strengthened people's relationship with the original song; the song took on a special meaning compared to its meaning before it had been used in the therapeutic context. However, research with adults who used song parody within a bereavement process concluded that using song parody can alter people's relationship with the original song in a negative way and lead to vulnerabilities outside of the therapy process (Gleadhill, 2014). For example, there were instances where the pre-composed song became a painful reminder of the songwriting process (the bereavement group), and the songwriters could no longer listen to this song. There were instances when the original song was played in public contexts, such as supermarkets where the songwriters were going about their daily business. On hearing the song, they were immediately taken back to the bereavement group. The process of creating original music eliminates the potential to influence people's relationships with pre-existing songs.

Moves people outside their comfort zone

Songwriting is a creative activity that has seldom been attempted by people when they are first referred to music therapy. For most, it is the first time they have been offered the opportunity to create lyrics and music – to create a piece of art that has personal significance and has the potential for contributing to health and wellbeing. Songwriting may also be an unusual experience for people who do not naturally share their inner selves with others; when they disclose, it moves them outside their comfort zone. Familiar existing song structures such as the blues provide songwriters with some security; the play 'givens' inherent in the structure of the songs allow for movement outside the comfort zone.

Allows for a songwriter's (musical) identity to be explored

In original songwriting, the high degree of originality of both lyrics and music allow the songwriters to express their own identity. The style, language use, meter, and flow of the lyrics created are generated entirely by the songwriters and results in a product that explores and reflects their identities. The freedom to create the music also permits the songwriters to have a high degree of control over all aspects of the song, ensuring that it explores and reflects their musical identity.

In the 1990s, I worked with Melinda, a 16-year-old girl with ABI following a road traffic accident. Pre-injury, she was popular at school with both girls and boys and enjoyed an active social life. She enjoyed weekly visits to the Sunday afternoon under-age disco, and her musical preferences reflected the 'Europop' style of music that was being played there at the time. Post-injury, she could walk with the assistance of an aid – but could no longer dance – and she had mild weakness in her left hand. While her physical impairments were evident, most problematic were her cognitive impairments. She had very limited anterograde memory and perseveration, and demonstrated no ability to initiate conversation. When responding to conversational interactions, her statements were short and closed. The main purpose of her therapy was to assist her in developing conversational skills so that she had topics to chat about with her friends post-discharge. Her songs were created in the 'Europop' style to reinforce her pre-injury musical identity, something that remained unchanged post-injury. At the same time, they enabled her to develop and expand her conversational skills on topics such as boys. The mnemonic properties of music and the meaningfulness of the process reached the threshold for memory, allowing these ideas and opinions to be more easily retrieved during interactions with her friends. I felt her motivation to engage in this task related to her knowing that she would create songs that were in her favorite musical style.

Limitations and contraindications

Original songwriting has its place in a therapist's practice, although it is not always suitable for every songwriter and for every context.

Original songwriting takes time

Creating both lyrics and music can be a time-consuming process even for the experienced songwriter (Zollo, 1997). Inspiration, incubation, illumination, motivation, and passion are not instantaneous processes. Further, a therapeutic process also takes time. The combination of songwriting and therapeutic processes is therefore indicative of a longer songwriting process when compared with a parody or FITB approach, which merely involves the therapeutic process and lyric writing. Sometimes a priming process of singing or listening to pre-existing songs, a guided imagery activity, or an improvisation may be needed to prime the songwriter before the creative process emerges and the core issue is identified – again, this takes time. In certain contexts, the therapist and songwriter are time-poor, deeming original songwriting as impractical even if therapeutically more appropriate than other approaches.

Original songwriting may be challenging for those with cognitive or language difficulties

Creating an original song, even with a supportive therapist, may be too challenging for those songwriters with significant cognitive or language impairments. Creating and completing a coherent story (lyrics) calls for intact cognitive abilities, particularly concentration and planning skills. Any impairment in these skills has the potential to slow down the creation of the song. Similarly, language difficulties as a consequence of congenital, degenerative, or acquired brain dysfunction also slows down progress in the activity. If the songwriting process moves too slowly for the songwriters, there is a risk that they will be bored and disengage, become frustrated and disengage, or become depressed and disengage. In such cases, original songwriting may be contraindicated.

Original songwriting may be unsuitable for those who need to be more grounded

Original songwriting is a free and flexible approach to creating a song. While this is definitely one of its strengths, it can be a challenge for those who need to be grounded. Having too much flexibility and openness may be detrimental for those who need to be focused on the present external world rather than becoming 'consumed' by negative feelings derived from their internal world. As original songwriting is more 'open' to an evolving process when compared with the more predefined structures of FITB and parody, the therapist has less control in keeping songwriters grounded. People who need to be grounded need to be presented with tasks that are 'safer' than original songwriting – less emotionally overwhelming, more concrete, and more predictable.

Section IV
Orientation

12
Outcome-Oriented Models of Songwriting

This chapter explores the ways songwriting is applied within orientations that are outcome-focused. According to Bruscia (2011, 2014), outcome-oriented thinking concerns approaches that lead to predictable, specific, and observable changes in a participant and align with medical, behavioral, educational, and cognitive–behavioral orientations. Bruscia suggests that therapy is focused on eliminating or minimizing 'problems'; the goals are predetermined and highly specific, and the outcomes are clearly observable and operationally defined as therapeutic. Within this paradigm, the therapist is recognized as and functions as an expert, planning the treatment approach for the participant based on scientifically or clinically proven methods. Further, the participant is viewed as a consumer or recipient of treatment. Music is understood as a tool applied to achieve a range of non-musical goals and typically functions as a stimulus to reinforce or to elicit measurable changes in behaviors or skills that are deemed to be of therapeutic value to the participant.

To fully explore the salient features of songwriting as practiced within Bruscia's broadly defined outcomes-oriented paradigm, I briefly describe the orientations and then how these influence the way songwriting is implemented in clinical practice. At the conclusion of the chapter, I summarize the different models in table form for ease of reference and so that the reader can compare between models.

Behavioral influences

Within the behaviorist paradigm, behavioral patterns (both adaptive and maladaptive) are understood according to early theories of learning: classical conditioning (Pavlovian) and operant conditioning (Skinnerian). As human behavior is learned, therapists can draw on the same learning processes that created the problem behavior in order to change it.

Classical conditioning states that when a neutral stimulus is presented just prior to a response, such pairing of stimuli will eventually lead to a reflexive response whenever subsequent presentations of that stimuli occur (Schaefer & Martin, 1969). In operant conditioning, desirable behaviors are learned, reinforced, or strengthened by providing a reward each time the desired behavior is produced (Schaefer & Martin, 1969). In other words, because behaviors are learned from reinforcement contingencies, changing the reinforcement contingencies that control behavior can also modify them. Today, the terms 'classical conditioning' and 'operant conditioning' are being replaced with 'contingency management' or 'systematic use of reinforcement'.

Only a few of the clinicians interviewed stated that behaviorist theories had a strong influence on their therapeutic songwriting practice. What was perhaps more interesting was that a number of other clinicians who claimed not to be behaviorists were using language that was indicative of behaviorist thinking. Words such as 'reinforcement' and 'reward' were being used intermittently throughout the interviews and provided indicators that the degree of subscribing to behaviorist songwriting practices varied.

Models

Contingency songwriting

Contingency songwriting is one approach to songwriting that has been employed within the behaviorist paradigm. Contingency songwriting is an application of any method of songwriting (parody, rapping over original music, original songwriting, and so on; see Chapter 9) where the songwriting session becomes the reward for the presentation of a desired behavior. Here, songwriting is used *in* therapy as opposed to *as* therapy (Bruscia, 1998). In a case study by Silverman (2003), contingency songwriting was employed to modify the combative and non-cooperative behavior of a man with schizophrenia. After identifying that participating in an individual songwriting session was of interest to the man, the treatment team developed a contingency songwriting program as a reward for non-combative and cooperative behavior on the ward and within group music therapy. Data on the man's behavior were collected on 34 separate days prior to implementing the contingency songwriting program. As soon as the contingency songwriting program began, there was an immediate and consistent improvement in his behavior in the group music therapeutic context, and a gradual improvement in his behavior on the ward. Importantly, the songwriter's clinical symptoms were so severe that he had no insight into his combative behavior. Insight-oriented approaches were therefore not appropriate and unlikely to lead to a change in behavior. What was needed was a clear cause–effect situation where the songwriter could act in a certain adaptive way which would subsequently lead to him receiving the songwriting session as a reward. Within a psychiatric or school setting, songwriting may be a reward for attendance, compliance, adaptive behavior, absence of inappropriate behavior, or higher level of effort.

Successive approximation songwriting

Successive approximation songwriting is a method of songwriting whereby skills or target behaviors of the songwriter are gradually molded or shaped through the songwriting process. For example, the skills being shaped might include turn-taking during songwriting or respecting other people's contributions during songwriting. As the songwriter's actions begin to closely resemble the behavior selected for modification, it is reinforced through some reward system such as writing an additional verse to the song, playing the song through multiple times, making a recording of the song, playing the song to friends or family, or writing multiple songs. Gradually, the desired behavior is refined through a continual reward process. Unlike contingency songwriting, the reward and general shaping of behavior takes place within the songwriting process itself – songwriting *as* therapy.

Lyric repetition technique

In the lyric repetition technique, the therapist suggests that a key point be repeated at least once in the chorus of a song that is being created on the target theme. This repetition highlights its importance and serves to 'reinforce' the statement. Through this repetition, the therapist encourages the songwriter to be more aware of the statement, and may increase the likelihood of a flow-on to changes in behavior, thoughts, and feelings. For example, some participants will communicate predominantly negative or sad material to include in the song. In such cases, the clinician will make suggestions or try to *influence* the song creation so that any positive (or at least the most bearable) statements are present in the chorus and are then repeated for emphasis. It is hoped that the repeated presence of these statements will change or influence thinking and behavior.

There is one contraindication that needs to be carefully considered here. If there are too many negative statements in the song, there is a risk that repeated singing/listening to the recording might reinforce the negative statements (Baker, 2013c).

Cognitive influences

Cognitive-behavior therapies (CBT) combine the earlier described principles of behaviorism with theories of cognition. The most significant difference between CBT and behavioral therapy is that CBT thinking proposes that our thoughts are an intervening variable between the stimuli and our response to it (Ledley et al., 2010). The way we act and feel is most often affected by our beliefs, attitudes, perceptions, and cognitive schema. They serve as a template through which events are filtered and appraised (SAMHSA, 1999).

Distorted or dysfunctional thinking is believed to underpin all psychological disturbances. Therefore, when a person responds to a stimulus emotionally, behaviorally, and physically, their response is a combination of the stimuli or the event and the person's interpretations of that event (Ledley et al., 2010). In this model, a person's thinking is understood to precede and inform feeling (Dilts, 2012). In other words, rather than a 'stimuli/event–response' relationship, there is a 'stimuli/event–thought–response' relationship.

In many cases, cognitive thoughts are irrational and can lead to experiences of depression and anxiety or lead a person to catastrophize his experience of events. These irrational assumptions, known as cognitive distortions, may be habitual and could occur when the world is viewed through a lens that is 'demonstrably false or incoherent' (Dilts, 2012, p. 206). Because cognition influences feeling rather than vice versa, a person's cognitive schemas require reframing before he begins to notice an improvement in his feelings.

Beck (1976) identified 14 types of cognitive distortions, which are summarized as follows:

1. Filtering: taking negative details and magnifying them, filtering out the positive;
2. Polarized thinking: thinking in terms of either black or white;
3. Overgeneralization: jumping to conclusions based on a single incident;
4. Mind reading: thinking you know things without proof;
5. Catastrophizing: expecting the worst;
6. Personalization: thinking that everything people say or do is a reaction to you;

7. Control fallacies: feeling externally controlled, helpless, a victim;
8. Fallacy of fairness: feeling resentful because you think you know what is fair;
9. Blaming: holding others responsible for your pain or blaming yourself;
10. Shoulds: holding inflexible rules about how people should act;
11. Emotional reasoning: believing what you feel must be automatically true;
12. Fallacy of change: expecting others will change to suit you if you pressure them to;
13. Global labeling: generalizing one or two qualities into a negative global judgment;
14. Being right: proving your opinions and actions are correct on a continual basis.

Unlike those who practice within the psychodynamic models, CBT does not explore the origin of cognitive distortions, and insight is only a valued outcome if it contributes to an increased awareness of a cognitive style or cognitive distortion (Dilts, 2012). The primary cognitive tool is restructuring, which involves a person identifying and reframing his maladaptive thoughts or the thought patterns identified by Beck (1976). The therapist assists the person to question his thoughts and to reframe them as irrational. From here, the therapist encourages the person to move toward constructive positive and adaptive thinking. In essence, CBT concerns the relearning of distorted cognitive schemas, which when altered to healthy rational cognitive schemas ultimately flow through to feelings and behavioral changes.

Cognitive restructuring

As mentioned, the main purpose of CBT is to facilitate cognitive restructuring, a process whereby participants increase their awareness of their cognitive distortions, are challenged to change, and eventually transform their dysfunctional cognitive structures (schemata) into healthy functioning ones (Twohig & Dehlin, 2012). Such cognitive restructuring involves first deliberately eliciting the dysfunctional thought patterns. The therapist then assists the participants to formulate rational responses to these negative automatic thoughts. By identifying and removing cognitive distortions, correcting false beliefs and assumptions, and reinforcing those beliefs that are positive and healthy, participants can begin to develop healthy patterns of thinking (Twohig & Dehlin, 2012, p. 137). This may involve identifying and recording cognitive errors, decatastrophizing situations, reattribution, cognitive rehearsal, and listing rational alternatives to their current thinking patterns (Huppert, 2009). Labeling distorted thinking is also a part of the process, including labeling 'all or nothing thoughts', jumping to conclusions, emotional reasoning, and 'should' statements (Huppert, 2009).

Problem-solving

Addressing poor problem-solving skills is a main concern for those practicing in the CBT model. Problem-solving is based on two separate, partly independent dimensions: problem-orientation and problem-solving style (Nezu & Maguth Nezu, 2012). Problem-orientation is the term used to describe whether people typically view problems as solvable challenges (positive problem-orientation) or unsolvable threats (negative problem-orientation). In contrast, problem-solving refers to the cognitive-behavioral strategies people engage in when attempting to solve problems. Both impact how successful participants are in challenging situations. D'Zurilla and Nezu (2007) propose that there are three main problem-solving styles:

1. *Rational problem-solving*: a constructive, systematic, planned approach that involves identifying the problem and potential barriers to solving the problem, generating alternative solutions, deciding on the best (cost-benefit) plan, and then implementing and evaluating the outcome of the action.
2. *Impulsive or careless problem-solving*: a dysfunctional or maladaptive problem-solving approach where participants impulsively attempt to solve a problem without taking the time to think through the process first.
3. *Avoidant problem-solving*: another dysfunctional or maladaptive approach to problem-solving where participants typically avoid attempts to solve the problem and overly rely on others to assist in generating solutions.

By increasing the effectiveness of a person's problem-solving ability, it is expected that symptoms of distress and incidences of relapse will reduce (D'Zurilla & Nezu, 2007). The aim of therapy programs is to enhance attitudes toward facing problems, improve efficacy of problem-solving skills, and minimize dysfunctional problem-solving approaches. I would argue that in addition to these aims, there is a basic need to be able to identify current problem-solving characteristics so the participants can learn to recognize them when they are occurring. Many approaches are habitual and require an awareness of these habits (without specifically identifying their origin) to have a chance of adopting good problem-solving skills and attitudes.

Psychoeducation

Psychoeducation is an evidence-based CBT approach that assists people with mental health challenges to cope with their illnesses (Lukens & McFarlane, 2004, p. 205). Therapists educate their participants about their illnesses so that they better understand the course of recovery and the potential for relapse. They also provide them with information about their own internal and available external resources. The theory holds that the more knowledge people have about their illnesses, the more likely they will succeed in living with them.

Psychoeducation is influenced by several psychological theories. Ecological systems theory is relevant in terms of how people understand their (experience of) illness in relation to other systems in their lives. Many of the psychoeducational programs are practiced in a group setting to aid this process of understanding. Group dialogue leads to social learning, increased support, and group recognition and reinforcement of positive change (Lukens & McFarlane, 2004). A holistic model of practice is emphasized whereby the therapeutic focus is on the here and now, the development of participants' competencies, and the promotion of coping behaviors (Lukens & McFarlane, 2004). Within psychoeducation, the participants and/or their families are in partnership with the therapist to maximize therapeutic benefits. Psychoeducation combines problem-solving and role-playing scenarios within a safe setting to increase understanding of how their behaviors – both the positive and the negative – impact themselves and others. The identification of personal strengths and resources are often achieved through narrative approaches that are effectively incorporated within therapeutic songwriting approaches.

For people with chronic mental health conditions, Bäuml et al. (2006) suggest four components of psychoeducation:

1. Briefing the participants about their illnesses;
2. Problem-solving training;
3. Communication training;
4. Self-assertiveness training.

These tasks are directed toward ensuring that the participants are informed and able to manage their illness, while also empowering them to take responsibility for their wellbeing. Psychoeducation also aims to improve insight into the illness, improve treatment compliance, and minimize the potential for relapse (Bäuml et al., 2006). The therapist aims to stimulate hope and reassurance, encourage personal exchange of experiences, and create an opportunity to experience a 'shared fate' with other group members.

Acceptance

More recently, the concept of acceptance has emerged as a critical component of psychological health (Wilson et al., 2012). The concept deviates from traditional CBT notions of trying to restructure or control thoughts, feelings, sensations, and memories, and instead encourages people to increase their awareness of these and accept and embrace them. It encourages people to identify and clarify their values and to act on them, and in doing so people live more meaningful lives (Zettle, 2005). Harris (2006) suggests people should embrace their demons, accept their reactions to them and be present, choose a valued direction, and take action.

Readiness for change

People's readiness for change and motivation to adopt strategies drives the transtheoretical model of behavior change. Transtheoretical models draw on several therapeutic approaches that depend upon the stage of change a person is currently at, including the cognitive-behavioral (Prochaska et al., 1994). When in 'treatment', Prochaska et al. outline six phases that people will progress through in their journey toward recovery:

1. *Pre-contemplation phase*: the person is not yet able to see that he is a part of the problem or solution; is not yet ready for change.
2. *Contemplation phase*: the person has begun to acknowledge that a problem exists, but is still not yet ready to initiate and follow through with change; is getting ready for change.
3. *Preparation phase*: the person engages in the identification of solutions, tests out actions in safe contexts (e.g. role plays), and formulates an action plan; is ready for change.
4. *Action phase*: the person and/or his support system engages the action plan; is actively changing behavior and avoiding situations where he may relapse into unhealthy behavior.
5. *Maintenance phase*: the person is focused on relapse prevention, and spreading the moments of relapse further apart.
6. *Termination phase*: the person begins to let go of the old self and put in place support systems that will assist in preventing relapse.

Several strategies are used to assist a person to move through the stages of change (Prochaska & Velicer, 1997):

1. *Self-reevaluation*: providing opportunities for people to discover that they do want to act out healthy behavior.
2. *Environmental reevaluation*: finding ways for people to realize how their unhealthy behavior affects others.
3. *Consciousness-raising*: increasing people's awareness through the provision of education and personal feedback about demonstrations of healthy behavior.
4. *Positive reinforcement*: as described above, creating opportunities for people to see that rewards come from positive behavior.

The 'readiness for change' approaches such as motivational interviewing are widely adopted in mental health settings, particularly for addiction disorders.

Models

Songwriting for cognitive restructuring

Songwriting for cognitive restructuring is the use of therapeutic songwriting to directly correct the cognitive distortions and challenges to problem-solving skills that people present with. Here, the therapist draws on well-recognized cognitive restructuring techniques and incorporates them into the lyric creation process. As such, therapeutic songwriting sessions typically have a stronger focus on lyric creation (see Chapter 9). Twohig and Dehlin (2012) outline several therapeutic techniques that are relevant for therapists who are using songwriting within CBT frameworks. First, the therapist engages the songwriter in a process of identifying, monitoring, and categorizing his distorted automatic thoughts. Such an activity serves to increase awareness of the presence of these cognitive distortions. The therapist may select a theme pertinent to the individual (or group) on which to base the song lyrics, and then use the brainstorming and story-telling phases of the songwriting process to draw the songwriter's attention to distorted thought patterns. Once these are identified, they may or may not be incorporated into the song lyrics. At this point, the therapist may explore, through discussion and lyric creation, how these thought patterns impact the person's life – the costs and the benefits – and helps the songwriter to understand and recognize that there is no evidence to support the thinking he holds. For example, a statement such as 'I have done nothing of value in my life' can be challenged and critiqued and then transformed into healthier statements for inclusion into the song.

Baker et al. (2012) illustrate how cognitive restructuring can be incorporated into songwriting with a group of people with substance use disorder. During the initial part of the session, some of the group members contributed lyrics that reflected unhealthy patterns of thinking: 'I wanna be high, so high'. The therapist (Gleadhill) engaged the group in a questioning and reasoning process which challenged the group members to really reflect on their statements. The therapist used this opportunity to facilitate a group exploration about the negatives of 'being high' and what the consequences were for this activity. Through their process of 'group problem solving and personal reflection and reevaluation, a consensus was reached to create a lyric "I wanna be high, on life"' (p. 327). The subsequent incorporation of healthy statements into the song's lyrics added additional cognitive reinforcement.

Reitman (2011) also employed cognitive restructuring songwriting approaches in his work with a group of people with substance use disorder. His insight-oriented method is used to challenge maladaptive thinking related to addiction and negative emotions, and to address self-defeating behaviors. Each songwriting task, whether original songwriting, parody, or FITB (Chapters 10 and 11), is goal directed and targets thinking, feeling, and behavior. Each song created addresses a predetermined topic area, either under the broad headings of challenging addictive thinking or lifestyle repair. For example, on the topic identifying consequences of addiction, Reitman uses a 12-bar blues FITB approach (Figure 12.1). He facilitates the group members so that they progress through a three-staged discussion: (1) exploring the consequences of addiction, (2) identifying behaviors that maintain dependence, and (3) identifying behaviors that serve to maintain sobriety. Following the discussions, the group proceeds to complete the missing sections of the 12-bar blues songs with lyrics inspired by their discussions.

Psychoeducational songwriting

Psychoeducational songwriting involves the creation of a song that is inspired by the content from a psychoeducational session (often in a group). Silverman (2011a, 2012) regularly employs songwriting within a psychoeducation-based session with people admitted to an acute psychiatric ward. During the sessions, he leads and educates the group members about their illnesses and the typical challenges people with mental illness may face when trying to live independently. The dynamic material that emerged from those discussions is a starting point for the

Verse 1: (consequences)
 Been down so low, I felt _____
 Been down so low, I felt _____
 I felt _____

Verse 2: (weaknesses)
 I need to look at _____
 I need to look at _____
 Need to _____

Verse 3: (strengths)
 If I use _____, it will _____
 If I use _____, it will _____
 Got to use _____, if I _____

Figure 12.1 Example of cognitive restructuring via 12-bar blues
Source: Reitman, 2011, pp. 25–26. Reprinted with permission from Barcelona Publishers.

songwriting activity. In creating a song, Silverman helps people to identify strategies for managing and coping with the challenges they have identified. These strategies are reinforced through the construction and repetition of lyrics within the song.

Psychoeducational songwriting was implemented during group sessions with caregivers of people with dementia (Klein & Silverman, 2012). The purpose behind the song parody was to explore the concepts of stress, self-care, and support. Participants were asked to rewrite the words of 'With Love from Me to You' by Lennon and McCartney (1963), drawing inspiration from psychoeducation about the stress that had just preceded the session. Continued discussion emerged as a consequence of creating song lyrics.

Transtheoretical songwriting

Clinicians who subscribe to the transtheoretical framework will use songwriting strategically to assist with the movement through the six phases of *readiness for change*. During the pre-contemplation phase, when the person is not yet ready to acknowledge that he has a problem that needs to be addressed, the clinician may approach the songwriting experiences as a rapport-building exercise. In building trust and comfort through sharing between the therapist and person or with group members, the therapist is laying important foundations for future growth opportunities. The songs that are created may focus on nonsense themes or on themes that promote opportunities for self-expression but do not directly address the target problem behavior such as drug use. Such a rapport-building exercise and a little familiarity with the songwriting process itself can lay important foundations that will aid the songwriting activities in the subsequent phases of recovery.

When a person moves into the contemplation phase, the songwriting approach becomes more focused on facilitating insight into and encouraging acknowledgment of his behavior. In this phase, transtheoretical songwriting may focus on describing challenging circumstances and encouraging the person to reflect on how responses to those circumstances positively or negatively impact his life or the lives of others. In the contemplation stage, the songwriter is encouraged to imagine a life where his behaviors are healthy and where he is benefiting from the positive outcomes this behavior has led to. Analyzing lyrics of songs and then rewriting them to reflect his context can bring about new awareness and a desire for change. The songwriting process becomes the vehicle for insight into thinking and behavior.

During preparation, the songwriting focuses on problem-solving, identifying solutions, and testing these out. Through discussion, brainstorming, and the writing of lyrics, solutions can be identified and the range and scope of solutions outlined in the song. The song takes the form of an action plan that may be later actioned. The therapist's role is to ensure that the songwriter is able to identify multiple potential solutions so that he can select the action plan that is most likely to lead to positive and sustained change.

Songwriting during the action phase is beneficial in keeping the person from deviating from the action plan. As he faces varied challenges, the songs created are reminders to stay focused on the positive actions rather than engaging in maladaptive avoidance behaviors. Group song creations can also contain messages of support from other group members, so that the person is part of a 'group energy' and shares a camaraderie that will sustain him emotionally during the more difficult moments. A continued supportive approach during songwriting would address the potential for relapse, which is an essential component of the maintenance and termination phases of treatment.

Learning and neuroscience theories

Emerging evidence of the human brain's capacity for reorganization has led to outcome-oriented thinking in the field of neurological rehabilitation. Music therapists who practice with neurologically impaired people will frame their practices around helping people to: (1) compensate for lost function, or (2) restore lost function (Baker & Roth, 2004).

Behavioral compensation is defined as the adoption and development of new skills by undamaged neural systems to complete tasks that were previously activated by now damaged neural systems (Dixon & Backman, 1999; Prigatano, 1999). The idea is that people's functioning recovers by changing the strategy or method of completing an action, rather than by trying to ameliorate the deficit. Examples of compensation include the use of walking aids, modifying equipment, and using diaries, or modifying approaches such as dressing while sitting down or using positive self-talk before undertaking challenging tasks. This allows the person to continue to function to his fullest potential.

The discovery that the brain is plastic and capable of reorganization led to a change in practice whereby rehabilitation focused on restoration of function, particularly in the early stages of recovery from neurological damage. In other words, rather than using novel or alternative strategies to restore skills, rehabilitation focused on regaining lost function. The idea is that the brain can make use of surviving brain tissue and undergoes reorganization so that lost skills are regained (Kolb & Gibb, 1999). Practicing a skill repeatedly contributes to reorganization by strengthening neural connections. Importantly, rehabilitation is more effective when the tasks are not just a repetition of the same exercise, but varied so that synaptic interconnectivity is promoted (Nudo et al., 2000).[1] In practice, it is preferable that rehabilitation approaches aim to restore function rather than using compensatory approaches. However, if restoration of function does not return, compensatory approaches should be implemented.

Models

Restorative songwriting

Restorative songwriting approaches aim to restore executive functioning following neurological damage, as well as the capacity to generate ideas and engage in a conversation. During restorative songwriting, the therapist assists a person with significant cognitive deficits to use the songwriting process as a vehicle to practice planning, organizing, strategizing, focusing attention, and managing time – skills that he may have lost post-injury. Through the songwriting process, the songwriter needs to be able to create lyrics and assist in creating music (if not a parody) that is time-bound; he needs to be aware of time and complete the task within the timeframe. Critically reviewing his work and making corrections during the process address executive functioning.

In restorative songwriting, the skills of idea generation and the ability to develop and incorporate these ideas within the context of an original song are practiced. As outlined in detail in Baker (2005), several conversational skills are assessed and addressed during songwriting:

1. Topic specificity: are the ideas being generated for the song unambiguous?
2. Topic maintenance: has the songwriter deviated from the topic selected?
3. Relevance: are the songwriter's ideas relevant to the topic?
4. Conciseness: are the ideas focused and is there an absence of unnecessary detail?
5. Quantity: are the ideas fully covered by the topic? Is there any missing information?

Outcomes are observable and measurable in terms of a person's ability to plan and complete the songwriting exercise, as well as his level of ability to generate ideas, identify which points are most relevant and discard the irrelevant ideas, and organize the ideas into a logical format. It is important that the songwriter is able to identify the core theme or feeling of the topic and incorporate these into a chorus (see Chapter 11).

Behavior recall songwriting

In many settings, such as in neurorehabilitation, behavior modification is dependent upon self-monitoring, which is in turn dependent upon recalling what the desired behaviors are. Behaviors in this context can vary from using an impaired limb (due to neglect), recalling strategies to speak more clearly (e.g. participants with dysarthria or dyspraxia), or refraining from impulsive and inappropriate social behaviors. Behavior recall songwriting is a method whereby the therapist and songwriter identify the desired behaviors in a language that is understandable and useful for the songwriter. From here, these behaviors are collaboratively transformed into lyrics and set to music that is in the musical style preferred by the songwriter. In such cases, the music should be melodically, rhythmically, and harmonically predictable and easily learned, and then rehearsed multiple times until the participant is able to recall the target behaviors. The song then becomes a mnemonic aid.

An example of behavior recall songwriting becoming a mnemonic aid is in my own work with people with ABI. For example, for people with dysarthria, intelligibility of speech is dependent upon the person

I like to talk to my friends
I like to talk to them about fashion
But they don't always understand me
And don't comprehend my passion
But when I speak slowly
And separate each sound
Chanel, Dior, Gucci, and Gautier
Are better understood all round.

When I speak much louder
And keep my talking pace slow
My friends take the time to listen
It makes me feel ever so – Wonderful!

Figure 12.2   Example of behavior recall songwriting

adopting a series of strategies. These may include increased voice projection, speaking at a reduced rate, and focusing on the clear articulation of certain sounds. When people with dysarthria employ these strategies, their speaking intelligibility increases, but many of these people do not use these strategies because they cannot recall them. Creating a song with a key message about adapting their behavior enables them to more easily recall the specific strategies that will assist them to be more verbally intelligible to others. Below is a song composed by an adolescent in music therapy who presented with dysarthria – a speech impairment characterized by the partial paralysis of the oral musculature. During music therapy, the young girl co-created this song to assist her in recalling the strategies she needed to improve her speaking intelligibility (Figure 12.2).

One may ask: 'Why doesn't the music therapist just write a song containing the information to be recalled, rather than collaboratively creating a song with the person in therapy? Wouldn't merely practicing that specifically composed song achieve a good outcome for him?' In my experience, collaborating ensures that the language and music used is more aligned with the person's own language use and musical identity (Baker & MacDonald, 2013b), and the person is thereby more invested in the process.

Critical points and levels of depth in the therapeutic process

Within the outcome-oriented framework, the lyric creation process was overwhelmingly identified as the place where the most important 'therapy work' transpires. Clinicians influenced by CBT and working within the mental health field suggested that as the songwriter explores a topic fully, his beliefs, methods of perceiving or solving problems, and his habitual patterns of thinking are brought to the fore, reexamined, and new responses and actions identified. While this might occur during all phases of the songwriting process, it is most evident during the lyric creation process. As these approaches are focused on facilitating change in a planned and structured way, the lyrics contribute to shaping thought patterns and transforming behavior. Within the neurorehabilitation approaches, the lyrics created contain the information that needs to be later recalled (behavior recall songwriting). During restorative songwriting, the creation of lyrics is the primary place where executive functioning and conversational pragmatics are assessed and addressed.

Discussing the meaning of the song creation can be a vital part of cognitive-behavioral approaches. Sometimes as a person is creating lyrics, there is a stream of consciousness occurring; he volunteers thoughts, feelings, and images without too much reflection, and he shares the rapidly changing thoughts as they move in and out of his mind. This stream of consciousness reveals thought distortions and habitual thinking. Returning to the lyrics for reflection may result in increased awareness of and sensitivity to thought patterns. Without such awareness, there is little chance that cognitive distortions will be addressed because change is difficult if a person is not able to recognize faulty thought patterns.

The refining of the song stimulates further insight and cognitive reframing, and can lead to a commitment to action. Song lyrics are not typically long, rich, or detailed descriptions of a person's experiences or events, but are pithy and designed to tell his story. This brevity demands that the listener exercise a degree of interpretation to understand the meaning of the song. Given this, every word must count and communicate the songwriter's intentions as precisely as possible. With this in mind, and on the assumption that there is sufficient time available, the refinement process is an ideal space for the songwriter to critically reexamine the lyrics he has created and further reflect on his therapeutic journey and future actions. Sometimes the reflections on words such as 'try' or 'want to' can generate discussions about a songwriter's commitment to change. These words suggest a desire for change, but without full commitment to taking action. In changing these words to 'will', he is declaring his intention to act.

Sharing the song with others, particularly significant others, can be an important step in the process of readiness for change (Prochaska et al., 1994). When a person shares his songs, he is declaring his intention to act and change his behavior. Sharing can also be a means to communicate to family and significant others that he is about to embark on a difficult and challenging journey, and would benefit from support as he navigates a new way of being in the world. One of the actions needed for change may simply be to be genuinely honest with others; sharing a song creation may be the first step in this process.

Replaying or singing the song plays an important role in both behavioral and neurorehabilitative approaches. In behaviorist traditions, hearing or singing the song is the reward and a symbol of achievement. Conversely, for those subscribing to theories of neuroplasticity, replaying and/or singing the songs is a means for the songwriter to learn and recall important information.

Outcome-oriented songwriting within hospital environments is often brief, and focuses on strengthening a person's level of independence, functional abilities, capacity to cope outside the safe hospital environment, and to live a meaningful life. Clinicians practicing within outcome-oriented songwriting approaches consider deep exploration of what is underpinning the songwriter's life challenges as inappropriate and potentially contraindicated. Clinicians are therefore more likely to practice within supportive activities-oriented or re-educative insight- and process-oriented models (Unkefer & Thaut, 2002; Wheeler, 1983).

The behaviorist approaches to songwriting align most closely with the supportive activities-oriented therapy. Successive approximation songwriting, contingency songwriting, behavior recall songwriting, and lyric repetition approach songwriting as an activity that supports change at a very surface but functional level. These songwriting approaches are designed to directly modify behavior rather than address the causes of the behavior.

Insight- and process-oriented songwriting is evident during the implementation of transtheoretical songwriting. During the early stages of 'readiness for change', a songwriter uses songwriting to gain insight and become more aware of his behavior. As he prepares for and implements action, the songwriting program can take on a re-educative role. These approaches do not reach the depth needed for processing or correcting the underlying cause, but rather seek to assist the songwriter to have a better understanding of his present self and how it impacts on his life and the lives of others. Similarly, re-educative-oriented levels are reached during songwriting for cognitive restructuring and during psychoeducational songwriting. The emphasis on enhancing the songwriter's understanding of his illness and ways to challenge thinking patterns is very much in the 'here and now'.

The role of songwriting and the music

Outcome-oriented songwriting serves to change behaviors so that people can lead happy, healthy, and functioning lives. Treatment focuses directly on problem behaviors or on identifying alternatives to the maladaptive thinking that leads to problem behaviors. Songwriting is therefore used to:

1. Promote adherence to a treatment plan;
2. Follow the rules and regulations associated with the plan;
3. Minimize or eliminate maladaptive behavior;
4. Develop, reinforce, or reward desirable behavior;
5. Change maladaptive thinking;
6. Support relapse prevention;
7. Develop independent problem-solving skills;
8. Stimulate neuroplastic changes; or
9. Develop compensatory strategies.

For successful results, it is critical that goals are specific, unambiguous, measurable, clear, concrete, and understood by both the songwriter and the therapist.

Music created or played within the songwriting process is regarded as secondary to the lyric creation process. During behavioral or cognitive-behavioral songwriting approaches, music functions as the framework through which the lyric creation process can take place. People derive a sense of achievement from creating a song (as opposed to a poem), the realization of one's ability to create something aesthetically beautiful. Opportunities for producing something valued by society is important when trying to combat distorted thinking patterns such as feeling worthless or a failure.

To change thinking patterns and behavior and to learn skills, a person needs to be engaged and invested in the process. Music can provide that motivation for investing as well as strengthening a sense of ownership and connection with the material (Baker, 2013b). Hearing a songwriter say 'this is *my* song' is evidence of ownership, and may be a signal of his willingness to commit to the actions he may have communicated within the song lyrics.

When information needs to be learned and applied in everyday life, music functions as a mnemonic aid (Baker, 2013c). Research indicates that because music can be emotionally powerful, it can be strongly encoded in memory (Judde & Rickard, 2010). Further, music engages a much more distributed network of brain regions than language alone, so including music can stimulate neuroplastic changes (Menon & Levitin, 2005; Salimpoor et al., 2009) and thus improve overall recovery in cognitive function (Särkämö et al., 2008).

The role of the therapist and the songwriter

The role of the therapist in outcome-oriented approaches is to design and implement well-planned – and sometimes bordering on scripted – sets of procedures to ensure the songwriting intervention adequately contributes to functional change. In behavioral approaches, the therapist identifies information about the situational antecedents leading to the problem behavior. She explores the dimensions of the behavior and the negative consequences associated with it. In planning for a change in behavior, the overarching process begins with the identification of a new behavior to learn. From here, the therapist formulates the goals for the therapy process, designs the songwriting approach to achieve this goal, then evaluates, and later follows up to ensure the behavior has been maintained.

During behavioral and cognitive-behavioral-oriented approaches, the therapist may redirect thinking or behavior by inserting musical or verbal comments. The therapist aims to gently challenge the songwriter when he contributes ideas or specific lyrics, and provides feedback about his lyrics either by validating them when they represent healthy thinking or by guiding the songwriter to explore alternative ways of viewing the world and himself when the lyrics represent maladaptive thoughts.

Within therapy sessions, clinicians practicing outcome-oriented models prefer to use non-directive approaches to govern the songwriting process. However, this might not always drive therapeutic change or be feasible, particularly in a group songwriting session where each group member may present with his own agenda. In such cases, the therapist's role may be to contain those who steer the focus away from the theme, to draw out those who are passive, to ensure flow and prevent stagnation, to manage group conflicts, and to make progress with the songwriting process so that the desired outcome is achieved (Baker, 2013a). For those working within the neuroplastic framework, the therapist has a role in ensuring that the lyrics of the song comprehensively and accurately cover the information that needs to be learned and applied by the songwriter. They actively monitor and modify their facilitation techniques to ensure that behaviors are being shaped.

The songwriter's role within outcome-oriented therapy is to participate as directed, engage in the process, as well as comply with the rules, regulations, and treatment plans set by the music therapist or treating team.

Table 12.1 Salient features of outcome-oriented models of songwriting

	Behavioral	Cognitive-behavioral	Learning and neuroplasticity theories
Premise	All behaviors are learned through conditioning 1. Classical and operant conditioning 2. Systematic use of reinforcement (contingency management) 3. Successive approximation	Distorted thinking underpins all behavior 1. Cognitive restructuring 2. Insight and awareness of cognitive distortions 3. Psychoeducation about the illness, recovery, and relapse prevention 4. Readiness for change is a phased process 5. Coaching on effective problem-solving skills	The brain is plastic and capable of reorganization 1. Neuroplasticity leads to regaining of lost skills 2. Varied rehearsal can restore lost function 3. Behavioral compensation
Outcomes/ objectives	1. Specific and observable behaviors	1. Specific and observable behaviors and changes in thought patterns	1. Specific and observable behaviors and changes in functional abilities
Approach	1. Predetermined, specific, operationally defined	1. Predetermined, specific, operationally defined	1. Predetermined, specific, operationally defined
Songwriting models	1. Contingency songwriting: – songwriting *in* therapy – songwriting is reward for adaptive behavior 2. Successive approximation songwriting: – songwriting *as* therapy – behavior modified within the songwriting process 3. Lyric repetition technique: – repeated lyrics 'reinforce' adaptive behavior	1. Songwriting for cognitive restructuring: – increase awareness of distorted thinking – targets the restructuring of thinking 2. Psychoeducational songwriting: – process is educational – explores managing and coping 3. Transtheoretical songwriting: – focuses on different phases of 'readiness for change'	1. Restorative songwriting: – restores lost functioning in executive functioning and conversational pragmatics – songwriting *as* therapy 2. Behavior recall songwriting: – songwriting to encode information in memory – songwriting *as* therapy

Critical points in the process	1. Lyric creation 2. Replaying or singing song	1. Lyric creation 2. Reflecting on song's meaning 3. Refining the lyrics 4. Sharing the song	1. Lyric creation 2. Refining the lyrics 3. Repeated listening/singing
Levels of depth	1. Supportive activities-oriented	1. Insight-oriented or re-educative	1. Supportive activities-oriented
Emphasis	1. Strong focus on lyric creation	1. Strong focus on lyric creation	1. Strong focus on lyric creation
Role of songwriting	1. Changes or moderates maladaptive behaviors	1. Changes or moderates maladaptive thinking	1. Learn or relearn lost skills in executive functioning
Role of music	1. Provides framework for treatment 2. Recognition of capacities	1. Provides framework for treatment 2. Recognition of capacities 3. Strengthen investment in process 4. Ownership: of song and commitment to change	1. Mnemonic aid 2. Stimulate brain activity and connectivity
Role of music therapist	1. Process is therapist-driven 2. Redirect behavior 3. Monitor and modify facilitation to shape behavior	1. Offer feedback 2. Process is therapist-driven 3. Redirect thinking 4. Challenge negative or validate positive thinking 5. Manage group dynamics	1. Offer feedback 2. Prompt use of strategies 3. Monitor and modify facilitation to shape behavior
Role of songwriter	1. Follows instructions to complete task 2. Reliance on therapist as expert	1. Follows instructions to complete task 2. Reliance on therapist as expert	1. Follows instructions to complete task 2. Reliance on therapist as expert
Role of artifact	1. Functions as reward	1. Reinforces planned actions and/or adaptive thinking	1. Mnemonic aid

While active participation is a key component of all songwriting processes irrespective of orientation, within outcome-oriented therapy there is more reliance on the therapist to guide the songwriter through the process rather than on the process being songwriter-driven.

The role of the artifact

As artifacts can function as reinforcement, they are particularly relevant for those practicing within a behavioral orientation. The therapist may provide the songwriter with a copy of his song creation, which functions as a record of his achievements within or beyond the therapy setting. Playing and/or singing the song is a useful tool to reinforce the 'message' of the song. Through repeated listening or singing, the information to be learned or reminding the songwriter of healthy thought patterns is designed as a reinforcement strategy.

Conclusion

This chapter described the perspectives and models of songwriting relevant to clinicians practicing in outcome-oriented models. Table 12.1 provides a comparison of the salient features for behavioral-oriented, cognitive-oriented, and learning and neuroscience perspectives.

13

Experience-Oriented Models of Songwriting

Bruscia's (2011, 2014) second category of 'ways of thinking' about music therapy is experience-oriented. This approach aims to engage people in music-based experiences that present opportunities for processing issues as they emerge in the moment. Bruscia indicates that any musical arti-fact – improvisation, composition, song, or recording – symbolizes and becomes a record of the process and outcome of the therapy. Experience-oriented practice is inherently meaningful, pleasurable, and empower-ing as people interact with the therapist and/or the music. According to Bruscia, psychological orientations include psychodynamic, humanis-tic, and Gestalt. In experience-oriented music therapy, music is regarded as an art rather than a science, and as the artworks are created, people's engagement in the process allows for therapeutic alternatives to be made conscious. Approaches to therapy can be either problem-oriented or resource-oriented, as will be evident later in this chapter. Bruscia sug-gests that the efficacy of the musical experience depends upon its rel-evance to the person and the therapeutic matter being addressed at the time. Unlike outcome-oriented thinking, experience-oriented thinking understands therapeutic benefit from both objective and subjective evi-dence; it values the perceptions and lived experiences of the people who engage in the therapeutic process.

The therapist's role in experience-oriented thinking is to be the expert who guides the session and the therapeutic process. During sessions, the therapy takes place within the music where the person/s explore them-selves in relation to the therapist and the music. In other words, music is a medium for therapy, but therapy takes place within a therapeutic relationship. These experiences are essentially simulations of people's own ways of relating to others in the world (Bruscia, 2011, 2014).

Taking the same approach as the previous chapter, this chapter begins with brief descriptions of the orientations and influences that emerge in experience-oriented songwriting practice before describing the specific songwriting procedures and approaches.

Psychodynamic influences

Songwriting has emerged as a frequently used method in psychodynamic-informed music therapy practice. Psychodynamic concepts of the unconscious, preconscious, and conscious as well as concepts of object relations, resistance, free association, interpretation, and transference are all considered relevant to therapeutic songwriting and are briefly discussed before describing their influence on songwriting practice. While the mental structures of the id, ego, and superego are also relevant to psychoanalytical thinking, interviewees did not describe these ideas as an influence, which is perhaps a reflection of the decreasing use of Freud's metapsychology in music therapy practice and therefore not referred to in this chapter.

Unconscious, preconscious, conscious mind, and defense mechanisms

Freud proposed that the interaction of conflicts operating at the unconscious, preconscious, and conscious levels of the mind is what shapes behavior and personality (Frosh, 2012; Gabbard, 2010). Consciousness comprises of the mental processes that people are aware of in the present moment. The preconscious mind represents people's ordinary memories, memories that are easily retrieved and brought to conscious awareness on demand. The unconscious mind, however, stores the feelings, urges, memories, thoughts, and repressed material that are outside our conscious awareness and typically represent unacceptable, painful, or anxiety-provoking feelings or behaviors. Importantly, the unconscious is understood as a 'space of dynamic activity' (Frosh, 2012, p. 42) where ideas and thoughts, despite being hidden from awareness, create tension and are continuously searching for ways to be released.

Psychodynamic treatment aims to resolve unconscious conflicts, to uncover and understand the meaning behind neurotic symptoms, the cause of the behavior, and the repressed material. However, insight alone is insufficient for change, as people have a tendency to repeat learned patterns of behavior which are a product of activated defense mechanisms.

Defense mechanisms are the unconscious psychological strategies people engage in to manage their unconscious impulses and thereby manage anxiety (Corey, 2013). In short, their function is to prevent unconscious ideas from reaching consciousness (Frosh, 2012). While they can serve as a protective mechanism, they can also cause significant psychological problems. There are a number of defense mechanisms that have been defined and described by psychodynamic theorists, the most common being denial, repression, regression, projection, reaction formation, displacement, intellectualization, and rationalization (Corey, 2013; Frosh, 2012). These defense mechanisms have a tendency to become active as people respond to situations that evoke similar feelings as earlier experiences. Such events present an opportunity to identify unhealthy patterns and explore their origins.

Transference

Transference has been described as the unconscious displacement of feelings and fantasies that are reactions toward people in a person's past onto the therapist (or on to another thing, e.g. a song). It offers a small window into a person's unconscious and his approach to interacting with significant others (Temple, 1996). This transfer of feelings and fantasies enables a person to understand, work through, and resolve conflicts from past relationships by re-enacting and reconstructing the past and understanding it with more clarity (Frosh, 2012). The therapist facilitates this process by exploring the various forms of resistance and patterns of behavior together with the person until old patterns of behavior are acknowledged.

Free association

Treatment focuses on bringing unconscious material to the surface so that childhood experiences can be reconstructed, discussed, interpreted, and analyzed (Corey, 2013). The result of this process is an increased self-awareness of how the self operates and a potential to change and enhance personal relationships with others. One technique relevant to songwriting and described later in this chapter is that of free association. During therapy, people are encouraged to share with the therapist whatever thoughts or images come into their minds, without censorship. Freud viewed this process as opening the doors to unconscious wishes, fantasies, conflicts, and motivations, which may lead to recollection of past experiences and a release of intense feelings (catharsis) that were previously repressed.

As the person communicates the thoughts and images, the therapist analyzes these and directs the person to potential meanings of these free associations. This interpretation process enables the person to assimilate the new material and to accelerate access to additional unconscious material (Corey, 2013).

Object relations theory

Klein moved away from earlier ideas that humans were driven by pleasure seeking, and instead viewed the establishment of relationships as the primary motivator. 'Object relation' is a term used to describe interpersonal relationships as they are represented intrapsychically (Dilts, 2012). The 'object' refers to something or someone that meets a need, to a person (initially the mother) or to an object that is the target of a person's feelings or drives. The theory proposes that family experiences and interactions during the initial years of life influence how people relate to other people and situations as adults. The experiences they have of people are transformed into 'internal objects' or representations in the preconscious that influences their relationships and interactions with others later in life. It is important to note that while some clinicians still ascribe to these ideas, more contemporary theories of object relations move away from the notion of unconscious drives and shift toward the view that the relationship is internalized.

According to early object relations theory, people are motivated to seek out object relationships, and it is these relationships that are intrinsically rewarding. Expressions of aggression are the results of frustrating and inhibiting object relations (Frosh, 2012). As a consequence, therapy focuses on repairing damaged object relationships by working with and through the therapeutic relationship.

Winnicott's concept of the 'good enough mother' is a key concept in object relations theory. The theory holds that it is the mother's role to provide a 'holding' environment, which allows a child to feel safe and supported as he develops a 'true self' (Grolnick, 1990). A good enough mother is available to her infant when needed and able to 'separate herself sufficiently so the infant can develop into his own self' (Frosh, 2012, p. 111). However, inadequate or inconsistent mother-holding patterns can lead to the development of a false self as the infant attempts to conform with the mother's needs in an effort to gain attention and love. As adults, the true self contains repressed or dissociated feelings that they never felt safe enough to express as children. A simplified view of therapy is that the therapist creates a holding environment that resembles that of what a good enough mother would create so that the person in therapy can begin to transform into the true self (Winnicott, 1965).

Transitional phenomenon (Winnicott, 1999) is described as an area of experience that lies between a person's internal and external reality. The transitional object refers to an object that is both real and symbolic (such as a blanket or toy) and that represents this experience and provides comfort and safety. This object enables the child to live in reality and fantasy and to begin to recognize the 'me', 'not me' in relation to his mother; the child is learning that there is a world that exists in addition to himself and his mother. It functions as a bridge between the self and others and is believed to aid in the development and internalization of relationships, coping with separation, and facilitating the move toward independence (Winnicott, 1965). The object provides psychological comfort, a feeling of safety that would normally be provided by the mother. It plays an important role during anxiety-provoking contexts such as during periods of being separated from the mother or at the time of going to sleep.

Symbols and metaphors

Symbols and metaphors are incorporated into various psychodynamic therapy approaches as a therapeutic tool. Jung (1971) describes a symbol as something that represents something else by association, resemblance, or convention, especially a material object used to represent something invisible. Symbols can function as indirect, non-confrontational ways to 'communicate and transport thoughts and feelings to consciousness' (Frisch, 1990, p. 20), or as 'accumulators and transformers of psychic energy' (Priestley, 1994, p. 47).

Metaphors are typically words, phrases, objects, symbols, anecdotes, or stories that represent complex emotions or situations or that make a comparison between two different objects or situations (Esparza, 2001). Thoughts, feelings, relationships, and beliefs are transferred from one familiar experience to another that is unfamiliar, as a means of building understanding of that unfamiliar experience (Burns, 2001). Bonde (2007) suggests that metaphors provide possibilities to '(re)create and (re)interpret our life world by adapting meaning from one, well-known area of life and transferring it to another, lesser known' (p. 62). Metaphors are useful tools to apply in therapy because of their capacity to represent the essence of an emotion (Levitt et al., 2000) and to 'amplify the understanding and meaning, and represent the unconscious' (Thompson, 2009, p. 4).

Esparza (2001) summarized 22 main functions of metaphors. I identified the eight most relevant to therapeutic songwriting.

1. Metaphors make, demonstrate, explain, or illustrate a point;
2. Metaphors open up possibilities for strategies;
3. Metaphors facilitate new patterns of thought, behavior, and feelings;
4. Metaphors reframe or redefine a problem or situation;
5. Metaphors allow a person to process directly at a subconscious level;
6. Metaphors bypass ego defenses;
7. Metaphors stimulate memories of something or some event;
8. Metaphors allow a person to form a choice or find his/her own direction.

Bonde (2007) explains how metaphors in music therapy are illustrations of how people experience music-based interventions and 'how they experience themselves' (p. 66). For example, statements such as 'The melody hit me right in the heart', 'I felt beyond time and space', 'The music sounded like a sermon' provide important insights for people and their therapist about themselves and their experiences in music therapy.

Models

Songwriting within psychodynamic-oriented music therapy

Psychodynamic-oriented music therapy is an improvisatory approach to address psychological problems. Improvisations between the therapist and client[1] aim to uncover unconscious processes and help the songwriter to explore his inner self. Through these improvisations, music is used symbolically and provides opportunities for insight, reflection, growth, and enhanced self-knowledge (Priestley, 1994). As is evident with other psychodynamic therapies, music therapy may also use verbal processing post-improvisation to assist the client to find meaning from the improvisation.

In line with psychoanalysis, transference, countertransference, and the therapeutic alliance are phenomena that may emerge within the improvisations between therapist and client or in the associated dialogue that precedes or follows them. According to the music therapists interviewed, these same elements of therapy may also be present when therapists apply psychoanalytical principles within songwriting interventions. As outlined for improvisation by Bruscia (1987), the aims of songwriting within analytically oriented frameworks are to: (1) bring repressed conflicts under conscious control, (2) bring awareness and acceptance of previously unacknowledged aspects of the self, (3) free up energy trapped by repressive and defensive mechanisms, and (4) redirect energy toward positive aims (Bruscia, 1987, p. 119). As songwriters confront, become aware of, and resolve unconscious material, there is a flow-on effect to verbal communication and interactional skills, control over their unconscious drives and impulses, levels of frustration tolerance, and increased motivation, purpose, creativity, and spontaneity in life (Bruscia, 1987).

As is the case with many psychodynamic improvisation approaches, the music therapist may begin the songwriting process with a verbal exploration of what is important in the here and now. The songwriter first communicates the events, situations, or feelings that have transpired in the recent past during the previous week or the feelings or conflicts that are currently present or of ongoing concern (Bruscia, 1987). The dialogue is an important feature of the sessions because it offers possibilities for the songwriters to make conscious their inner thoughts and feelings in the absence of any musical interaction.[2]

Following the dialogue, the music therapist assists the songwriters to summarize and translate their verbal expressions 'into a title, one that captures the essence of the conflict or concern' (Bruscia, 1987, p. 125), and this title becomes the focus for the creation of an original song, an improvised song, free-style rap, or, less often, a song parody (see Chapters 8–11).

If a key issue or concern does not emerge from the initial dialogue, the therapist might suggest the songwriter and therapist engage in a referential-free improvisation. This improvisatory experience may evoke thoughts, feelings, or memories, and be the catalyst needed to find the focus for the songwriting session. Many clinicians begin a songwriting session with an improvisation to 'prime' the songwriter (see Chapter 8). This form of priming may help the songwriter to connect more easily with his feelings and unblock or unlock the unconscious. Given this, there are two approaches to using songwriting within analytical music therapy frameworks: (1) where the songwriting intervention is the sole agent for addressing the analytically oriented goals, or (2) where the songwriting interventions are preceded by improvisatory experiences.

Songwriting as a self-integration process

Jung (1966) suggests that the primary aim of therapy is to increase cohesion and wholeness of the self. His theories hold that the personal unconscious is organized around a common theme, which leads to a core pattern of emotions, perceptions, and memories (Schultz & Schultz, 2009).

He also introduced the concept of the collective unconscious and archetypes. The collective unconscious is a part of the unconscious mind that incorporates patterns of memories, instincts, and experiences shared by a society, a people, or all humankind. Archetypes are considered inherited patterns of thought or symbolic imagery derived from the past collective experience and present in the personal unconscious. These archetypes come to the fore during fantasies and dreams, and may take the form of a character that resembles the personal unconscious. Common archetypes include the orphan, the hero, the caregiver, the explorer, the rebel, the lover, the creator, and the magician. As the archetypes enter consciousness they are transformed, a process that contributes to the individuation process (Stevens, 2006).

Importantly, creative processes are vehicles to activate the unconscious and where archetypal images can then be represented in creative works (Jung, 1966), including original songs. Viega (2012) describes how some rap and hip hop songs are representations of the archetype of a hero/heroine and his/her transformative journey to 'fully realizing the Self' (p. 59). As a focus, he draws on Campbell's stages of a hero's journey: (1) the call to adventure, (2) the supernatural aid, (3) crossing the threshold of adventure, (4) trials and tasks, (5) reaching the nadir, (6) receiving the boon, (7) the return, and (8) the crossing of the return threshold (Campbell, 1949/2008 cited in Viega, 2012, p. 58). Other archetypal figures may feature in this journey – a wise old man, a person or thing with supernatural powers – that play a role in the hero's journey (Viega, 2012). This overall hero's journey is a representation of the self-discovery process – a strengthening of the ego, becoming real, and returning within ourselves with a stronger sense of our true identity or self (p. 59).

Songwriting is a creative activity that can be an agent to represent and transform archetypal images and rediscover and reconnect with the authentic self (Borling, 2011). In a study of women who had experienced abuse, Curtis (1997) published several songs that the women had created in music therapy. While Curtis practices using feminist music therapy frameworks, one song by participant 'Ann' illustrates how she perceives herself according to three archetypes – the gypsy/traveler, the lover, and the Christian warrior (Figure 13.1). Ann's lyrics suggest a conflict between positive and negative aspects of self-perception.

Cohesion and wholeness are inhibited by internal ambivalence. Songwriting can be a vehicle to identify this ambivalence and work toward a resolution. Such ambivalence is clearly illustrated in the lyrics of a 27-year-old woman diagnosed with a major depressive disorder

"Ann's song"

This is a song about Ann
Gypsy, traveler
Lonely, weary, and pretty
Caring daring, enchanting, romancing, Ann
This is a song about Ann
Crazy, lover
Naughty, unstable, and happy
Caring, daring, enchanting, romancing, Ann
This is a song about Ann
Christian warrior
Rebel, heartless, and cold
Caring, daring, enchanting, romancing, Ann

Figure 13.1   Songs with archetypal images
Source: Curtis, 1997, p. 315. Reprinted with permission from Sandra Curtis.

Just when I feel all the pain's been discovered
Another new memory sends me to depths of
Despair and confusion well up all around me
I am drowning and sinking – I panic
The voices of daddy, The silence of mommy. . .

Figure 13.2   Example of lyrics illustrating internal conflict
Source: Hudson-Smith, 1991. p. 490. Reprinted with permission from Barcelona Publishers.

and borderline personality disorder (Hudson-Smith, 1991). The woman was experiencing internal conflict concerning feelings of guilt and disloyalty, and simultaneously feeling rage toward her parents. Her songwriting experiences were aimed at freeing herself from her destructive thoughts and living independently, exploring both the positive and negative parts of the self, and moving toward better self-integration (Figure 13.2).

What is important here is that the ambivalence is expressed in words rather than purely in the music. The concretizing of ambivalence aids in bringing it to awareness, as it can be viewed and reviewed in the repeated playing of the song.

Transference in songwriting

In music therapy, transference and countertransference experiences occur within musical improvisations between therapist and client and/or during the verbal interactions that are associated with the musical experiences (Priestley, 1994). During verbal interactions, feelings and desires unconsciously retained from childhood are no doubt transferred to the

therapist and, following the therapist's reflections of the clients' interactions, the transference provides opportunities to bring these to the
clients' conscious awareness. However, sometimes these transference
experiences occur entirely within the musical space, allowing for the
expression and exploration of transference emotions (Priestley, 1994).

In songwriting, transference experiences are made possible both during the songwriting exercises and through the ensuing dialogue between
therapist and songwriter. During the creation of the song, the songwriter
may transfer his unconscious thoughts, feelings, and experiences to the
song creation. This could be through the music itself, the lyrics, or the
accompaniment (Hakomäki, 2013). This transference is most likely to
occur through a process that mirrors free association – spontaneous verbalization of lyrics that occur during improvised songs or through free-
style rap, as outlined later in this chapter.

Austin (2008) suggests that when the therapist and songwriter engage
in a two-way improvised song creation, the possibility for transference
and countertransference emerges. Improvised songwriting is an invitation to share an intimate experience, opening the space for 'a natural flow
of energy, including sensations, feelings and images, to be exchanged
between the songwriter and the therapist. Improvising with one another
requires leaving the safety of the structured song behind and plunging
into the unknown together' (Austin, 2008, p. 97). Through this experience, the songwriter's and the therapist's unconscious thoughts and
feelings can coalesce and commingle (Hakomäki, 2013).

Frisch Hara (2012) recalls that when her songwriters create spontaneous rap music, it often contains swearing and/or violent content. In
such cases, the therapist assists in the transference process by listening
to and reflecting back to the songwriters how these words and images
affect the therapist and what she thinks the songwriters are communicating. Rather than attempting to edit the language or content, the
music therapist uses the expression as an opportunity for therapeutic
dialogue. This can be problematic, however, when working with youth
where certain words symbolize one thing in one subculture, and something completely different in a different subculture. For example, in one
American city, the term 'bodies' in one group represents people a songwriter has killed, but in a different subculture it is indicative of people
the songwriter has had sexual relations with.

Kowski (2003) described a songwriting experience which enabled at-
risk African American children to explore their unconscious feelings
about goodbyes. These young songwriters had experienced parental
issues of drug use and violence and had been emotionally/physically

It's hard to say good-bye
Why?
Because it seems like the person
You say bye to gonna die
Some people will cry when they say bye,
But be strong and say "Hi"
Just be like me
And don't cry
Act as if you was gonna see the person again and say bye.

Figure 13.3   Lyrics of song illustrating transformation to healthy resistance
Source: Kowski, 2003, p. 100. Reprinted with permission from Barcelona Publishers.

neglected or abused. Kowski's therapy was primarily aimed at acknowledgment and expression of feelings, anger, self-esteem, and conflict resolution. Transference during songwriting transpired during her final session with the group. Kowski was leaving, and the children were angry with her as it unconsciously aroused their feelings of abandonment. These feelings resembled those felt previously when neglected or abused by their parents. Kowski provided the children with an explanation for her departure and the possibility to accept it. Through songwriting, their resistance was transformed into a healthy resistance, as they were able to acknowledge their feelings of abandonment (p. 101, Figure 13.3).

Frisch's (1990) experiences with an adolescent girl illustrate how feelings of abandonment were communicated to the therapist and within the song creation itself. The 16-year-old female had been admitted to hospital with depression and had childhood experiences of being abandoned by her mother (Frisch, 1990). She created a verse within a group song creation titled 'Leaving', expressing her sadness about her anticipated cessation of music therapy. However, the presenting issue of separation described in the song stimulated insight into the feelings associated with her mother's acts of abandonment. She (initially unconsciously) transferred her feelings on to the therapist and the song created. Later, her identification of the unconscious issue of abandonment was a pivotal moment for the adolescent, and became the focus of her verbal psychotherapy. Frisch indicates that the adolescent would sing the song every day as a tangible approach to keeping the issue present in her awareness.

Free associative songwriting

Free associative songwriting – akin to Austin's (2008) free associative singing – encourages the unconscious images, memories, and feelings to emerge during an improvised song creation process. Austin suggests that this free association creates a 'musical portrait of themselves or parts of themselves', revealing the songwriter's 'strengths, vulnerabilities, conflicts and feelings' (p. 141). A song is created as songwriters verbalize and sing aloud their stream of consciousness. During synchronous rapping or improvised songwriting, a direct connection is made to the unconscious through the process of free association (Hudson-Smith, 1991; Lightstone, 2012; Viega, 2013). Here, the therapist (with or without input from the songwriter) may spontaneously create the music or a backing track for the songwriter to lyricize over the top. The combination of the emotion-arousing and holding effects of the music creates a context through which there is direct access to the unconscious and possibilities for free association to follow. Unlike dialogue, the musical context allows for a socially acceptable repetition of statements or expressions, which serves to increase the intensity of affective expressions (Austin, 2008) and allow them to be fully felt, processed, and released.

As introduced earlier, Hudson-Smith (1991) worked with a 27-year-old woman diagnosed with a major depressive disorder and borderline personality disorder. Within music therapy, the songwriting process enabled the woman to access unconscious material and unlock repressed memories of rape incidents. In later sessions, the woman listened to an instrumental piece of music and simultaneously created an improvised song based on images of her life that were evoked by it. She first allowed the images of her life (both positive and negative) to be brought into conscious thought, and on the second and subsequent playing of the instrumental pieces she began to spontaneously sing words in a free association. It took her 10 weeks to create the entire song.

Songwriting using symbols and metaphors

Songwriting provides a perfect context for people to transform symbols and metaphors into a concrete object in the form of lyrics and music (Erkkilä, 2011), and in doing so strengthen the ego (Frisch, 1990). Through improvised songs, the symbols and metaphors used will reveal important information about the internal world of a person, allow them to illustrate their thoughts and feelings, and offer the songwriter an opportunity to process at the subconscious level (Oldfield & Franke, 2005). In using these symbols and metaphors, the songwriter has the possibility to reframe or redefine his situation and make plans for introducing new ways of thinking and feeling and new ways to act.

Song creations that utilize symbols and metaphors can go beyond just expressing the inner world of a person to also transforming it. Aigen

(1991) worked with a gifted boy with behavioral issues, creating long blues and rap songs with improvised lyrics. The boy drew on fantasy – wizards and witches, fairies and monsters – to represent good and bad polarities. The characters were transformed, which Aigen suggests is an indicator of how the boy was able to manage his inner conflicts through the use of his own resources.

Many songwriters not only use metaphors but also may write their lyrics in the third person. This can be understood as a defense mechanism, where they may not be fully ready to completely 'own' or acknowledge the lyrical content of the song. By writing in the third person, they are not writing about themselves but recounting someone else's story or context. This serves to protect them from acknowledging feelings or experiences that they are not yet ready to face. In telling this story through the eyes of another character, they are bringing the issues to conscious awareness in preparation for facing them at another point in the future. An alternative perspective is to consider this action as using the song as a container for their emotions because they are conscious of their thoughts as they create lyrics.

Initially, it may be difficult for the therapist and songwriter to understand the meaning behind the symbols and metaphors expressed in the lyrics or music. Barba (2005) suggests that cryptic or mysterious symbols and metaphors, often told in the third person, may only be able to be understood after time has passed and the songwriter and therapist have had a period of reflection. At times, the artifact plays an important role in facilitating the full understanding, relevance, and significance of the song for the songwriter.

The symbolic and metaphorical elements of music (Bonde, 2007) are also a reason why music assists in ego strengthening and facilitating developmental transitions (Frisch, 1990). The music people create – including the lyrics and accompaniment of songs – is a symbolic projection of a person's unconscious self. People experience growth when they make the connection between the symbols expressed in their music and their internal world (Erkkilä, 2011). However, for the same reason some songwriters tell their own story in the third person, some songwriters may not be emotionally ready to make the connection between the symbols and metaphors emerging in the songwriting process and their reality. Further, verbal processing of the significance or meaning of the song creation may not be necessary, particularly if the songwriting process itself led to relief at the psychic or symbolic level (Erkkilä, 2011). Ambivalence, conflict, and paradox can be subtly or dramatically expressed within song creations. Erkkilä (2011) describes his work with one young person (Punker), indicating that the lyrics expressed symbols and emotions of loneliness, anxiety, love, family relationships, and dreams, but were hidden in the very noisy and fast music and a shouting singing style. This leaves the listener confused over what is being communicated.

In my own clinical experience, songs contain verses and choruses, and each of these (depending upon their subject matter) can represent different events, feelings, or emotions and the subsequent transition to new events, feelings, or emotions. There is a movement through the verses from beginning to end (or sometimes the reverse), with the chorus often acting as the transitional point, the bridge between one emotion, feeling state, or event and another. Often lyrical symbols and metaphors are present in the choruses of songs, where repetition is more common and where the music contains greater emotional intensity.

The music created can be shaped to enhance the imagery and symbols communicated by the lyrics. Sound painting is often used to highlight these. One adolescent girl in Viega's (2013) study created a song titled 'Butterfly Wings'. The lyrical themes of the song are of self-love, redemption, and renewal (p. 188). Her song incorporates symbols of the phoenix being rebirthed, butterfly wings, a cheetah, a dove, and a doe. Viega describes how the musical elements are also symbolic of the theme – the harmony never resolves to the tonic, so there is never any harmonic closure 'as if it is moving perpetually into the future' (p. 184). He describes how the synthesized textures create a feeling of 'floating through space, creating the illusion of flight' (p. 185), just like the phoenix and butterfly might do in the song.

Songs as transitional objects

Transitional objects were described earlier as important in creating safety and comfort, a defense against anxiety. And while toys and blankets provide safety and comfort for infants, adolescents and adults may still have a need for the safety and comfort of a transitional object, but one that is more age appropriate and relevant. Musical transitional objects such as a favorite song may function as an alternative to a toy or blanket for adolescents and adults as well as for children. For example, rap music may function as a transitional object that provides safety for adolescents as they navigate their way through tasks during the maturation process (Frisch, 1990; Frisch Hara, 2012; Viega, 2012).

According to Frisch (1990), O'Callaghan (2005), and Baker (2013c), a person's own song creation may take on the role of a transitional object. As the songwriter engages in song creation and repeatedly plays it during the refining stage, it becomes increasing familiar and can be transformed into a transitional object that provides safety and comfort. One clinician reported that songs were useful in helping the songwriter to manage his anxiety during the transition from the therapy room to his everyday life because it gave her 'a voice in his treatment from day to day rather than once or twice a week for 30 minutes' (Baker, 2013c, p. 44). In other words, her capacity to have her songwriters feel safe could be extended past the therapy room via the use of this transitional object – the song. The song becomes the connection between the therapist and the outside world, assisting the songwriter to internalize something of the therapeutic relationship (just like the child internalizes something of the mother in a Winnicottian sense).

Hudson-Smith (1991) described how a woman who had been abused used her own song creation as a transitional object to assist her to manage her anxiety about leaving the therapist and the safety of the hospital. Her songs functioned in the same way as a comforting blanket – to calm her anxiety. The content of the song was central to achieving this, as it expressed her feelings and appreciation for the hospital, the therapist, and the music therapy group who she reported had supported her. The importance of the song for her ongoing coping is evident, as she had made multiple copies of the recording so that she could play them repeatedly without fear of having the recording deteriorate after repeated use.

Song creations can assist people to transition and cope constructively with anticipated loss. Frisch (1990) reported that a group of adolescent inpatients used a song created within group music therapy to prepare them for the discharge of one of the adolescent girls with whom they had developed an attachment. The group members could be heard singing their song during their free time in the days leading up to this girl's discharge and for several days after. In this way, the song functioned as a transitional object, allowing the girls to process their loss during the transitional period.

Reality contemplation songwriting

Songwriting approaches informed by psychodynamic thinking may lead to insights about the underlying cause of the songwriters' problems, internal conflicts, and unresolved issues. The next step for the therapist is to assist the songwriter to process and resolve these conflicts. Confronting these issues head-on is one approach clinicians reported using what I have coined 'reality contemplation songwriting'. The purpose of this approach is to encourage a person to confront the situations that cause him fear, anxiety, destruction, and ambivalence. In this context, the therapist guides the person to create songs about the reality he is facing and that is causing him distress. In line with Priestley's (1994) use of improvisation, during songwriting the person creates lyrics and music that address the challenging issue, while simultaneously inwardly experiencing the negative feelings associated with this imagined reality. The therapist then facilitates a verbal discussion of the meaning and felt experience of the song creation process.

Critical points and levels of depth in the songwriting process

Psychodynamic-oriented music therapists vary in their perspectives of where critical points in the songwriting process occur. Unlike outcome-oriented approaches, all interviewees practicing psychodynamic-informed approaches agreed that songwriting was rarely introduced in the initial few sessions of meeting a new songwriter. Rapport is needed before people will open themselves up to deep, probing songwriting experiences. Further, many songwriters engage in improvisations immediately prior to commencing songwriting, as a form of priming where the unconscious material is brought to the surface (Chapter 8). The cognitive and emotional responses are then transformed from the abstract non-verbal to more concrete verbal expressions – lyrics.

While awareness and processing of unconscious material can occur at any stage during the songwriting process, clinicians tended to agree that the most significant work emerges during the middle to later stages of a song creation (after a number of sessions) and/or after the song has been created and its meaning and significance are discussed. Time is needed to develop that deep and trusting therapeutic alliance so that the songwriter feels safe to open to himself and to the therapist.

When working with people with acute mental illness, there is a tendency to stay at a more supportive and insight-oriented level, because there is a need to establish security, a sense of belonging, a sense of integrity, and to experience intimacy. Many clinicians reported that the songwriters they were working with were just too 'unwell' and 'unstable' to create songs at a deep and transformative level.

Songwriting attempts to be reconstructive and transformative, bringing about a conscious awareness of the songwriter's inner world and processing it. However, there are many circumstances that may prevent a truly deep and reconstructive songwriting experience to emerge. Time to verbally and musically explore issues may not be available, and songwriting subsequently reaches only supportive and insight-oriented levels. For example, some psychodynamic clinicians may only have the possibility to see people once or twice. Probing too deep with these people is contraindicated when a trusting relationship has not yet been established or when there is insufficient therapy time available to devote to processing highly sensitive and painful feelings. When people are expected to attend therapy for multiple sessions, the songwriting process has the possibility to take on a transformative role. The therapist has the time to develop a strong therapeutic alliance and have the songwriter feel safe to open up, and also have sufficient time to give issues the space to be processed and resolved at a pace that meets the songwriter's ability to move forward.

At times the spontaneous improvised song creations that occur in therapy may be transformative, clearly connecting with unconscious thoughts, feelings, or events. However, engaging the songwriter in a process-oriented verbal dialogue following the song creation may be too confronting for some songwriters. They may not be ready to 'own' the expressions contained in their lyrics and music; just having them expressed may be sufficient at this point. When using improvised songwriting approaches with children, one clinician recounted:

> One seven-year-old boy created many songs about ice hockey, and the ice hockey images were symbols of his inner feelings. There's a term called 'a sudden death in ice hockey' (which refers to a point in the game when one act can end the game) and this was used in a song that was about his brother's death. The song really served a function of not owning the feelings at the time because he was not yet able to emotionally live those feelings . . . His first song was very closed. He said that this first piece about ice hockey described the moment when he saw his brother dead (following an accident at home). Over time, he created more songs. . . . The transformative moment occurred when he created a song and gave it the title of his dead brother. This is the saddest piece I've ever heard. We were having Music Therapy almost exactly a year after that piece was created and I said to him 'Would you like to play the piece you made a year ago about your brother?' He said 'Okay. Yes, I will play it' and he played it and then he said, 'I want to compose a new one about my brother.' He composed a piece, a totally different kind of song. Less than two months later, he wanted to play it again and then he changed the ending of it. He also wanted to change the title of the piece. He went to the computer, and letter-by-letter he changed the letters of his brother's name and replaced it with his own name. This was the transformative moment in this process.

The role of songwriting and the music

Within psychodynamic orientations and depending upon which school of psychodynamic theory a therapist subscribes to, songwriting strives to resolve unconscious inner conflicts, identify defense mechanisms, work through past relationships, integrate a fractured sense of self, and help the songwriter to find meaning. The efficaciousness of the songwriting process is in part dependent upon how relevant the musical experiences are for the songwriter and for his particular therapeutic needs. For example, if the clinician is able to facilitate the creation of a song where the music closely resembles that of the songwriter's preferred style, then the experience may be more meaningful than music created in a less preferred style. Imitating modern pop genres is easier in the present day since the introduction of inexpensive technological software and devices such as GarageBand.

While creating lyrics is important in transforming thoughts, feelings, and emotions into a concrete form, the music also plays an important role in the change process. Music may be the catalyst for therapeutic growth (Austin, 2008) or may weaken censors so that a person is able to fully express unconscious fantasies (Noy, 1966). More importantly however, the symbolic aspects of music (Bonde, 2007) are able to express or access unconscious content and also express a number of thoughts and feelings at the same time (Noy, 1966). This allows the music to express and/or symbolize the inner conflicts that the songwriter may be experiencing. For example, hip hop and rap music is often multitracked and multilayered, and therefore has the potential to 'take on juxtaposition of order and chaos, control and out of control' (Frisch Hara, 2012, p. 19).

Several clinicians interviewed proposed that songwriting was a much safer approach to explore issues than was improvisation. They reported that many of the people they were working with were too emotionally unstable to employ improvisatory techniques. They recounted how the lack of a predictable musical structure in improvisation was unsettling for those with a weak ego or those who were experiencing psychotic episodes. Songwriting offered an alternative to improvisation, with the musical structure providing stability and much needed containment. At the same time, a songwriting structure does not inhibit the exploration and expression of issues; instead, its predictable structure allows the songwriters to feel relaxed so that they can take risks and experiment with new ways of 'being'.

Creating contexts where 'play' can take place are central tenets of Winnicottian theory (Winnicott, 1999) and inherent in the improvisatory experiences provided by many psychodynamic clinicians (e.g. De Backer & Van Camp, 2003). Improvised song creations (such as those described in Chapter 10) offer the songwriter the possibility to 'play' with the music, either individually or collaboratively with the therapist. It is only through this play that the songwriter uses his whole personality creatively and discovers the self.

In some cases, the music provides a frame to 'hold' the songwriter in an emotion so it can be experienced fully, reach a climax, and potentially be cathartic; a 'container for in-depth processing to occur' (Austin, 2008, p. 118). Once the music has been created, it can be played repeatedly. If the accompaniment is grounding but not constricting, controlled but not controlling, supportive but not irresponsible, responsive but not over-involved, suggestive but not directive, and strong but not overpowering (Bruscia, 1987, p. 130), the music can allow the songwriter to experience the emotions fully in a safe and contained manner. One clinician interviewed described this experience:

> In my work with Andrew, we wrote a song grieving the loss of his family. His wife left him when he was diagnosed with Parkinson's disease. He was also estranged from his three children. He wrote a song that chronicled his life from the time he met his wife, married, and began a family. He acknowledged that writing the song was difficult but extremely cathartic. The accompaniment held the client in the space to discuss with me his feelings, grief, and loss. We played the song multiple times in one session and the client took an active role in singing as many of the lyrics with me that he was able to in his condition. The accompaniment was fairly simple, but utilized the preferred style of music the client desired. I think this deepened the client's experience and allowed or facilitated further connection with the lyrics and music. Preferred music provided a safe place and container for the emotions to be explored.

In her work with young people, Khare (personal communication, April 18, 2014) recounts how a song allowed songwriters to feel emotion while also being contained:

> The song was titled 'Someone 2 Love'. The frame that 'held' the songwriter was the Chorus lyric . . . 'I am starting to understand just who I am – and what I'm capable of – I need to say how I feel 'coz it keeps me real – I am Someone 2 Love . . .' This lyric came from the previous week's therapy dialogue. We had finished our first song 'Choir Boy' and were considering our next song project. The songwriter began

to talk about 'having things I want to say but just can't say them.' In talking about this what was understood was that the youth knew what they wanted to say, but weren't sure about the delivery and didn't believe they would be listened to. So I offered 'that sometimes it's not about being heard, at first, but it's about being given the space to express what we feel – and that we could create that space for their expression and then *we* could listen.' The songwriters loved this idea . . . In talking about what would be written, the songwriters identified that they felt they were at a new place, one that could be a new beginning (I am starting to understand just who I am – And what I'm capable of).

This notion of space is an example of Winnicott's ideas of 'potential space', an inviting and safe interpersonal space where a person can be playful but at the same time connected to others.

Uhlig (2011) offers a rich description of the case of Richard, where the young boy transformed his aggression into something positive through the medium of rap. Initially he was shouting sounds or screaming words, but as he engaged in the process his vocalizations were transformed into rap lyrics. Importantly, Uhlig incorporated a simple repetitive chord progression on the keyboard to hold him in the space and allow him to express his deep frustration and anger to his fullest potential. A feature of Uhlig's approach was her musical mirroring of his rapping, where she contained his aggressive expressions when needed.

The role of the therapist and the songwriter

The therapist plays a crucial role in guiding the whole songwriting process and operates as expert musician and therapeutic guide. Particular to psychodynamic-oriented songwriting, the therapist has responsibility for structuring the songwriting experience so that the songwriter can explore unconscious or conscious conflicts safely and effectively. The therapist must provide the level of structure needed – too little structure can create anxiety within the songwriter, whereas too much structure can inhibit expression and reduce the potential for therapeutic change (Bruscia, 1987). Setting specific songwriting play rules such as how the lyrics and music should be created may provide structure. If the songwriter is more grounded, the music therapist may be less directive, allowing the songwriter to shape the songwriting experience more freely.

The clinician also creates structure through her musical contributions. As the songwriter creates lyrics, and in doing so expresses inner conflicts, the music therapist aims to 'hold' the songwriter so that the emotions and blocked energy can be fully released. This may consist of an improvised accompaniment to the songwriter's spontaneously created lyrics, or in assisting the songwriter to create an accompaniment that may heighten the emotion expressed in the lyrics (Baker, 2013e).

Much of the therapeutic work transpires during the interactions with the therapist where transference and countertransference events emerge and the songwriter's defense mechanisms are activated. As the songwriter creates his song, the clinician can play a surrogate role, resembling a person in a past relationship, often a parent or primary caregiver, and then use this reconstruction of a past relationship to work through issues. Songwriting offers possibilities for the therapist to 'mother' the songwriter, and calls for the therapist to act as listener and responder to the songwriter's lyrics, music, and dialogue. A clinician working with at-risk youth reported that when young people have experienced chaotic and frequent changes to home circumstances, they might not have had a consistent adult in their life for any length of time. These young people are experiencing loss and struggling to understand what is going on. This is compounded by the reality of approaching adulthood and the anxiety about what will happen to them next. During songwriting, the therapist offers support and nurturing and at the same time provides a meaningful experience of enjoying something together.

Khare (personal communication, April 18, 2014) described her therapeutic role as a nurturer during the creation of a song titled: 'The Darkest Pain'.

'Darkest Pain' explicitly references the songwriter's relationship with his mother who had passed away from AIDS, and discusses how he is moving through transition with support. I was definitely a nurturer, someone who believed in him and was there for him – someone he could trust and have as a resource to leverage the personal strength to look at his pain. The harmonic and melodic themes in 'Darkest Pain' were my place in the mix – the place I would say, 'Is this what you need? Does this hold the pain? Does this create the space you need to feel this through?'

Post-creation verbal processing is a vital part of psychodynamic songwriting, particularly for improvised song creation experiences. The therapist's role here is to elicit the songwriter's verbal reactions to the songwriting process and the product, encouraging the songwriter to identify and verbally share internal feelings and thoughts. The therapist may comment, augment, or respond to what the songwriter is expressing in the song or remain silent to receive the full assault of the songwriter's verbal projections (Bruscia, 1987). This is epitomized in the example offered by Khare (personal communication, April 18, 2014):

> The song 'The Real in Me' was written by a group of youth. They had attended a youth leadership conference during the summer. In one of our weekly group meetings, I asked about a subject they had started talking about at conference – the challenges of medical transition and how care providers (CP) aren't always supportive of their choices. These youth have grown up with these CPs, so the CPs sometimes struggle with seeing them as 20 year olds and letting them independently make choices regarding their medication adherence. The youth needed to vent – needed a song where they could just sing it like it is for them – with no concern for repercussions. They needed to express their feelings of anger and then listen back to their song and determine and process if this is how they felt. So there was much discussion about the song/lyrics after it was initially written. There were changes and adaptations to the song and then it was finalized. I then led a discussion asking them to consider how the CPs feel – which is not listened to – and they were able to realize that both parties were feeling the same way, but for different reasons – and that both parties wanted the other to listen. We talked about how maybe listening was the path to being heard. That being able to say 'I hear what you're saying, and realize you're saying this because you care. I want you to hear where I'm coming from.' Then we processed dealing/accepting when others won't listen but how we can still hear ourselves.

The songwriter is always active during the songwriting process, whether that is through free association, creating lyrics, music, or dialoguing about the meaning of the song. As he creates songs, feelings, fantasies, and anxieties are projected into the lyrics and/or music from deep within the psyche. Through his active exploration of the self and the interactions with the therapist, the songwriting process becomes a simulation of his own life (Bruscia, 2011). Some songwriters have more difficulty achieving this than others when their defense mechanisms are strongly activated.

The role of the artifact

While most clinicians reported that the creation of the song was the most important phase of the songwriting process, many believe that the experience of listening to recordings deepens the meaning of the song creation experience (Baker, 2013c). Repeated listening allows the songwriter to re-feel, further explore his reactions, and give voice to his feelings. Barba (2005) suggests that as a songwriter sings back his own song, he is transported back into himself where he can 'feel centered, calm, composed and fully present to the world' (p. 101). Singing helps the songwriter to reconnect with his body and emotions (Austin, 2008). Again, Kimberly Khare shared a vignette that illustrates this:

> So, there is listening and re-listening as that's an important part of the recording process and songwriting intervention. Hearing yourself is powerful, and when done right in music therapy, is empowering. 'Miracle' is a song from the artist who wrote 'Choir Boy' and 'Someone 2 Love' [mentioned earlier in this chapter]. 'Miracle' is the third song, where she began to feel centered, calm, composed and fully present in her world. Through listening to her song she was reconnecting within herself and her emotions. (personal communication, April 18, 2014)

Clements-Cortes (2009) recounted her experiences of a couple where the wife was in palliative care. The songwriter (wife) wrote a song cycle for her husband, celebrating and thanking him in an effort to facilitate relationship completion. After singing all the songs, the therapist encouraged the songwriter and her husband to process each song individually in subsequent sessions. This sharing and re-listening enabled the couple to discuss memories, feelings, and emotions central to their need to complete their relationship.

The quality and timbre of the songwriter offers insights into his emotional state and psyche, and may signal the meaningfulness of the song for the songwriter. The vocal tone communicates pain, joy, relief, intimacy, anger, or sadness. However, as singing is very connected to the self, the songwriter may refuse invitations to sing his own songs or he may do so with trepidation. Singing words is associated with ownership of the voiced issues, and in many situations the singer/songwriter may not be ready to own the material. Further, he may have been previously traumatized by unsolicited critique of his voice, so any invitation to sing may trigger unnecessary anxiety.

Humanistic influences

Humanistic psychology, founded by Abraham Maslow and Carl Rogers, emphasizes concepts such as self, self-actualization, individuality, creativity, authenticity, being and becoming, and meaning as important for a happy, healthy, and fulfilling life (Schneider & Krug, 2010). A focus on the lived experiences and the establishment of authentic relationships are integral to humanistic psychology. This theory is grounded in the assumption that people are inherently trustworthy, have potential for understanding themselves, and have the capacity to grow. Subscribers of humanistic thinking emphasize working with the present rather than uncovering and resolving the past.

In terms of behavior, Rogers suggests that people act in response to their perception of reality (which may not be the absolute reality) (Rogers, 1959), and which serves a function in assisting them to cope and live in their world. However, people's reality may cover up and make 'inaccessible other experiences' (Polkinghorne, 2001, p. 83) and they may need opportunities to become aware of alternative realities. So in humanistic psychology, change in behavior is in part determined by increasing people's awareness of an alternative reality.

Maslow's hierarchy of needs (1943) is another key concept associated with humanistic psychology. This hierarchy indicates that once physiological and safety needs are met, people need to feel loved and feel a sense of belonging. Self-esteem, confidence, respect for people, and the need to be respected by them then become important. At the top of the hierarchy is self-actualization, which is understood as a motivation to reach one's own fullest potential. It is often associated with expressing creativity and spontaneity, acceptance of facts, quests for spiritual enlightenment, and morality. People are self-actualizing when they are growing toward an ideal self. Indeed, not being true to the self or being inauthentic is understood as being the source of problems (Rogers, 1986). Psychological problems are viewed as the result of inhibited ability to make 'authentic, meaningful, and self-directed choices' about how to live (Substance Abuse and Mental Health Services Administration, 1999, p. 103). Importantly, Rogers believed that a tendency 'to grow, to develop, to realize full potential' (p. 200) is present in all people so long as the conditions for self-actualizing are present.

Given the above, interventions embedding humanistic psychological principles are aimed at increasing people's self-awareness and self-understanding, and encouraging the expression of feelings. Therapy is directed toward opportunities for acceptance and growth and to free them of beliefs and attitudes that restrict them from leading fulfilling lives. Through insight-oriented interventions, people are encouraged to be courageous and take responsibility for their own actions. The interventions focus on bringing to conscious awareness thoughts, feelings, and perspectives in the here and now. Therapeutic approaches are growth-oriented, typically non-directive, and an organic process that may journey in a number of different and non-predetermined directions.

The primary role of the therapist is to create a therapeutic relationship that is warm, accepting, and communicates an empathic understanding of the person's subjective experience and context. This will lead to the development of a trusting relationship where alternative realities can be explored safely. Another key concept in humanistic psychology is the notion of 'unconditional positive regard' (Rogers, 1961), sometimes referred to as person-centered (Carr, 2013) – an unconditional acceptance and support for a person, irrespective of how he acts or communicates. For some people in therapy, this experience of unconditional positive regard is new, as they have never experienced that from previous child or adult relationships. The therapist's empathic listening serves to communicate this unconditional positive regard, thereby inviting the person to open and share his feelings with the therapist. In time, the therapist and person begin to collaborate and develop a working alliance which research suggests is the single best predictor of positive therapeutic outcomes (Krupnick et al., 1996). In summary, the aim of therapy and therapeutic encounters is to create the conditions that will enable people to engage in meaningful self-exploration and to grow.

Positive psychology

Positive psychology focuses on building positive human functioning so that individuals, families, and communities can thrive (Seligman, 2002). Seligman initially proposed that positive human functioning was built on three principles: The Pleasant Life, The Engaged Life, and The Meaningful Life. Happiness was understood from within the theory of hedonism (Bentham, 1978), where feelings of pleasure are maximized and feelings of pain are minimized (Seligman, 2002). According to desire theory (Griffin, 1986), engagement is associated with states of being engaged and absorbed, while object list theory (Nussbaum, 1992) proposed that meaning and purpose are derived from experiences of freedom, civic spirit, beauty, knowledge, and good conscience (Sirgy & Wu, 2009). Seligman (2011) later revised his theory and suggested that to flourish in life, people need to move toward Positive emotions, Engagement, Relationships, Meaning and purpose, and Accomplishments (PERMA). A flourishing life is one where people experience mastery, accomplishment, and a sense of belonging.

Positive psychology emphasizes that people are drawn to consider the future. However, the past and present are not ignored or even forgotten; instead, therapists work to help people become content with the past, happy in the present, and optimistic about the future (Magyar-Moe, 2012). Recognition and satisfaction of a person's own past is an important contributor of authentic happiness (Seligman & Csikszentmihalyi, 2000). Positive psychology draws from several theories including the broaden-and-build theory, strengths-based theory, and peak experiences and flow to explain how people can flourish in life.

Broaden-and-build theory

The broaden-and-build theory (Fredrickson, 2001) asserts that positive emotions broaden momentary thought-action repertoires, and consequently open people to a wider range of possibilities (thoughts and actions). In turn, increased positive emotions lead to a building of physical resources (physical health), social resources (friendship, social skills, and support), intellectual resources (knowledge, problem-solving), and psychological resources (creativity, optimism, and resilience) (Magyar-Moe, 2012, p. 358). The theory also holds that increasing positive emotions has the potential to 'undo' enduring negative emotions. The combination of increased positive emotions, reduction in negative emotions, and a strengthening of resources builds resilience and overall wellbeing.

Strengths-based theory

Strengths-based theory proposes that growth and wellbeing are promoted by drawing on people's strengths, potentials, resources, and abilities to overcome challenges, rather than focusing on their weaknesses or deficits (Grant & Cadell, 2009). Within the strengths-based approaches, people are understood to have increased confidence to approach challenges when they begin by using the resources and strengths that they already know and recognize (Clifton & Nelson, 1992). Therefore, strengths-based interventions focus on helping people identify their resources and character strengths and then assisting them to utilize these in resolving their problems. For example, if someone has been subjected to a traumatic experience such as abuse, a natural disaster, racial persecution, or war, the therapy may focus on assisting this person to identify what strengths have developed as a result of the trauma, such as displayed pro-social behaviors. By raising this awareness of their strengths, there is an increased potential for the person to purposefully utilize this strength in other contexts he encounters in life.

In strengths-based interventions, the therapist works to strengthen people's resilience. Resilience emerges from developing effective coping strategies and feeling a strong sense of hope, optimism, self-esteem, and competence by learning how to set realistic goals and expectations, and recognizing what they can and cannot control in their lives (O'Neil, 2005). To achieve this, the therapist must first create a trusting relationship that allows those in therapy to feel confident and safe to try out new ways of being. They should be encouraged to take responsibility for their own lives, to be empowered. Carr (2013) suggests that there are three important phases to achieving this. The first is the engagement phase where the therapist aims to develop a strong and respectful collaborative therapeutic alliance with those in therapy. The second phase involves the assessment of people's strengths. The third phase involves the development of a plan, which contains the actions needed to achieve people's personal goals.

Peak experiences and flow

Two concepts subscribed to by those following the humanistic traditions and positive psychology are the notions of peak experiences and flow. Peak experiences are described as personally valued moments of true happiness and joy and are characterized by an intensity of perception and depth of feeling (Maslow, 1971). They stand out as significant moments when contrasted with other experiences, may be 'turning points' in people's lives, and may be transformative in nature. Maslow (1962) suggests that peak experiences are triggered by activities such as 'art, nature, sexual love, religion, exercise and movement, and creative work' (1962, p. 492). Relevant to songwriting, peak experiences are commonly triggered by music (Maslow, 1971).

Flow is used to describe a state of consciousness where people are intensely immersed in an activity that is enjoyable; it is a state of optimal experience. According to Csikszentmihalyi's (2000), people move into a state of flow when their skills match the skills needed for the task, there is a merging of action and awareness, when they have a sense of what is expected of them and that the goals are clear. During flow, people receive immediate and unambiguous feedback, become totally involved in what they are doing, and lose self-consciousness. The person experiences a sense of control and an altered sense of time. During flow, the experience becomes autotelic, and the task is intrinsically rewarding. As both flow and peak experiences are linked to wellbeing (Asakawa, 2010; Maslow, 1971; Privette, 2001), activities and interventions that arouse these experiences are valued.

Narrative influences

Narrative approaches to address growth and wellbeing draw on the beliefs that people use story-telling as a way of giving meaning to their past, understand the present, give direction for their future (Krippner & Feinstein, 2008), and 'actualize their inherent potentials' (Polkinghorne, 2001, p. 96). When people experience unexpected life events such as psychological or emotional abuse, or diagnosis of a life-threatening illness, people's narratives in the continuum of past, present, and future are thrown into chaos (Pennebaker et al., 1997) and there is a need to re-author and reconstruct their stories (Neimeyer, 2000). As people tell their stories, they expose how they feel, what they believe in, and the meaning of their experiences, rather than offering factual accounts of the events themselves. Their stories are more than just descriptions of events in chronological order.

In humanistic psychology, therapists who make use of narrative approaches have a role in guiding a person to author a 'new chapter in life' (Substance Abuse and Mental Health Services Administration, 1999, p. 107). As people tell and retell their stories, the therapist provides feedback and assists them to identify or recognize alternate explanations and understandings of the events in their lives. She assists people to discover how life events have assumed particular significance and to identify how these events have impacted on patterns of thinking, relating, or behaving. The therapist's role is to gently challenge people to rewrite their lives 'according to alternative and preferred scripts' (Substance Abuse and Mental Health Services Administration, 1999, p. 144).

Existential influences

Existentialism originated from the philosophical work of Kierkegaard, Nietzsche, and Sartre. Supporters of existentialism view people as a product of their choices in life rather than as victims of circumstance (Corey, 2013). There is a focus on the here and now rather than on recovering or overcoming past experiences (May & Yalom, 1995). Existentialism is grounded in the belief that people's inner conflicts arise from confronting what Yalom calls the 'givens' of existence (Yalom, 1980, p. 9): mortality, isolation, meaninglessness, and freedom. When inner conflicts become overwhelming, extreme existential anxiety develops, leading to dysfunction. Constructing meaning, purpose, and values are important components to healthy living, without which people experience emptiness and are at risk of isolation (Corey, 2013). Further, without meaning, there is a risk that people will not be living fully authentic lives. Therapists subscribing to existentialism therefore focus treatment on assisting people to find meaning and purpose (Yalom, 1980), help them resolve their existential conflicts, and enable them to redefine themselves so that they are able to live authentically. Through participation in existentially oriented therapy, people reflect on the lives they are living and the factors and motivations that influence them, increase awareness of alternative interpretations, and begin a journey where they consciously make decisions and shape their lives (Corey, 2013).

Gestalt, one school of existentialism, focuses on what is being done, thought, and felt in the moment rather than focusing on what was, might be, could be, or should be (Yontef, 1993). The person actively 'works' with the therapist to increase awareness of various areas, including the environment, responsibility for choices, self-knowledge, and self-acceptance. Simple strategies such as using probing questions like: 'What are you aware of now?' 'What are you thinking/feeling?' can encourage a person to focus on the here-and-now experiences. There is a firm emphasis on supporting people to find their own solutions to their problems. The therapist typically provides feedback on how a person is seen, heard, experienced, and how the therapist feels about him.

Creative music therapy influences

Music therapy clinicians locating themselves within the creative music therapy (CMT) tradition incorporate humanistic principles into their practice and principally work within a music-centered framework. Pioneers Nordoff and Robbins used music *as* the therapy; music is the primary means to engage people in personal growth experiences and identity work (Aigen, 2005a). Music-centered practitioners regard the musical structures within music therapy as fundamental to understanding the therapeutic process (Aigen, 2005a). While music-centered approaches may be adapted to varied theoretical stances (Lee, 2013), there is a long tradition of these being aligned with humanistic thinking.

Recognizing the importance of concepts such as peak experiences, intrinsic learning, and self-actualization (Bruscia, 1987), CMT therapists draw on various music-centered techniques to foster self-confidence, to encourage expressive freedom and independence, creativity, communication, and to develop relationships with others. CMT therapists use music to help people explore and bring their present inner experiences to conscious awareness.

CMT practice is essentially non-directive, and allows feelings, impulses, inhibitions, and fears to be transformed into action, and in doing so made conscious (Bruscia, 1987). These therapeutic transformations are driven by the therapist-person relationship that is built *in* and *through* music. Bruscia (1987) proposed that in CMT the therapist's role is to be the mediator of therapeutic music and to establish a relationship with the 'client' that was based in musical interactions. Through the creation of a musical-emotional environment, the therapist creates music that 'conveys acceptance and engenders feelings of trust and security' (Bruscia, 1987, p. 60).

In CMT practice, verbal interactions are kept to the bare minimum and comprise predominantly of instructions, prompts, or reflections of events in the moment. People's actions, reactions, and experiences are not discussed within the session; instead, the music and musical interactions are used to work through people's issues (Aigen, 2005a).

Models

Narrative songwriting

Narrative songwriting may be described as an approach that facilitates the telling of a person's or a group of people's story. This could be an historical account of someone's life, the story of a particular event or relationship, or the construction of an imagined future life story. Therapists facilitate narrative songwriting through the use of interview techniques. Here, the therapist facilitates the story-telling process by asking questions (as in an interview) and transcribing the responses verbatim. The therapist's role is to help the songwriter to create lyrics that include as much of the songwriter's original wording as possible. This ensures the song is authentic and that the intended meaning is preserved. As the therapist listens to the story, she communicates her 'availability' by responding to and validating the material shared.

The songwriter may choose one of several songwriting approaches to tell his story, depending upon the songwriter's musical preferences, time available to create the song, and the context (see Chapters 3–6).

My own clinical and research practice with people with brain injury uses songwriting within a positive psychology framework during the acute and early stages of rehabilitation. This approach (Tamplin et al., 2015) promotes an acceptance of the past, contentment with the present, and optimism for the future via the telling of three stories. Songwriters create three songs: the first about the past self, particularly focusing on identity and self-concept, the second about the present self, and the third about an imagined future self post-rehabilitation and hospital discharge. By examining their stories and examining parts of the self-concept – such as the personal self, social self, physical self, academic self, and moral self – the songwriters are able to identify their character traits, strengths, and identity, which ultimately leads to a more fulfilling and meaningful life. In a study in progress, we (Felicity Baker, Jeanette Tamplin, Nikki Rickard, Raymond MacDonald, and Jennie Ponsford) have been collecting data about the effects of this approach on self-concept, identity, flourishing, self-efficacy, satisfaction with life, and affect in adults who have acquired severe brain injuries or spinal cord injuries. Preliminary data suggest that there is a trend toward improvement in all of these areas over a six-week songwriting program over 12 sessions. Table 13.1 presents excerpts from the three songs created by three participants in the study (participants 4, 5, and 10). Song 1 about the past self shows clearly how these songwriters have created songs with statements that accept the past and at times highlight positive aspects of it. Song 2 presents a mix of emotions. These songs are mostly descriptions of the here and now, with acknowledgments of the negative aspects of sustaining brain injuries present, but interspersed with moments of positivity. For example 'my body may be broken, but my mind has been set free' is an example of how the songwriter views his life through the lens of someone who has a deeper self-understanding and inner strength post-trauma. Despite a voiced struggle, Song 3 presents examples of optimism for what lies ahead for them.

In their research with older adults, Baker and Ballantyne (2013) investigated whether group songwriting could embed principles of positive psychology and promote happiness, satisfaction with life, and flourishing in old age. Six songwriting sessions focused on creating song parodies about the past, the present, and an imagined future life. After the songs were created, they were performed at a concert held at the retirement village where the members were living. This had the purpose of allowing the group members to contribute back to the community as well as derive a sense of accomplishment and pride from their musical engagement. A combination of video footage, focus groups, observational journals, and song lyrics provided Baker and Ballantyne with a rich dataset to identify moments of pleasure, engagement, and meaning (Seligman, 2002).[3] They found songwriters experienced all three forms of happiness (Figure 13.4).

Insight-oriented songwriting

Insight-oriented songwriting may be incorporated into therapy when the main purpose of therapy is to stimulate personal insight about one's current context, feelings, and behavior, and gain an understanding of the true self. Songwriting can lead to insight when the lyric

Table 13.1 Lyrics of past, present, and future self-focused songs created by people with SCI

	Song 1: Past	Song 2: Present	Song 3: Future
4	Looking back. . . . I didn't know what I had I didn't appreciate my freedom My family . . . were always there for me But I was blind, I just couldn't see	When I look in the mirror, it doesn't look like me Subtraction of my hair and addition of a chair My body may be broken, but my mind has been set free And it's improved my personality Some days are good, some days are bad But I'm grateful for each day that I might never have had	When I look into the future, I see a new and different me More focused on the things that count, like my friends and family This accident has changed me, but not in the obvious way New priorities have come into play I wanna have a stronger role as part of my family
5	Happy memories, these were the good times When we started out We enjoyed all the seasons, all the colours of the spring Nothing to weigh us down	I live in the same body, but it can't talk to me anymore All my friends are different now People try to sympathize, but I must be strong inside Time is the healer and I know I will survive	I can see myself walking and jumping Doing what I could before Might have to make sacrifices I've come so far, but there's so much more to go
10	I'm just an average bloke Always loved a beer and smoke Doing just what most blokes do Having a drink and playing up too	Feel like a burden, stuck in this chair And no amount of bourbon's gonna take away this fear I don't know who I am now, and how I'll provide I've lost my motivation, but not my will to survive	Don't know yet, how much movement I'll get back Don't know how I'll support my family We won't be able to live like we used to Gotta change my life and do something new

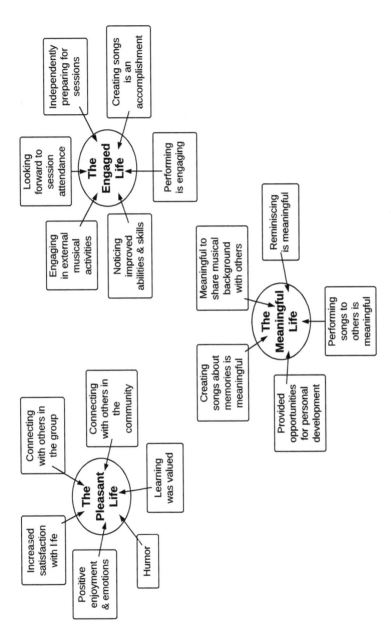

Figure 13.4   Positive psychology themes that emerge from group songwriting with retirees

and/or music creation process elicit rethinking, re-knowing, re-feeling, or re-experiencing (O'Callaghan, 2005, p. 125). To facilitate the process, the therapist encourages the songwriter to explore an issue through empathic listening and by using probing questions. Once the lyrics are created, the therapist assists the songwriter with music that purposefully matches or contrasts with the specific issue expressed in the lyrics. Insight-oriented songwriting tends to focus on a feeling or specific situation such as love, pain, loss, anger, abandonment, and disappointment. A music therapist interviewed described one case, which illustrates clearly how songwriting facilitated insight into the source of a young boy's previous criminal act:

> He had committed a carjacking and was later picked up and arrested by the police. At the hearing, the judge had determined that his grandmother who the adolescent was very close with had recently passed away and that the adolescent seemed to have a lot of anger about that. So astutely, the judge thought that there may be some unresolved anger issues surrounding the death of his grandparent. The judge referred him to our adolescent bereavement program. The adolescent attended weekly music therapy as a condition of his sentence. . . . he revealed during his first or second session that he was very angry, but it wasn't about the death of his grandparent. His ex-girlfriend had become pregnant by him that nobody else had known about it and she had miscarried or had an abortion. . . . So he wanted to write a song for the baby that might have been. He became very emotionally invested in the relationship between himself and this baby that he had never gotten to meet. So I remember the song, 'Baby Sleeps Tonight', was about this baby and being peaceful, being in heaven, and being safe. That story (or the song) was never shared with anybody else. I think the experience for him was reconstructive because he was changing his relationship with himself as well as the relationship with this unborn child. He gained insight that the reason that he did the carjacking was to get away from all the stress and all this pressure . . . So get a car and drive.

Music-centered songwriting

Music-centered songwriting has evolved from the principles of CMT whereby therapeutic change occurs predominantly in the music itself – music *as* therapy. Through and during the creation of original song material, the therapist–songwriter relationship can develop and the therapeutic environment constructed so that the conditions for therapeutic change are created. As the songwriter expresses his identity in the lyrics and music created, he engages in expressive freedom, independence, empowerment, and creativity, and subsequently grows. In keeping with CMT, verbal interpretations are typically not encouraged, although some therapists will engage in verbal dialogue if the songwriters initiate it (Viega, 2013).

When working with adolescents and young adults, engaging people in creating songs based on groove-based genres (rap, hip hop, etc.) is ideal because those genres inherently emphasize authenticity, self-expression, and self-reflection (Aigen, 2005b; Lightstone, 2012) and therefore assist young people to form or reform identity (see Chapters 9 and 10). For example, as songwriters build multitrack songs, they may make subtle manipulations of rhythms, sound effects, or instrumentation which serve to actualize their music potential, function as a motivating force, and allow the songwriters to explore different ways of being in the music and different identities, often without an awareness that they are engaging in this process. One illustrative example was with a young boy who was seen in music therapy just prior to a surgical procedure to remove the halo traction. While his parents, who were often present, preferred he listen to classical music, the therapist convinced them to give their son and the therapist some space to work together on their own. The therapist says:

he wanted metal, so he started choosing the GarageBand loops and he organized the whole song. I was the technical guide, but he made all the choices and he wrote this amazing song and the lyrics. The song was about feeling numb over his body as the halo traction was beginning to cause that lack of feeling in his left side . . . So the song was 'I feel numb all over my body, I feel numb'. He told me he liked it: 'it's crazy good'.

The therapist recounted that this boy was inadvertently saying, 'I want to test out who I am and I always wanted to experience this music'. The therapist stated:

I had this amazing moment with this kid where he let loose and had fun and the music came out of him to say, 'it's crazy good'. There was this great playfulness about it and it was just a very powerful thing, but he made all those choices. That song was his.

When adolescents are exploring their identity during music-centered songwriting, they may start by imitating their favorite pop star and then build to greater future possibilities. One clinician indicated that some young people begin by intentionally creating songs that resemble the sound of their favorite artists:

> It's the beginning of identifying and saying, 'well this is me and this isn't me, so let me explore this character'. . . . when I feel like it's moved out of the imitation phase and has moved into a phase where they're actually working on their voice and sculpting the music into their own creative sound, there's some kind of authenticity; as if they are saying, 'I know where I want to take this'. Then I feel like we've entered into a new phase of identifying myself; 'who I am, what my voice is'. Some people it comes kind of naturally to them like they've had this artist with them the whole time, while others need to start with saying, 'I want to sound like this person; let's find a beat that sounds like this'.

Strengths-based songwriting

Strengths-based songwriting draws on the principles of strengths-based theory and involves the creation of a song that utilizes or brings into focus the songwriters' strength, potentials, and resources,[4] and in doing so increases people's confidence, competence, self-esteem, resilience, effective coping strategies, and sense of empowerment. When people create songs, they experience a sense of achievement, pride, and self-esteem in having created a socially admired and beautiful artifact (Baker, 2013c). They have a 'voice' when they choose what to say and what not to say musically and lyrically, an action that engenders a sense of power and inner strength.

To facilitate the recognition of their strengths, the therapist may subtly direct them to reflect on 'what is there', 'what is not there', 'what they can move forward with', 'what works', and 'what are the limitations' (and to be comfortable with the limitations). Dialoguing during and post-song creation allows the therapist to validate the strengths of the songwriter and identify whether these are musical or personal strengths. Acknowledging and validating these strengths is a demonstration of positive regard, which in turn supports the songwriter to reflect deeply, create a song that has meaning, and journey toward healing.

When interviewing a clinician about her strengths-based approaches to songwriting with children and adolescents, it emerged that the key to her practice was to 'get at the essence of who these people are, what their perspectives are, and what they are experiencing, to really try to get to the core'. By observing their body language, movements, energy levels, and the way they interjected themselves into or withdrew from a group, she identified which 'musical roles would best fit'. She then used her therapeutic skills to draw out the strengths she recognized in them or pushed them to grow 'into something past where they are right now'. At the same time, she allowed the songwriting process to organically unfold and left the final decisions to them, so that their own voices were authentically present in the song.

Existential issue-based songwriting

The search for meaning is the main aim of existential issue-based song-writing. Within this approach, there are three main principles that drive the songwriting process: (1) meaning can be created by creating a work or doing a deed, (2) meaning can be created through experiencing something or encountering someone, and (3) meaning is derived from self-transcendence. Within existential issue-based songwriting, people construct meaning through their creation of a song, their experiences of working with others on a meaningful topic, and their transcendence from illness through the creation of a beautiful artifact (Cordobés, 1997). Cordobés recounted how a group of people used group songwriting to express their inner world in a meaningful way that transcended the HIV infection. Through the creation of songs on specifically chosen issues, the group members worked collaboratively to shape their ideas into a song form that had meaning for them. Through the engagement in a songwriting activity, group members developed relationships, expressed emotions, and felt supported. In this study, Cordobés drew on Clark's (1993) conversational model of coping to inform his approach whereby assimilation and organization occur through engaging in talking and writing. Such conversational models 'encourage coherency of language, multiple perspectives, insights, and emotional reaction. In turn, these actions lead to problem solving, appraisal, and finding meaning' (p. 50). During issue-based songwriting, group members first verbalize their experiences, thoughts, and feelings, which are then transformed into lyrics, and in doing so become more integrated and organized.

Sung imaginal dialogue and empty chair songwriting

Sung imaginal dialogue is a direct translation of the empty chair tech-nique used by Gestalt therapists (Wagner-Moore, 2004). Here, the song-writer creates a dialogue by singing, which directly addresses a part of himself or a person who is physically not present. This approach is used to explore external or internal conflict. In traditional Gestalt empty chair interventions, unresolved issues and feelings such as grief and anger are explored by talking to an empty chair, a form of imaginal exposure (Diamond et al., 2010). The approach seeks to restructure emotional memories, with the purpose of accessing and expressing 'previously inhibited painful feelings, and acknowledging and legitimizing previously unmet needs' (Greenberg & Malcolm, 2002, p. 406).

Sung imaginal dialogue (Iliya, 2015) involves a person singing an imaginal dialogue to a part of himself or to another person. In Iliya's study of creative arts therapists who had experienced a recent death, the sung imaginal dialogue involved the participants singing directly to the deceased person, as an opportunity to communicate thoughts and feelings that may have been left unsaid. The therapist created a two-chord harmonic structure to support the participants' sung dialogue. Later in the session, the participants were asked to 'switch chairs' and respond using a sung imaginal dialogue, as if singing from the perspective of the deceased person. Iliya notes that if the participants became overwhelmed and ceased singing, she would continue the music and singing as a support. Importantly, Iliya reported using various grounding exercises to assist people to transition from the sung imaginal dialogue back to the present moment.

Empty chair songwriting takes Iliya's process a step further and transforms the (sung) dialogue into a more structured song form. The songwriter creates a song that 'speaks' directly to another non-present person. In a study with university students and refugees (Baker & MacDonald, 2013b), one young female university student created a song that was an apology to her grandfather about not training to become a doctor. In this song she expressed her reluctance to disappoint him, but also used the process to resolve her own feelings about her choices (Figure 13.5).

Critical points and levels of depth in the therapeutic process

In humanistic and positive psychology songwriting practices, the therapeutic relationship is regarded as a key component in the songwriting process. The songwriting process has the potential for maximum therapeutic benefit when rapport has been established. At what point this therapeutic relationship is established, however, is somewhat difficult to articulate with certainty, as it will be depend upon numerous factors, including the setting, the diagnosis (if relevant), the therapist's characteristics, sociocultural factors, and length of the proposed treatment

"Grandpa, I'm sorry"

Verse 1
Grandpa you were my very best friend
You were also a great dentist
You showed me your love in lots of ways
You bought me candy and let me wear your white coat
You made me want to be a doctor as well
We would pretend that I was a dentist and you were my assistant:
You would say, "What do you need doctor?"

Chorus
But I'm sorry Grandpa I just couldn't make it
I wanted to be like you
I'm sorry Grandpa but I just can't fake it
Maybe that's not the right path for me
Maybe I'm meant to be like me

Verse 2
At high school I tried my best
I was sure I wanted to be like you
I studied real hard I took extra courses
Medicine was what I really wanted to do

Bridge
But you remember Grandpa how I used to scream when I saw
    blood
You tried to make it better with your words but even now I'm
    still afraid of blood
And I still scream

Verse 3
So now I'm doing psychology
I can still help people without seeing their blood
Maybe I can still be a doctor
Yes maybe a doctor of psychology is what I'll be

Figure 13.5   Example of sung imaginal dialogue

plan (see Chapters 3–6). For example, one clinician reported that building a trusting relationship sufficient for songwriting takes longer when she works in mental health when compared with her work in palliative care. Therefore, the initial stages are a very important part of the songwriting process, where the therapist is establishing this safe space for the songwriter to express himself in song when he is ready and able. Some clinicians begin the therapy process by asking songwriters to create a 'lighter', less personal or emotional song as a way of introducing songwriting as a possible journey in their recovery.

Being empowered to have a voice is a fundamental principle of humanistic thinking. When a therapist is sitting next to the songwriter and acting as a scribe, the songwriter has the freedom, support, and safety to create lyrics and/or music. The songwriter experiences this therapist attention as a form of unconditional positive regard, of being heard, acknowledged, and validated. These feelings of validation might prompt the songwriter to take more risks with disclosure and uncensored material, and share, process, and potentially release tension associated with internal or external conflict. The songwriter may experience similar feelings of empowerment and validation when his song is being performed or shared (Baker, 2013d).

Performing to and sharing the song with significant others can be a critical step in the songwriters' therapeutic journey, affording greater transformative power than the creation process itself. For example, for children grieving the loss of a family member, sharing the song creation with others can lead to additional grief processing. One clinician stated:

> The kids were great creating songs for or about their lost family member and we would record them on a CD. Sometimes the child wanted to share it with the rest of the family, often mum and dad, sometimes the whole family, aunts, uncles, grandparents will all come along. There'd be tears and there'd be hugging; it was really powerful. Then they would all start processing what had happened to them, and doing it as a family.

For those working on identity issues with adolescents, a critical point in the songwriting process occurs when the adolescents start to replace the imitation of their idols with their own voices and sculpting the music into their own creative sound. One clinician suggests it is this authenticity in sound that signals the entry into a new phase of 'identifying myself; who I am, what my voice is'.

Some clinicians assert that self-growth is associated with self-disclosure. As the songwriter works through therapeutic issues, he may feel vulnerable, exposed. There are moments of baring oneself in front of other people, having to own what has been created, and risking being exposed to whatever feedback or reactions might follow. It is through the therapist's support that songwriters courageously share themselves through lyrics and music, and become catalysts for self-actualization.

Experienced humanistic and positive psychology-oriented clinicians differed in their views of the level of depth achieved through therapeutic songwriting. Levels of depth depended upon time available, therapeutic needs being addressed, and the age and abilities of the songwriters and context. Songwriting at the supportive level is practiced when its purpose is to support the songwriter in whatever is prevalent in his life at that moment, whether the focus is on accepting the past, being content with the present, or looking toward the future. In the medical setting, for example, songwriting would be supportive when a person is about to undergo a medical procedure or is in pain. Supportive levels are appropriate when the songwriters are preparing for discharge and exploring feelings and concerns about the future. In the palliative care setting, songwriting is supportive when children or adults feel a need to express their here-and-now feelings – feelings that may be transitory and not necessarily ongoing issues.

A humanistic-oriented clinician working with an eight-year-old boy from the Dominican Republic recounted an example of songwriting at the supportive level. The young boy had received a burns injury and had travelled to the United States to receive reconstructive surgeries. He had large keloid scars and limited movement in his hands due to scarring, and his disfigured appearance led to social isolation at home. During one of his first music therapy sessions, his nurse interrupted the session to undertake a procedure involving a needle. The music therapist noticed the boy presented with symptoms of post-traumatic stress disorder during the needle part of the procedure. The mother reported that ever since he had been a baby, he had had a needle phobia (and these procedures were to occur weekly during his treatment period). The music therapist offered to support the boy and addressed his phobia in various ways, including offering the boy a space to express how he felt about needles. Using songwriting, the child wrote a song called 'La Aguja Mala' (The Bad Needle). The music to accompany it was created to support the negative emotions he expressed about the needle, thereby acknowledging his negative feelings. The boy and the music therapist sang together when recording the song, with the boy playing percussion and the music therapist on guitar. The song (Figure 13.6), composed in Spanish, included repeated lyrics to highlight certain thoughts and feelings.

In this case, the use of songwriting during distressing procedures illustrates its effectiveness in addressing the here-and-now feelings.

People who have experienced trauma or who have a mental illness may experience catharsis as songwriting releases stress and tension, and insight may result as they move toward a new realization about their lives. For example, a songwriter's lyrics might express 'I may have lost the house, I may have lost some books, I may have lost some photos, but I haven't lost my life'. As children with disability or people in palliative care tell their story through the lyrics and music, they concretize their abstract feelings, and this verbalization process contributes to increased insight into themselves and their contexts.

La Aguja Mala (The Bad Needle)

Chorus:

La aguja mala, Puya mucho   (The bad needle pokes a lot)
La aguja mala, Puya mucho
La aguja mala, Puya mucho
Ooo me duele   (oh, I hurt)

Verse:

El miércoles, que visito la alguja mala   (every Wednesday, I visit the bad needle)
La aguja mala
La agula puya
Grito   (I scream)
Tengo Dolor, Ou ou ou   (I have pain, ouch ouch ouch)

Figure 13.6 Example of song composed at the supportive activities-oriented level

Source: Permission to transcribe and print song 'La Aguja Mala' (The Bad Needle) given by Annette Whitehead-Pleaux.

Songwriting at the reconstructive or transformative level was less frequently reported for those practicing within the humanistic traditions. Transformations occurred during the processing of some form of loss – for example, loss of a loved one through death, loss of a relationship, or loss of a physical self – and also led to the capacity for some people to genuinely forgive others. As one clinician reported: 'I think so many transformative things can happen during songwriting. You know you can forgive others, you can forgive yourself and you can express emotions that you never knew existed. You can say things like I love you, thank you, you can assess regrets, pathways that you've chosen in life.'

One clinician recounted her experiences of working with a 16-year-old girl from the Dominican Republic who received significant burns and relocated to the United States for treatment. She described the girl as having a significantly altered appearance due to the severe burns on her face, upper limbs and hands, chest, and feet. Her family tried to protect her by not giving her an opportunity to see herself in the mirror during her initial hospitalization. Internalizing the message that she was hideous to behold, she hid in her room in the dark, afraid of her appearance and afraid of having others see her. Additionally, her eyelids contracted, limiting her ability to blink, which resulted in cataracts that blinded her. Upon admission she was referred to music therapy to focus on her pain management, anxiety management, and coping. During one of her sessions, the music therapist introduced the idea of songwriting. The adolescent girl wrote many songs, starting with song parody and then moving to writing lyrics and original music. Her songs were a way to bridge her 'three lives': life before the accident, life since the accident, and her life when she returned home. She saw the third life as a joining of the two first lives. Outside of her music therapy sessions she created the song 'Chica Diferente' (Different Girl), which explored her feelings of being different, and she brought it to her therapy session. It was a significant step for her in the integration of her two 'lives'. In this sense, the songwriting process was transformative.

The role of songwriting

When a person creates a song that emerges from a therapeutic interaction with a therapist, it offers an opportunity for that person to explore the self. For example, if the focus of the songwriting experience is to create a song about a recent challenging experience, there is an opportunity for the person to examine the different facets of the experience – his feelings, actions, and perspectives about the context or other people's actions (or lack of actions) – which are then transformed into lyrics. As the therapist validates and reflects the songwriter's contributions, there are opportunities to discover the true and false self as they unfold in the lyrics. Sometimes it is not until the songwriter begins to create the music to accompany the lyrics that the self – true and/or false – becomes evident. Regardless of whether the lyrics or the music are created first or simultaneously, the combination of the two allows for feelings to be evoked (and sometimes intensified), brought to conscious awareness, and made concrete through the use of words and music. This experience may or may not be cathartic or transformative, but still contributes to growth and an enhanced self-understanding.

Related to self-discovery is the notion of the reconstruction of identity. As people tell their stories, they re-author their lives through the narrative process (Baker & MacDonald, in press). Similarly, as championed by Viega (2013), creating songs allows for young people to 'try out' different identities. Here, by creating songs using different genres, children and young adolescents can take on the different voices as expressed by favorite artists until they resolve conflicted identity and construct an identity they can comfortably own. While not discussed in terms of identity, Aasgaard (2002) describes the case of 'Mary's' second song. Mary was a young girl being treated for cancer in a Norwegian hospital. Over time, she wrote several songs with Aasgaard. For one of the texts, she created different versions of the song set to different musical styles, including Punk-style, priest-like style, and jungle-style. Through her exploration of different musical genres, she was experimenting with different identities, to see which one might fit her best at that moment.

Songwriting aims to give people a voice, build confidence and resilience, and assists them to feel empowered to make decisions about their lives. As the songwriters are guided to make decisions about song content and have control over the music created, they are presented with opportunities to have a voice – sometimes for the first time in their lives – authentically expressing themselves. Songwriting (when sensitively guided by the therapist) provides a forum for taking such a risk.

Clinicians subscribing to positive psychology focus on bolstering positive emotions so that people can become aware of their internal and external resources. Songs focus on meaning, relationships, and accomplishments, and offer opportunities to be engaged in life. The songwriting experience offers the songwriter the potential to explore meaning through the creation of a song.

The role of the music

Music takes on a central role in humanistic-oriented songwriting; it is the medium through which change takes place. Humanistic philosophy values individuality, creativity, and authenticity, as well as the being and becoming. All of these are inherently present during the creation of the music. Whether the music is created pre-lyrics, synchronously, or post-lyrics, the songwriter expresses his identity (or emerging identity) in the musical style, instrumental choices, tonality, and other components of the music. Viega (2013) describes cases where musical identity is explored and transformed through the recording, mixing, and editing techniques used. Songwriters gain a sense of mastery, confidence, and autonomy as they are supported to create an aesthetic art form that essentially says 'this is me'. As was evident in the research of Baker and MacDonald (2013a), original song creations were perceived as significantly greater expressions of identity than lyrics created without music.

Musicing (Elliott, 1995) is embedded in music-centered approaches and is understood as the expression of a person's aesthetic agency in action (Abrams, 2014). The being and becoming are present as the songwriters experiment with sound, harmony, tempo, and rhythm, learning about themselves and outwardly expressing that to others. Further, the music processes allow for the development of relationships with the therapist through the music creation itself, by listening to the song product, or by discussing the music.

The musical components do allow for multiple feelings to be expressed simultaneously, such as tension, stability, ambivalence, and the like (Baker, 2013e). Music adds an emotional backing to the lyrics and provides possibilities to heighten climaxes and strengthen the release of tension at the musical resolution (see Chapter 7). People are generally more motivated to engage in the process when they create music, and also to invest more in the process.

The role of creativity, peak experiences, and flow

Creativity and flow are central to humanistic and positive psychology thinking. Studies by Baker and MacDonald (2013a, 2013b) focused on experiences of flow and meaningfulness of the songwriting process in healthy university students and retired older adults. The songwriters reported that they enjoyed the freedom and excitement of creating original works that were based on their own personal experiences. All participants experienced some or all of the nine dimensions of flow (Csikszentmihalyi, 2000a). They experienced achievement without effort and were pleasantly surprised at what they were able to accomplish. It was challenging without being over-challenging. Participants also recounted that they were so engaged in the experience that they 'lost track of time'. One participant stated:

> I just find time passes so fast. I looked at my clock as you went out, and it had been an hour. I was like, 'Are you serious?' It felt like it was only like 15 min.

Participants described becoming fully focused, 'fully absorbed and in tune . . . lost in the music', unaware of other things going on around them in the environment, and that everything around them seemed to disappear. Mood and energy levels increased, and many reported feeling more relaxed and happy when they had completed a song. About a quarter of the participants found creating personally meaningful songs was cathartic. It allowed them to vent their frustration and anger, and to cry. An important finding of this research was the relationship between the strength of flow experiences and the meaningfulness of the songwriting process. The measures indicated that increased strength of flow was a predictor of how meaningful the songwriter found the songwriting experience.

The role of the therapist and the songwriter

The principle role of the therapist in humanistic-oriented songwriting is to empathize with the songwriter, reflect the songwriter's feelings (either musically or verbally), and meet the emotional needs of the songwriter in the moment. The therapist should encourage the songwriter to bring forth what he has to share. Clinicians need to take responsibility for creating an environment where the songwriter feels confident to express those thoughts, feelings, or experiences and take responsibility for ensuring that the words sung are in the songwriter's own words wherever possible. In sum, the role of the therapist is to facilitate the songwriter's discovery of his essence, of who he is as person, what his perspectives are, and what he is experiencing. The clinician is there to help the songwriter discover his 'core' self. Clinicians embedding positive psychology principles into practice assess the songwriter's strengths and, in collaboration with the songwriter, develop an action plan aimed at achieving the songwriter's personal goals.

In Baker and MacDonald's (2013a, 2013b) study, songwriters commented on the relationship they had developed with the music therapist facilitating the sessions, the support that the music therapist offered, and her therapeutic presence. Participants found it 'easy' to share themselves with the therapist and valued her skills in helping them to shape their thoughts, feelings, and experiences into a meaningful song.

By reflecting the lyrics or music created, the therapist validates the songwriter, communicating unconditional positive regard and developing therapeutic alliance. Humanistic therapists emphasize that there is no right or wrong when creating a song. The therapist may offer comments such as 'I would just so love to hear more about this' or 'I think that would make a great song' to reassure the songwriter that his contributions are valued.

Ideally, music therapists support the songwriters so that all decisions concerning the song content, lyrics, and music flow from the songwriter (empowerment). One clinician's work with bereaved children uses statements such as 'I'm going to help you create the music', 'You can do this', 'You're in charge', 'I'm here to facilitate, but you're the boss of this song' to affirm that it's the songwriter's own voice that is valued.

One clinician shared her story of her sessions with the spouse of a lady who was in palliative care. She states:

> One of the projects that I did last year was just so rewarding to me – a spouse of one of my female clients brought in this box of memories that they'd collected. My client was dying. I originally offered her music therapy as a relaxation. And despite a brain tumor, she was able to sing. So it was positive. But as she got more and more frail the therapy became about him [the spouse] coming to music therapy with her. One day he brought me this box. I think he just wanted to share the poetry he'd written her with someone. They were love letters. We turned them into a song cycle of nine songs and I sang them at her memorial. We made a CD of it that he gave to everyone at the memorial.

Many of the songwriters who are creating songs in therapy lack confidence in their musical skills and ability to create a song. It is the music therapist's role as expert musician to offer the songwriters musical choices to select from as they build their songs. They need to do so in a manner that ensures the songwriters still experience their songs as their own and not that of the therapist. However, it can be argued that the songs created within a therapeutic relationship are never truly owned by the songwriter because they were a product of a dynamic interaction with the therapist – a product of a collaborative process.

Clinicians interviewed described various approaches to shaping the music to ensure the songwriters experience ownership of their songs.

In her work with children who have disabilities, one clinician used statements such as 'What should it sound like?', 'When do you want it to change?', 'What do you think of this?', 'Where do we go from here?' to allow the children to have control over the final product and leave them with a strong feeling of ownership. In deciding what musical suggestions to offer, clinicians take into consideration the intended meaning of the lyrics, the overall mood of the songwriter at that time, the intonation of their voices, their body gestures or energy, and their musical interests. The clinician then reflects on these and translates these into musical ideas to present to the songwriter for consideration.

Integral to the humanistic approaches is the emphasis on movement toward health being the responsibility of the person in therapy. The therapist does not take an authoritarian role, but is a support person who is present and accessible and functions to ensure the person focuses on here-and-now experiences (Rogers & Wood, 1974, cited in Corey, 2013). The songwriters are viewed as beings who are encouraged to retain basic agency, 'the capacity, condition, or state of acting or of exerting power' (Abrams, 2014, p. 151). Therefore, the songwriter is encouraged to take an active role in exploring the self in relation to the music being created. He will actively engage in creating lyrics on a topic of his choice that is appropriate and relevant at the time.

The role of the artifact

The song product may play a pivotal role in the therapeutic process, either at the relational level (between therapist and songwriter) or at the internal level of the songwriter. At the relational level, the therapist's unconditional positive regard and 'care' is clearly demonstrated as she types up the lyrics or makes a recording of the song and presents it to the songwriter as a record of their process together. This may be perceived as a 'gift' from the therapist and can bolster the therapeutic rapport between songwriter and therapist (Baker, 2013c). It is at this moment that the songwriter may experience being fully validated and have his voice not only heard but also valued – something that should be made permanent.

Insight may be gained from subsequent performances of the song, repeated listening to recordings, and/or discussing the meaning of the song (Baker, 2013c). The therapist may ask: 'What did you learn about yourself from creating this? What did you learn about yourself through doing this together with me (or others)?' In this way, the experience of creating a song is emphasized as much as the meaning of the product. So, process and product are both relevant.

For those songwriters who used songwriting as a tool to experience empowerment or to assist with coping in the face of adversity, the song products can become powerful reminders and sources of inner strength. One clinician described his work with a young Indian girl whose song gave her inner strength to manage her response to ongoing events in life:

> I wrote this song with a young girl. Her family is very reserved and very secretive about stuff, and she'd been raped by her father, uncles, cousins, and so here she is, she's sitting in front of me . . . when she puts on make-up, the males say 'you're a slut', and it gives them more of a reason to abuse her. We wrote this song called 'I'm Pretty on the Inside Looking Out'. It became a mantra to her, that it doesn't matter what they do to me physically, verbally, spiritually, whatever, as long as I'm strong within myself I'll get through this.

At other times, strength is derived from just knowing that their own song is there, as a marker of their achievements:

> [I]f they come to a point emotionally where they are struggling and they can use this song to listen to and think 'Well I've been here before and I've been feeling really crap before, but I got through it. I processed it through music'. Like a tool that might only come out once in a blue moon or might not even be listened to. It's just there as 'that's something that I did'.

While there are numerous benefits associated with the artifact and its ongoing life, there are also a number of concerns clinicians should consider prior to giving the songwriter a permanent record of his song (Baker, 2013c). For example:

1. Listening to the song may stimulate the recall of painful emotions.
2. Dissatisfaction with the song product leads to negative outcomes such as disappointment, reinforcing feelings of worthlessness, and the like.
3. Over-listening hinders moving forward in songwriters' recovery.
4. Sharing song creations with others places songwriters in positions of increased vulnerability because others may ask the songwriter difficult questions about the meaning or intentions of the song.
5. Song creations may find their way into the hands of the wrong people and be misused.
6. Song creations are only a synthesis of process and dialogue and do not represent the whole process.

Table 13.2 Salient features of experience-oriented models of songwriting

	Psychodynamic	Humanistic	Positive psychology
Premise	People's behavior is shaped by inner conflicts arising from unconscious past: 1. People's response to events is influenced by defense mechanisms 2. People seek intrinsically rewarding relationships 3. People use symbols and metaphors to understand themselves and the world and communicate this to others 4. Transference allows people to re-enact and reconstruct and resolve past and understand it with more clarity	People act in response to their perception of reality in the 'here and now': 1. People are inherently trustworthy 2. People have potential for growth	Wellbeing is a result of accepting the past, being content with the present, and most importantly optimistic about the future: 1. Positive emotions broaden momentary thought-action repertoires 2. Positive emotions build resources and increase resilience 3. Building on strengths rather than focusing on minimizing weaknesses builds resilience 4. Peak experiences and flow are linked to wellbeing
Outcomes/ objectives of songwriting	1. Resolution of unconscious inner conflicts 2. Awareness of defense mechanisms 3. Release of psychic energy 4. Increased wholeness and cohesion 5. Reduction in anxiety/depression 6. Resilience	1. Self-actualization and authenticity/ true self 2. Creativity 3. Increased awareness of reality and conscious thought 4. Confidence self-esteem, acceptance, resilience	1. Positive emotions 2. Engagement 3. Relationships 4. Meaning and purpose 5. Accomplishments

Approach	1. Process and problem-oriented 2. Partially directive 3. Emphasis on understanding through symbols/metaphors/free association/transference	1. Process-oriented 2. Non-directive 3. Emergent/organic process, 4. Emphasis on meaning, pleasure, and empowerment, collaboration and therapeutic alliance	1. Outcome and process-oriented 2. Partly-directive
Songwriting models	1. Free association songwriting SW as/in therapy – improvised songs or synchronous rap songs, metaphors, free association Reality contemplation songwriting SW in therapy – songs which deal with confronting situations Songwriting as a transitional object SW in therapy – songs created to manage anxiety about separation and transitions	1. Insight oriented songwriting Rethink, re-know, re-experience, re-feel gain insight into present feelings 2. Narrative songwriting SW as therapy – retelling and reconstructing one's story 3. Music centered songwriting SW as therapy, authentic lyrical and musical expression with focus on making music/songs rather than dialogue, musical identity 4. Strengths-based songwriting SW in therapy, aimed at recognizing and developing strengths/resources, develop coping mechanisms, empowerment, 5. Sung imaginal dialogue SW as therapy – sung dialogue to empty chair to resolve internal/external conflicts 6. Existential issue-based songwriting SW in therapy – SW to explore specific predetermined issue	1. Narrative songwriting SW as therapy – retelling and reconstructing one's story 2. Strengths-based songwriting SW in therapy, aimed at recognizing and developing strengths/resources, develop coping mechanisms, empowerment,

(continued)

Table 13.2 (continued)

	Psychodynamic	Humanistic	Positive psychology
Critical points in the process	1. After rapport building 2. After a priming activity 3. Free association 4. Discussing/interpreting the song's meaning	1. Development of trusting relationship 2. Feeling empowered and being heard 3. Sharing the song with others 4. Finding one's own voice 5. Growth from self-disclosure	1. Development of trusting relationship 2. Feeling empowered and being heard 3. Sharing the song with others 4. Finding one's own voice 5. Growth from self-disclosure
Levels of depth	1. Supportive-activities level 2. Insight-oriented or re-educative 3. Transformative/reconstructive	1. Supportive-activities level 2. Insight-oriented or re-educative 3. Transformative/reconstructive	1. Supportive-activities level 2. Insight-oriented or re-educative 3. Transformative/reconstructive
Emphasis	On both lyric and music creation, free association, symbols and metaphors	On both lyric and music creation, free association, symbols and metaphors	On both lyric and music creation, free association, symbols and metaphors
Role of songwriting	1. Process unconscious issues 2. Facilitate stream of consciousness 3. Express self in symbols and metaphors	1. Express authentic self 2. Gain insight into self 3. Gain confidence, strengthen self-esteem, acceptance, resilience, and coping 4. Tell the songwriter's story	1. Promote positive emotions 2. Explore purpose and meaning of life 3. Experience accomplishments
Role of music	1. Weaken censors to allow unconscious fantasies to emerge 2. Symbolically express unconscious content 3. Expresses juxtaposition of order and chaos 4. Structure, containment, grounding, play	1. To express individual or collective identity 2. Pride association with creation of a work of art 3. Express aesthetic-agency-in-action 4. Provide context 'to music' with others 5. To express complex and/or conflicting emotions	1. To express individual or collective identity 2. To be work of art of social value 3. To express complex and/or conflicting emotions

Role of music therapist	1. Assess and balance freedom and structure 2. Provide surrogate/mothering/nurturing experiences 3. Facilitate verbal processing 4. Creating holding accompaniment to facilitate full release of blocked energy	1. Create a therapeutic relationship 2. Unconditional positive regard/empathy 3. Focus on and be present 4. Engage songwriter in meaningful self-exploration 5. Create conditions for songwriters to be empowered	1. Create a therapeutic relationship 2. Encourage positive thinking and challenge negative thinking 3. Focus on hope and optimism for the future 4. Dialogue that targets purpose and meaning 5. Create opportunities for mastery and accomplishments 6. Focus dialogue on identifying strengths and resources
Role of songwriter	Actively self-explore through dialogue, music, and lyric creation processes	To take responsibility for growth, share feelings openly and honestly	To take responsibility for growth, share feelings openly and honestly
Role of artifact	1. Transitional aid 2. Replaying recordings or singing to revisit, reconnect, and re-explore feelings, experiences and the response to them	1. Function as relational tool between therapist and songwriter 2. Validation through performing or sharing 3. Source of strength and comfort, a coping tool during challenging times	1. Reminder of a journey from past, present and imagined future 2. Validation through performing or sharing 3. Document of ability to accomplish and master new activities

Conclusion

This chapter described the perspectives and models of songwriting relevant to clinicians practicing in experience-oriented models. Table 13.2 provides a comparison of the salient features for psychodynamic-oriented, humanistic-oriented, and positive psychology orientations.

14
Context-Oriented Models of Songwriting

This chapter provides an overview of the songwriting approaches that have been broadly grouped into context-oriented approaches as defined by Bruscia (2011, 2014). These comprise feminist music therapy (FMT), community music therapy (CoMT), and resource-oriented music therapy (ROMT). This chapter has perhaps been the most challenging to construct in terms of teasing out the salient features of songwriting and trying to identify which orientations many of the participants I interviewed aligned with. This was problematic because (1) many components of the philosophies (such as empowerment) are shared between orientations, (2) much of the songwriting literature which I have categorized as context-oriented does not make explicit their orientation, so in some cases I have been challenged to determine the overarching orientation of the authors, and (3) many of the music therapists I interviewed and the literature on songwriting subscribed to a more eclectic practice and borrowed from more than one context-oriented orientation (e.g. O'Grady, 2009). Faced with this conundrum of being able to present distinguishing practices, I initially decided to present these in an integrated format, but after discussions with colleagues this overly simplified integration of concepts seemed too general and did not achieve my original intentions of being able to have songwriting described according to different orientations. Hence, I reverted to constructing this chapter in much the same format as Chapters 12 and 13, even though it might appear that there is significant repetition and overlap in content. Where appropriate, some orientations only briefly touch on influences that would be well argued as central to those practices. In these cases, the influences have been described in detail under a different orientation within this chapter. For example, the concept of empowerment in songwriting is not described in the section 'Community music therapy'.

This is not because it is not relevant to CoMT, but because it is covered in detail in both the 'Feminist music therapy' and 'Resource-oriented music therapy' sections.

Music therapy *in* context, *as* context, and as *interacting* contexts

It was timely that as I was constructing this chapter, Rolvsjord and Stige's (2015) paper had just been published in the *Nordic Journal of Music Therapy* (first published online in 2013), a journal which now has a long history of publishing philosophical discussions on context-oriented approaches. Rolvsjord and Stige claim – and I soon discovered this was also evident in the literature and interviews on songwriting – that there is no single shared definition of context; some understand context as elaborations 'on contextual worldviews, others on theoretical perspectives, and others again on adjustments of practice to specific cultural, social, or political contexts' (p. 2). They labeled and defined three types of context awareness:

1. *Music therapy in context* – refers to 'an awareness of the surroundings of music therapy' (p. 8) and describes the notion that music therapy always exists within a social, academic, and political context. Its focus is on how music therapy can impact on and is used in non-music therapeutic contexts. The focus might be on developing musical skills, social skills, access to music, or enablement and cultural capital.
2. *Music therapy as context* – 'refers to an awareness of the ecology of reciprocal influences within a music therapy situation' (p. 8). They recognize that music therapy is a context through which people can develop and change.
3. *Music therapy as interacting contexts* – describes an 'awareness of the ecology of reciprocal influences between various systems that music therapy is a part of and relates to' (p. 8). This notion of context awareness views music therapy practice as operating with and in connection to a 'broader ecology of contexts' (p. 12). These contexts might span the institution that the music therapy participant is a part of, their local community, the musical culture they belong to, and the healthcare system they are linked in with.

These distinctive definitions are important to keep in mind as one reads the context-oriented practices contained within this chapter.

Feminist music therapy

The influence of feminist theory on music therapy practice – and therefore on songwriting practices – is beginning to emerge in the literature, and certainly several music therapists interviewed in this study reported feminist theory as having an influence on their songwriting approaches. Feminist theory is complex and diverse, and just like the many orientations presented in the previous chapter, the diversity of perspectives and positions of feminist theory are too numerous to describe in detail. Instead, I outline the relevant key principles of the theories as adopted in the songwriting practices described by interviewees.

Theoretical frameworks, aims, and objectives

Feminism is a sociocultural, political, and philosophical movement originally 'created by and for women's liberation/emancipation from various forms of male hegemony' (Hadley, 2006, p. 7), a critique of male superiority and centrality. Today, feminism has moved from focusing purely on women, to one that critiques marginality and partiality (Evans, 2014, p. xx). Identities of gender, race, ethnicity, religion, social class, or sexual orientation (in some combination) are emphasized in feminist theory (Lorber, 2005) and in FMT (e.g. Veltre & Hadley, 2012). Feminism proposes that the political climate and socially constructed beliefs create disadvantage to certain groups. For example, in some societies, social class determines who will be most likely to obtain a university education as universities are increasingly driven by money (Lorber, 2005), and therefore those from lower socioeconomic groups are disadvantaged and maybe unable to obtain an education. This then limits their employment opportunities, thereby perpetuating the cycle of disadvantage.

It is well recognized that cultural and social expectations directly contribute to a person's and cultural group's beliefs about people, personalities, and behaviors (Ballou et al., 2007). There is a notion of contextual identity, which suggests that a person's own identity (and therefore that person's behavior) is multifaceted and dynamic, and determined by an individual and society. Therefore, a person's sense of self is not only individual but also relational; an understanding of the self in relation to other people. This sense of self is socially constructed and based on (a combination of) social units such as skin color, sexual orientation, gender, ability/disability, and the like. The sociocultural group within which a person is born and lives influences how that person is perceived by others within her own family and cultural group and by society (Ballou et al., 2007).

Feminist-informed therapists work to combat issues of patriarchy, systematic oppression, and discrimination, and strive to cultivate a culture of openness to difference and appreciation and nurturing of difference (Hurtado, 2010). Issues of power, oppression, and discrimination are also of paramount importance in FMT practice (Curtis, 1997; Merrill, 2006; Veltre & Hadley, 2012), where music therapists use music to 'transform all levels of society by supporting the participants through their process of healing as well as confronting and changing systematic oppression' (Adrienne, 2006, p. 57). Political factors that influence and impact their participants are taken into consideration, while simultaneously pursuing ways to influence political and social change on the participants' behalves (Merrill, 2006) – a sociopolitical transformation (Curtis, 2006). During FMT practice, the music therapists combat oppression by assisting participants to understand societal influences and to develop strategies to navigate societal expectations (O'Grady & McFerran, 2006).

FMT practices tend to reject medical models (O'Grady & McFerran, 2006) and instead share many humanistic beliefs such as being person-centered, offering acceptance and unconditional positive regard, and striving to be empathic. The therapeutic process calls for participants to actively engage to achieve insight, introspection, and self-awareness if they are to change their lives (Corey, 2013).

Because of the underlying assumption that people's behaviors are shaped by their own individual histories, cultures, and the society of which they are a part, feminist music therapists avoid working with people in isolation from their context. Therapists acknowledge the culture-centered perspective where health and illness are in part influenced by the cultural context (O'Grady & McFerran, 2006). Participants' independence, interdependence, and empowerment are core principles of FMT. They are guided to understand their own individual situations within a sociopolitical context, challenge those conditions that are oppressive, and engage their resources while working toward both personal and social transformation (Hadley, 2013). Such activity exemplifies the notion of music therapy as an interacting context (Rolvsjord & Stige, 2015). In her work with abused women, Curtis (2006) facilitates music therapy programs that enable the women to value women's perspectives and value themselves. The focus is on the identification of internalized socially constructed beliefs and replacing them with their own beliefs and helping them trust in their own intuition (Curtis, 2006).

Models

Feminist focused song parody

Feminist issues such as oppression, discrimination, disempowerment, domestic violence, sexualization of adolescent girls and women, division of domestic labor, and women's struggle to rebel against these have been the subject of many songs written and performed by females, particularly in the hip hop scene. 'Respect' (Aretha Franklin), 'Unpretty' (TLC), 'Tramp' (Salt n Pepa), 'You Oughta Know' (Alanis Morissette), 'Bag It Up' (Geri Halliwell), and 'Flawless' (Beyoncé), are just some of the many examples of songs sung by women about women's issues. Engaging in an analysis of gender and power issues expressed in such songs allows women to identify with and reflect upon the issues they face at a societal level[1] (Veltre & Hadley, 2012). It validates their experiences while simultaneously illustrating the power of song to express gender issues and tell personal or social stories.

Originating from interviews with participants, I have labeled one songwriting approach 'feminist focused song parody', a form of song parody that specifically addresses gender-based issues. The therapist, with or without the collaboration of the songwriter, selects a song that resembles the issues and situations that the songwriter may be experiencing. Feminist focused song parody relies on careful selection of an original song; to be successful, the song must in some way resonate with the songwriter's own experiences. The chosen song is played and the songwriter subsequently guided through an analysis of the lyrics. She is encouraged to reflect on the ways the original song is similar or different to her own story. Once the analysis of the song has been completed, the songwriting process progresses to the songwriter rewriting the lyrics to authentically represent or express her own experiences and story. It is through this rewriting process that her individual experiences, feelings, and stories can be voiced.

Feminist individual songwriting

'Feminist individual songwriting'[2] involves a songwriter creating an original song that narrates the songwriter's story and/or embodies the feminist beliefs as understood and valued by the songwriter herself.[3] The therapist is present as a guide, offering support so that the songwriter's own voice is present in the song that is created.

Informed by the interviews, the overarching aims of feminist individual songwriting are to address the oppression of women (and other minority or marginalized groups), facilitate the healing from harm caused by systematic oppression, and enable them to deal with the internalization of oppression (Curtis, 1997). Literature and analysis of interview data led to a collection of goals and objectives associated with the feminist individual songwriting approach:

1. Increase understanding of the songwriter's sociopolitical context;
2. Examine gender-role socialization;
3. Develop the songwriter's self-image to include independence, self-esteem, and freedom from gender-role stereotypes;
4. Empower songwriters;
5. Increase independence of songwriters;
6. Achieve optimal functioning as defined by each songwriter (not society); and
7. Develop relationships that are characterized by mutuality and equality (Curtis, 1997).

Through the process of creating a song, the therapist will guide the songwriter to identify the gender and power messages that have been received and internalized, and to understand the impact these have on the songwriter's life (Curtis, 1997, p. 33). As the songwriter narrates her own stories, she is called upon to either accept or reject these internalized messages and develop a plan that will incite internal transformation. The song created may also communicate a plan to change the external world (Curtis, 1997). The role of the artifact in this process will be further explored later in this chapter.

In her work with women who have removed themselves from situations characterized by domestic violence, Curtis (1997) argues that songwriting enabled these women to share their story of domestic violence and experience a sense of having a voice and being heard. Women utilized the songwriting process to give voice to their anger, explore and work through their grief and loss, and importantly, to construct new lives as survivors rather than as victims. Curtis' process of facilitating is illustrated in Figure 14.1.

Figure 14.1   Model of feminist individual songwriting

During the initial phase, the therapist engages the songwriter in an analysis of gender-role, power, and oppression as expressed within the lyrics of pre-existing songs (e.g. 'Flawless' by Beyoncé). Following this, the therapist provides education and training to develop the songwriter's skills in songwriting such as by creating hooks, musical form, instrumentation, and melody. Once skills have been developed, the songwriter and therapist work together to select a feminist theme or a narrative for the song and identify a musical style that would appropriately reflect the theme and the songwriter's identity. Lyrics are then created which authentically represent the songwriter's voice and story. Finally, the music is created to accompany the songwriter's lyrics.

In Curtis' dissertation, she reported on her analysis of six women who had engaged in feminist individual songwriting to address their needs associated with experiencing domestic violence. In one case, a 25-year-old African American woman with a six-month-old daughter had sought refuge in a shelter to escape her abusive boyfriend. She created a song titled 'Not Anymore' in the style of Jody Watley's 'When a Man Loves a Woman'. In examining the lyrics closely, the songwriter's story is one of recognizing and acknowledging the reality of her context and voicing her inner strength and beliefs about her strength, beauty, and capacity to cope on her own. She expressed anger toward her partner as well as toward herself for having not seen the situation through this lens sooner (Figure 14.2).

Feminist group songwriting

'Feminist group songwriting'[4] (FGS) involves the embedding of feminist principles within a group songwriting context. It often (but not exclusively) involves facilitating the creation of songs with marginalized or oppressed groups of people. FGS uses a group therapy approach and aims to raise awareness of how societal and cultural views and practices impact the songwriters' lives, while simultaneously working toward freeing them from their feelings of oppression, strengthening their sense of self and self-love, and empowering them to make choices about how they live their lives. Discussion and dialogue stimulate group members to share experiences of marginalization or oppression. Through the identification of commonly shared experiences, the group establishes a sense of unity and a culture of collaboration. Once the experiences and issues have been identified, the therapist supports the group to challenge their held views so as to create opportunities for change. A group story is constructed and transformed into lyrics and music in various

"Not anymore"

There comes a time in a woman's life when she doesn't want to be alone
She wants that peace of mind, the need to be touched
By a strong man with strong hands, the kind that turns her on
But not anymore

There comes a time in a woman's life when she feels like time is running out
She needs stability, a husband, and a family
But not anymore

I thought I found that man of my dreams
But roses turned blue and milk got sour, the grass wasn't green
Not anymore

Who do you think you're calling a bitch?
I was good to you from day one, and never stopped
I should have recognized the signs, but I was blinded by love, you see
But guess what baby
Not anymore

You see I realized the day I left you
That roses are red, only violets are blue
So you can kiss my ass and the baby's too

I don't have to take your shit
I am Black, I am beautiful, I am strong, I am proud
And we don't need you
No, not anymore.

Figure 14.2   Example of feminist individual songwriting
Source: Curtis, 1997, p. 350. Reprinted with permission from Sandra Curtis.

ways using original songwriting methods (see Chapter 11) so that the final song encompasses the group's shared experiences and/or story and communicates a need for action or a plan of action.

FGS was incorporated into a songwriting program with women who had experienced childhood abuse (Day, 2005). The program aimed at breaking the cycle of child abuse by enabling the women to develop an awareness of how their abuse affects their behavior, in particular their parenting behavior. The group members brainstormed ideas and lyrics and in the process, through sharing their stories of abuse with others, worked collaboratively to process grief associated with a lost childhood and to identify solutions. Day's research indicated that their self-esteem and sense of self improved, and they began to trust themselves and other important people in their lives. In FMT thinking, trust is an important component of healthy, fulfilling relationships.

Feminist principles are evident throughout Day's program, from the self-referring nature of enrolling in the songwriting program to the extent of commitment and effort she made to increase societal awareness of the impact of abuse (Day et al., 2009b; see later discussions). The two-hour 12-session format with a closed consistent group membership enabled group cohesion and belonging to be established, providing the necessary safe conditions for disclosure (Yalom, 1995). Day reports that commonly expressed issues present in final versions of the songs comprise descriptions of the effects of childhood abuse and domestic violence on the women and their children, the effects of verbal abuse on children's self-esteem, children's rights to feel safe and loved, social isolation, self-esteem, self-harm, body image, suicide, anger, trust, and managing stress.

'Tears of a Child' (Figure 14.3) is one group-composed song by women in Day's program. The song is a synthesis of the women's thoughts, beliefs, feelings, and wishes. It conveys the enduring pain, feelings of betrayal, and grieving over the loss of a childhood. However, this is

"Tears of a child"

My tears as a child I have not cried dry
I hold in my heart a pain that tears can't take away
By the people I trusted I have been betrayed
Trust, a cherished gift that should never be broken
I longed for something to set me free
Open your eyes why can't you see
Please, please help me

Our memories keep us a prisoner,
   blocks like bricks you can't break
No matter how hard you try
Triggers that bring up the pain
Places and faces I'll never forget
I remember them well

I want to be a natural child at ease and free
For you to be gone and not watching over me
You denied me of my dignity, I was just a child
Too young to know it wasn't right

I want to build a better wall
One with friendship and trust
Face everything and recover

Figure 14.3 Example of feminist group songwriting

Source: Strength to Strength © 2000. Permission to transcribe and print song given by Toni Day.

balanced with expressed desires for a different life free of the perpetrator and one filled with positive relationships.

O'Grady (2009) implemented a songwriting study with seven female prison inmates who worked together to create and perform a musical. While O'Grady (2009) views herself primarily as a CoMT practitioner and this is clearly exemplified in the structure of her approach (O'Grady, 2011), her dissertation describes how the work is informed by feminist theory – the songs tell stories from women's perspectives and is therefore relevant to FMT practice. The group context allows the women to receive positive feedback from other group members, validation from voicing their experiences, and increased courage, confidence, pride, and motivation. The group context provided opportunities to connect with other women in the prison and foster a culture of sharing and reciprocity between the group members.

Critical points and levels of depth in the songwriting process

The song creation process can be the catalyst for changing perspectives and feelings, and planning for action. There was a consensus among the feminist self-identified music therapists that the telling of a songwriter's story is the most important component of the songwriting process.

Chaplin (1998, cited in Merill, 2006) reports a seven-stage plan for feminist counseling, which, through my analysis of interviews and information from literature, I have adapted to suit the therapeutic songwriting process and reflect a synthesis of interviewees' perspectives. First, there is a getting started and building trust phase. Trust is fostered when songwriters tell their stories and through this story-telling process experience a sense of being heard. The initial discussions and sharing of experiences as songwriters offer ideas for the song material provide the conditions whereby the music therapist (and other group members) can verbally or non-verbally validate the songwriters' experiences. After trust, the therapist assists in facilitating the identification of themes. This takes place via an analysis of song lyrics and the subsequent offering of ideas for individual or group songs. During the songwriting process, themes of power, gender, oppression, and societal expectations are reviewed and reflected upon. The third phase concerns an exploration of the past and developing an understanding of the opposites and inner hierarchies. Here, songwriters explore feminist themes further in relation to their own history and changes in societal views over time. As the songwriters prepare for the creation of the song, they begin to connect their own story with that of other songwriters, and importantly, identify the feminist themes that have ultimately shaped their own stories.

Here, the focus of lyric writing is on retelling their past histories within the context of feminist themes. The process then moves toward breaking down the inner hierarchies, facing their ambivalence, and accepting opposite possibilities. During this stage, the lyric writing process offers opportunities to challenge views about power and hierarchy. This leads on to the fifth phase of the process, making changes and living with the opposite possibilities. Creating song lyrics that present an alternative reality to that told in earlier lyrics offers possibilities to imagine a different future to how things may be in the present. During the sixth stage, the therapist assists the songwriters to create lyrics that communicate an action plan for making changes to their lives. Finally, women may be empowered to follow through on their planned changes as they perform or share their songs with significant others or in more public spaces. This process is depicted in Figure 14.4.

Ideally, songwriting programs as practiced within a feminist framework aim to be reconstructive and transformative. Through verbal or music-evoked probing and priming, songwriters' stories provide the conditions whereby a deep understanding of power and control issues can lead to an active rejection of dominant societal views. The process is transformative when the songwriters recognize when and how external forces influence their behavior and contribute to anxiety and defensive behavior patterns. Reconstruction occurs when internalized societal messages are replaced with healthy messages that reflect the songwriters' own values and meaning of life. As a major goal of feminist songwriting practice is empowerment, the process is transformative when songwriters accept themselves as worthwhile people, feel confident and empowered to act, and reach self-actualization. Lyrics and music often illustrate and represent these reconstructive and transformative experiences.

The role of songwriting and the music

As feminist approaches utilize story-telling to enable people to have a voice and be heard (Curtis, 1997; Day, 2005), the primary role of songwriting is to be the vehicle for the songwriter to construct a story. The song structure of a beginning, middle, and end provides the focus for a story to be told, and the optional use of a chorus may serve to highlight the key message or feeling portrayed in the story. For example, several songs on Day's album offer detailed descriptions of sexual abuse, stories of intense pain, disempowerment, and an abuse of trust. Similar stories pervade the songs of women in Curtis' (1997) study.

Songwriting offers opportunities to voice both internal and external conflicts that the songwriter has become aware of as a consequence

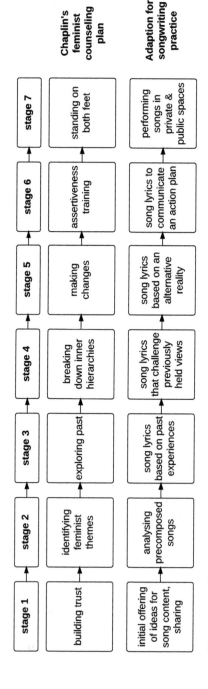

Figure 14.4 Phases of the feminist songwriting processes

of telling her story. As the songwriter identifies destructive internalized perspectives and actively works toward rejecting these and replacing them with constructive views, she may experience some resistance as she holds on to enduring views. Rejecting oppressive thinking and assimilating new and healthy thinking is a complex process of negotiation whereby the songwriter moves continuously between the healthy and destructive perspectives before completely committing to a full rejection of oppressive thinking.[5] These emerging conflicts can be represented by using explicit and contrasting lyrics. Alternatively, the conflict can be communicated through the deliberate misalignment of feelings expressed in the lyrics and music.

The songwriting process can be viewed as political activism. To voice one's feelings and opinions and to tell one's story is imperative, a step toward being empowered to change one's internal and external worlds. The contents of the song can be an explicit rejection of gender-role socialization or of oppression, or in contrast might describe healthy self-images such as independence, self-esteem, and freedom from gender-role stereotypes. For example, in the song 'Not Anymore' detailed earlier (Figure 14.2), the lyrics 'I am black, I am beautiful, I am strong, I am proud' are examples of affirmations of self-worth that contrast with the songwriter's internalized social messages. Songs created in therapy therefore become political statements which can be recorded and stored for future political use.

The music created during feminist-informed songwriting takes on quite defined roles. Most importantly, as the song tells a songwriter's (or group of songwriters') story, the music serves to express the songwriter's identity, her true self. This authentic expression of identity is a key feature of FMT, as it embodies the notion of empowerment. To create one's own music is an emphatic statement of who one is as a person. As alluded to earlier, music has the potential to express the ambivalence experienced by the songwriter as she attempts to replace her long-held internalized messages with new ones. In such cases, the music can aid in the expression of strong feelings of anger, frustration, or disappointment, or can express the songwriter's emerging inner strength.

The role of the therapist and the songwriter

Feminist music therapists reject the medicalized view that the therapist is the expert and the 'client' is a passive recipient of treatment. They suggest this reinforces the power relationships that feminists are committed to dissolving. Power relationships are evident when the songwriter is expected to disclose but the therapist does not. Such unequal exchanges create barriers to the therapeutic process through the establishment of hierarchies. During feminist songwriting practices, the therapists strive to flatten or equalize hierarchy (Merrill, 2006). They emphasize an egalitarian relationship by sharing more of themselves with the songwriters in an effort to increase reciprocity and normalize the relationship (Curtis, 2006; O'Grady & McFerran, 2006; Purdon, 2006). Importantly, the therapist's role is to demonstrate an attitude of respect, understanding, patience, and support.

During songwriting, the music therapist facilitates an analysis of power so that the songwriter gains an increased understanding of how society has led to experiences of powerlessness (Curtis, 2006). These analyses occur as the therapist responds to the lyrical contributions of the songwriter, or rather during the analysis of lyrics from a pre-existing song. For example, Lesley Gore's song 'You Don't Own Me' contains lyrics that communicate a message that a woman's 'lover' does not own her and that she is not an object to be put on display. In the past, this song has been an inspiration for young women and has played a significant role in the feminist movement. The analysis of the lyrics of the song presents an opportunity to discuss the held view that some men have of women.

When original songs are created, the songwriter is actively contributing (Merrill, 2006), taking responsibility for sharing her story, giving voice to her experiences, engaging in decision-making, and taking action for more permanent changes to her thinking and life situation. The therapist supports the songwriter to take an equal role and to negotiate what roles each of them will take during songwriting. This process combats passivity and dependency, behaviors that the songwriter may have developed as a consequence of being disempowered throughout life. Action might comprise making decisions about the structure of the song, the central issue to be communicated in the song, the genre, or the content. Being an active participant in creating the song is empowering and creates the conditions for taking ownership for the message the song communicates.

The role of the artifact

Recording and performing the songs post-creation is regarded as an important component of feminist-informed songwriting. The songwriters in Day et al.'s (2009a) study commented that having their songs recorded provided a tangible outcome from the songwriting workshops and, in one songwriter's words, 'the closing of a book'. In creating the song product, there is a sense that 'this was my life, I am finished with it, and I am moving on to a new narrative'. It was also viewed as a means of creating something positive from all their negative experiences.

The song is a product that may be laden with political messages – statements on a topic that may be relevant for others who have been disempowered due to similar circumstances. When presented to public audiences, the therapist and songwriters hope that audiences will view the songwriters through a different lens and, in some way, effect a gradual change in societal views (Amir, 2006; Baker, 2013c; O'Grady, 2009; O'Grady & McFerran, 2006). One music therapist I interviewed had been working with adolescents with mild to moderate autism. She regularly employed songwriting as one of several interventions in her practice. This music therapist reported how one young man created songs about his experiences of being a person with autism. He clearly communicated statements directed at the 'autism experts'. His song suggests that the experts should cease making assumptions about what people with autism feel and need, and that it would be more beneficial to ask them directly. This young adolescent felt so strongly about his political message that he sent his song to Tony Attwood.[6]

When sharing the song in a public forum, the direct impact on the songwriters is derived from the shift in focus from 'internal responsibility to external forces' (O'Grady & McFerran, 2006, p. 76). O'Grady and McFerran (2006) suggest that they 'objectify the cause of their struggle', and in doing so 'decrease their sense of victimization in responding to it' (p. 76). Women in Day's study (Day et al., 2009a) recorded and produced an album with the specific purpose of having it function as an educational resource about childhood abuse (Day et al., 2009b). In launching the album, the women performed their songs to an audience that included policy makers and government representatives. O'Grady (2009) understood the performance of the female prisoners' musical as a form of social action. The women's stories were shared with an audience that included government representatives and health professionals. There was a belief that the performance would give the audience an increased understanding of the issues affecting the female prisoners, which may have a flow-on effect to changes in policy.

The songs and the shared experience of the audience and performer seek to challenge hierarchy and power differentials. By actively engaging the audience, the song performance may play a role in shifting the thinking away from what the song means to what it does. As one interviewee stated:

When most songs are performed the entertainers are the experts, akin to a therapist being an expert in psychodynamic thinking. But when

folk artists or political activists share songs, the songs are the catalyst of change not the performer. The performer creates the space for
shared expression and the audience must somehow become active
in the performance . . . The song and the musicking experience challenge the praxis-oriented nature of the event, shifting to poiesis,
what it does. The purpose and primary intention of the song is to
shift consciousness of the group.

Community music therapy

Theoretical frameworks, aims, and objectives

CoMT is a value-based theoretical perspective that aims to give voice and
access to the disadvantaged and promote musical community engagement in arenas where people face barriers to participation (Ansdell,
2010; Procter, 2004). There is an emphasis on the ecology of the community, social capital, and changing the relationships that link people,
places, and events (Stige, 2003/2012; Stige & Aarø, 2012). It is a contextual practice that considers and often actively engages with the context
of the participants beyond the individual setting of therapy, is participatory in nature, and where individuals are considered in relation to
their gendered, social, cultural, and political environment (O'Grady &
McFerran, 2006, p. 64). Music is understood as an action, rather than
an object, that is largely performative – musicking (Small, 1998) – and it
is through collaborative musicking experiences that relationships with
others and transformation of communities can take place. CoMT strives
to cultivate musical communities (Ansdell, 2002) that are inclusive and
accessible to those who may have limited access to musicking opportunities due to various forms of marginalization (Bolger, 2014).

CoMT perspectives evolved from contemporary views of music and
health, where health, illness, and treatment are understood from within
the social context in which they are experienced and practiced. CoMT
has been influenced by emerging ideas of health musicking, ecological practices, social capital, culture-centered practices, empowerment,
and affordance and appropriation. The degree to which each of these
perspectives influences practice differs from practitioner to practitioner.
What follows is a brief description of these perspectives to set the frame
for discussing songwriting practices within CoMT perspectives.

Health perspectives and health musicking

CoMT perspectives reject the medicalized view of health and perceive
health as a biological, psychological, social, and cultural phenomenon

(Stige, 2003/2012). Influenced by Antonovsky's (1987) salutogenic orientation, health is understood along a continuum whereby the state of health is a measure of how a person is coping. Being free from disease does not imply health; health is a state of ecological wholeness (Bruscia, 1998, cited in Stige, 2003/2012). To have health is to have the capacity and opportunity to participate in social and cultural activities. Therefore, health extends beyond the individual and is also dependent upon the resources of the community and the relationships between them (Stige, 2003/2012). Building on this premise, the primary aim of CoMT is to stimulate health-promoting relationships, and build the resources in both the individual and the community to ensure that those who are disadvantaged have access to social and cultural activities that promote health and healthy relationships (Stige, 2003/2012).

Musicking (Elliott, 1995; Small, 1998) is a term that describes music as a process, not an object. Small states: 'To music is to take part in any capacity, in a musical performance, whether by performing, by listening, by rehearsing, or practicing, by providing material for performance or by dancing' (p. 9). It is a music-making in action (Stige et al., 2010). Musicking is inherently a social process, an activity where relationships are performed and meaning is derived. It is through this idea of musiking that the concept of 'situated health musicking' (Stige, 2003/2012) emerged. Stige (2002, p. 211) conceptualized health musicking as 'the appraisal and appropriation of the health affordances of arena, agenda, agents, activities, and artifacts of a music practice'. Here, through planned musical participation that is inclusive, people can participate in an ecology of situated activities that promote health (Stige, 2003/2012).

Ecological systems and approaches

Ecological practice, as informed by Bronfenbrenner (1979), is a core facet of CoMT (Stige & Aarø, 2012). Its practice is directed toward health promotion 'within and between various layers of the sociocultural community and/or physical environment' (Bruscia, 1998, cited in Rolvsjord & Stige, 2015, p. 12). In planning activities, practitioners consider all levels of the system – the individual, family, schools, broader community, and so on. It is critical for success that the health of the whole system is considered, as it may well be that health at the individual level is not the one in most need of attention (Bruscia, 1998).

Music activity is regarded as an ecological practice (Stige, 2003/2012; Stige & Aarø, 2012) where relationships between the layers are activated. Stige (2003/2012) suggests that the interactions between the layers have a transactional character; the participants, the musical activities, and the music that has been created change and develop through a 'process of mutual influence' (p. 194). Individuals and communities are shaped through bidirectional processes of interaction and reciprocal influence. Therefore, collaboration is a shared interactive process between the therapist, the participants, and the community. Such collaborations are examples of working *with* participants and not *for* them. In turn, these actions empower participants as their active roles influence the change process.

Social capital

The concept of social capital is integral to CoMT perspectives (Procter, 2011) and has been linked with the health and wellbeing of communities (Stige & Aarø, 2012). The term is used to define the features of a social organization such as trust, norms, and networks that enable a society to function effectively and facilitate collective action (Kawachi & Berkman, 2000, cited in Stige & Aarø, 2012). Bonding and bridging are two distinct forms of social capital (Putnam, 2000). Bonding refers to social networks of homogeneous groups of people, while bridging refers to social capital of groups of people from across social dividing lines (Putnam & Feldstein, 2003).

Social capital theory has relevance to CoMT because music-making 'offers experience of loose social networks within which people have the opportunity to experience trust and reciprocity' (Procter, 2011, p. 243), thereby establishing and strengthening social capital. From a health perspective, the development of such musical capital facilitates the development of social support networks, and more broadly contributes to the reduction of physical and mental health vulnerabilities. Consequently, CoMT works toward reducing social exclusion and marginalization to build social capital and therefore enhance the health of communities (Stige & Aarø, 2012).

Culture-centered influences

The importance of a culture-centered perspective is also a marker of CoMT practice. It is a term used to identify people and relationships within a context (Stige, 2002). According to Stige, culture is the 'accumulation of customs and technologies enabling regulatory human coexistence' (2002, p. 381). Customs are defined as the beliefs and behaviors that develop over time (e.g. rituals), whereas technologies are physical or symbolic tools that belong to the culture (e.g. music, language). Importantly for CoMT, the ways people relate to each other are culturally organized. 'Culture is what happens when people spend time together. They act and they interact, they produce artifacts, and they use artifacts, and they do this as they make rules and break rules, if only to make new rules' (Stige, 2003/2012, p. 188). The concept of culture combines the process of social interaction with the products that represent the lifestyle and customs of a network of people (Stige, 2002).

When community music therapists embark on projects directed toward opening up arenas for marginalized groups to participate, an awareness of culture (including musical cultural practices) is needed. At the macro level, it demands an awareness of factors such as history, environment, race, language, beliefs, and values from an individual (O'Grady & McFerran, 2006). At a micro level, there must also be sensitivity to cultural practices. For example, in Bolger's (2014) study (see later in this chapter) a CoMT program within a shared house for marginalized young people was framed around the already pre-existing practices and the behaviors of those residing there.

Empowerment

Empowerment is a concept that has its roots in community psychology and emerged from the civil rights movements of the 1960s and 1970s (Rolvsjord, 2010). Individuals and communities that are empowered feel they have the economic, political, social, educational, gender, or spiritual strength to act. Empowerment[7] is a process of developing skills and self-power or collective power to influence other people, institutions, or society and to overcome obstacles in the environment. Within CoMT, a community level of empowerment is often (but not solely) emphasized whereby the community instigates actions that aim to increase opportunities for citizen participation, respond to threats concerning the quality of life of the community, and more generally improve the wellbeing of the community (Zimmerman, 2000). Importantly, empowerment calls for changes at both the individual and community levels, because empowerment at the individual level does not automatically correlate with enhanced empowerment at the community level and vice versa (Dalton et al., 2001). As CoMT is focused on empowerment at all levels, it can function as a mechanism for change. As will be discussed in more detail later in this chapter, empowerment in music therapy relates primarily to the increased awareness and development of strengths and resources (Procter, 2011; Rolvsjord, 2010).

Affordance and appropriation

DeNora (2000, 2011) introduced the term 'musical affordance' to the music sociology discourse, a notion that music affects people in a way that is linked with their social and cultural context. She claims that musical activity has the potential to afford a number of benefits for people, but these benefits are dependent upon how these potentials (affordances) are used (appropriated) and on the individuals and their contexts (Ansdell, 2004). How music is appropriated may vary from one person to another. While musical affordances are the properties and structures within music and musiking, musical appropriations describe how these affordances are used by participants (Ansdell, 2004). The way in which a person seeks to use musical opportunities and experiences will in part determine what benefits will be derived.

Models

While CoMT does not comprise a predefined set of procedures and techniques (Pavlicevic & Ansdell, 2004), songwriting and the performance of song creations have taken a prominent place in its practice to date. In fact, with the exception of Silverman's CBT songwriting approaches, songwriting within CoMT currently dominates contemporary literature. This may be because songs and songwriting appeal to and can be appreciated by a large proportion of society, and the affordances they offer are more widely understood when compared with other music therapy methods such as improvisation.

Stige and Aarø (2012) present the acronym PREPARE (see below) to represent seven qualities that characterize CoMT. While these characteristics may not be exclusive to CoMT orientation, they argue that these qualities are emphasized, to different degrees, in the diverse range of practices represented by CoMT. They suggest that practices informed by these CoMT qualities can support individuals to participate in their community through music and prepare the community to accept and support each individual.

1. **P** – *Participatory*: How processes afford opportunities for individual and social participation, how participation is valued, and how the idea of partnership is supported. It seeks to enable *all* participants' voices to be heard and valued.
2. **R** – *Resource-oriented*: Focus on mobilization of personal strengths and social, cultural, and material resources. Resources can be of different types – for instance, the personal strengths of participants (such as musical talents and interests), relational resources (such as trust and emotional support), and community resources (such as music organizations and traditions).

3. **E** – *Ecological*: Working with the reciprocal relationships between individuals, groups, and networks in a social context.
4. **P** – *Performative*: Focus on human development through action and performance of relationships in ecological contexts. An 'outwards and around' approach (Stige et al., 2010, p. 283) as an indication of efforts made to engage participants with their surrounding communities and contexts.
5. **A** – *Activist*: Recognizing that people's problems are related to limitations in society, such as unequal access to resources, and being willing to address this limitation. It is a forum for social action.
6. **R** – *Reflective*: Dialogical and collaborative approaches, with an emphasis on reflecting with participants in accessible ways. Acknowledging lay and local knowledge as central.
7. **E** – *Ethics-driven*: Human rights of freedom, respect, equality, and solidarity are central to health, wellbeing, community, music, and CoMT practice. (pp. 18–20)

These qualities are present in varying degrees in the songwriting practices described below.

Songwriting as a health musicking practice

Songwriting is a form of musical activity that allows people to perform relationships and engage in cultural activities, and as such has participation and health musicking at its core. McFerran and Teggelove (2011) led a CoMT project with young people who were survivors of the Australian Black Saturday bushfires of February 2009. A series of bushfires raging across the Victorian countryside led to the largest loss of human life (173) and injuries (414) in the nation's history. Twenty-six young secondary school students from a school located in one of the areas hardest hit by the bushfires participated in one of three small music therapy groups over 10 weeks – a group of young males (12–15 years), a group of young females (13–15 years), and a mixed group of upper secondary school males and females (15–16 years). The CoMT program epitomizes the notion of health musicking where songwriting[8] is an active form of participation and performing relationships.

While the songwriting activities were offered in a closed group context, McFerran and Teggelove assert that their approach was multisystemic, with school staff and families 'intertwined in the drama, without actively involving them at the outset' (n.p.), evidently an outward and around approach (Stige et al., 2010). It was the participatory nature of 'group' songwriting that characterized it as a health musicking practice. The young people had opportunities for creating their songs in a collaborative structure, with the process being directed toward a singular but common purpose – to create songs. The emphasis of the program was on normal social processes – being a young person, having fun, expressing the self – rather than 'healing trauma'. Musicking manifested through the creation of words and music, and later during the rehearsal of their songs – their activities were in essence performative (Stige & Aarø, 2012). This led to bonding within groups and bridging across the different age groups (Putnam, 2000). Collaboration with the community included the engagement of a community musician who assisted with enabling the young people to record their songs and produce a high-quality album. Here, health musicking was evident in the relationships built between the members creating the songs, in performing the songs to members of the community, and in the creation of an album with a community musician.

Songwriting as an ecological practice

Songwriting as a musical activity affords possibilities to work with the many layers of a community. Bolger's (2014) study of marginalized young people in three different contexts also illustrates how ecological practices can be incorporated into songwriting activities. Bolger's study examined the concept of collaboration within three contexts involving young people:

1. A *drop-in group*: a program for young people residing in public housing. Many had challenging or traumatic life experiences, such as refugees from their countries of origin, victims of violence, or systemic poverty, among others. The main aims of the community program were to connect the young people and promote positive cross-cultural interaction. A drop-in group indicated that people could come and go as it suited them. This flexible drop-in approach therefore had potentially different weekly attendance.
2. The *share home*: a network of community homes housing young people who had experienced extended periods of homelessness. Many had left their homes due to physical, verbal, or sexual abuse, violence, and abandonment. The CoMT programs were implemented within the existing culture of the house.
3. The *therapeutic camp*: a camp-based program for young people engaged in the foster system. These young people may have lacked stability and security, had engaged in drug abuse and criminal activity, and were at risk of living in out-of-home care. The camp was

aimed at providing support for these young people and to foster positive connections with peers.

Each of the groups drew on songwriting as one of the main music therapy methods. With support from the community workers (some of whom identified themselves as musicians) and a professional sound technician, the drop-in group created and recorded an original song. The therapeutic camp used songwriting as its primary activity, also recorded original songs as a means to explore their experiences of the camp, and performed their songs to a large audience comprising peers and families.

Bolger recognized the importance of staff as important contributors to the process and was concerned with engaging community organizations as key supporting players. She argued that they brought 'their local knowledge and skills, and their existing relationships with the young people and the community' (Bolger, 2014, p. 60).

In his work with children being treated for cancer in a pediatric hospital in Norway, Aasgaard (2002) developed a method of songwriting that he describes as music environmental therapy, where there is a clear focus on interplay between the individual songwriter and his environment. This ecological perspective incorporates the creation (and performance) of songs within the context of society, culture, and environment. Aasgaard studied the songwriting process and the resultant products by examining their 'geography' – who are the people who participate? Where do the song creation activities take place, when, and for how long are songs developed and performed? (p. 141). Ecological practices are exemplified by song creations and performances occurring in the songwriter's isolation rooms, open areas of the hospital, the hospital school, the songwriter's home, the local school or kindergarten, and occasionally on free-to-air television. Songs were created with input from doctors and nurses, other hospital staff, and school teachers and/or school friends, and members of the family. Figure 14.5 is an illustration of the geography of the song creations and the people who participated either by adding lyrics or by listening to a performance of the song (adapted from Aasgaard, 2002, p. 148). One example Aasgaard describes is the case of Mary and her first song 'A Suspiciously Cheerful Lady'. After Mary writes the song, it has a life that moves beyond the hospital room. The following summarizes the events:

1. Three months after the text was created, the music therapist creates a melody and records the song for Mary. She plays the song in her room. Her parents learn to sing the song.

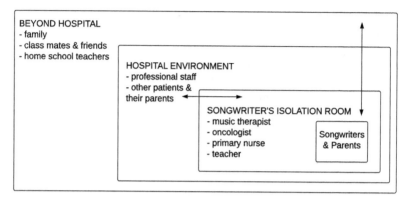

Figure 14.5   A 'map' of potential song participants and audiences
Source: Aasgaard, 2002. Permission to adapt given by Trygve Aasgaard.

2. Four months after the text was created, the local school teacher visits
   Mary and she lends the recording to the teacher to play to her school
   friends. The school friends reciprocate by creating their own recording and sending it to the hospital for Mary to listen to.
3. Six months after the text was created, Mary's younger brother has
   learned to sing the song and adapted the text. Mary learns the
   brother's version. A copy of Mary's song is given to family members
   as a Christmas gift.
4. Nine months later, Mary is playing the recording to unfamiliar staff
   and the physiotherapist is using the song in his sessions with her.
5. Twelve months after the text was created, the hospital staff band
   arranges for the song to be performed for patients, relatives, and staff.
6. Sixteen months after the text was created, Mary sings the song on television and interacts with TV producers, describing her experiences
   of hospitalization.

This case study of Mary's song illustrates how there were bidirectional
processes of interaction between the individual and the various layers
of her ecological system. As illustrated in Figure 14.5, the songwriting
activities involved parents and siblings, Mary's treatment team, other
health professionals within the hospital, and her classmates.

Songwriting for building social capital

Collective benefits are derived from the solidarity, reciprocity, and collective strength of groups of people or organizations with common interests, purposes, and visions. Social capital can be strengthened through

bonding members of homogeneous groups together, or through bridging networks between groups and individuals from heterogeneous groups. Group songwriting as creative activity has the potential to build social capital by bonding or bridging groups and individuals.

In a CoMT project with female prison inmates in an Australian prison, O'Grady (2011) facilitated the creation of a musical, which functioned to bond and strengthen relationships within the prison, and to bridge the prison with the outside world. She also viewed the musical as a form of community cultural development (O'Grady, 2009), whereby increased creative and cultural capacity could be fostered within the community. The project involved a collaboration between the music therapist (musical director), some community musicians, and female prison inmates. O'Grady et al. (2014) described the working framework as 'collaborative workshops', which were focused on writing group and individual songs while simultaneously verbally and musically processing the overarching themes emerging from the song creation process. O'Grady et al. (2014) outline a cyclical process of play, reflection back to the group, transformation of ideas, negotiation with group members, and collaboration. The collaboration then moved to a second phase of learning the song material for the public performance. This included orchestration and arrangement of the song. The community artists then created a script that would connect the songs together, and each song was choreographed. Finally, there were full rehearsals, which included props, costumes, lighting, sets, songs, and script (see Figure 14.6). The process had a strong emphasis on musical creativity and performance, an example of building musical capital (Procter, 2011).

An important consideration in the collaborative approach of O'Grady's work (2011), which incorporated the continuous exchanges between the artists and participants, was the notion of ownership. Creative exchanges are characterized by the artists creating material, playing it to the group, and followed by negotiations between artists and participants as to the emerging material. As the artists were actively involved in creating material alongside the participants' contributions, there was a shared ownership of the material, which was openly acknowledged. This is in direct contrast to the experience-oriented approaches whereby music therapists strive to ensure participants experience full ownership of the created material (see the previous chapter). Notably, participant ownership is enhanced by the focus of the songs' contents, which are stories based on the lives of the participants.

In O'Grady's (2009) study, the performative component of songwriting played an important role in bridging the inside life of the prison

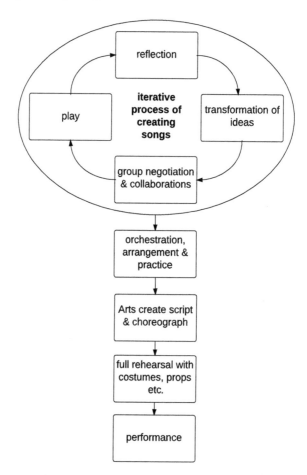

Figure 14.6   Illustration of O'Grady's (2009) process of creating a musical

with the outside world. They experienced a sense of connection with the audience and of being supported. There was an experience of sharing and reciprocity (O'Grady, 2009). Some of the women in the prison noticed that their involvement in the program had afforded them more freedom and access to the prison compound as a result of enhanced trust from prison staff. O'Grady's (2009) study exemplifies the role of songwriting in building social and musical capital through the bridging and bonding that occur at many levels of the system. As songs were created and performed, the songwriters' common purpose enabled them to cross the dividing line and bring their prison experiences to the outside world. The song creation activities enabled them to develop trust with the prison staff and enhanced the health of the prison community.

Songwriting as a culture-centered practice

Integral to CoMT perspectives is the notion that culture is a resource for action. For an outward and around approach to flourish within a songwriting program, the music therapist needs to be sensitive to the cultural practices of the targeted community and view these cultural practices as possibilities and opportunities for engagement. At the microsystem level, Bolger (2014) accommodated the individual culture of each community into her songwriting approach. For example, the share house described earlier was a culture unto itself. When attempting to plan her program for a home of four adolescents with varied lifestyles and commitments, she needed to work with the 'inherent chaos' culture (p. 66) that existed in the house. These young people had school and work commitments, had visiting boyfriends, and rotating staff. Merely planning the time of day for songwriting sessions was a cultural consideration. In other words, 'Working with existing community cultures also involved working with existing constraints and boundaries in each community' (p. 85). Therefore, songwriting need not be set in an arena which may be more characteristic of outcome-oriented or experience-oriented approaches, but may take place in a lounge room (Bolger, 2014) or in a car park, perhaps at times of the day that are outside of business hours. In other words, for success, the songwriting activities had to fit into the culture of the community.

When it came to participation, the culture of each community influenced the form of choices Bolger offered. For the 'drop-in' group, there was a necessity to offer the young people the freedom to choose their level and mode of participation. Here, the community had a 'come and go as you please culture', which needed to be considered when planning songwriting activities. The culture of an inconsistent and ever-changing group membership has a different atmosphere in songwriting sessions when compared with a consistent group (Baker, 2013a).

In a songwriting project with Mexican migrant farmworkers in the United States, Schwantes (2011) considered a range of cultural considerations in designing her program. She adapted her therapy approach to support the Latino cultures and the marginalization of the Mexican migrant farmworker (p. 23). For example, she recognized that music for this Latino farmworker culture was not only a bridge between the therapist and local community, but also between them and their families back in Mexico. She identified cultural strengths such as dignidad (dignity), respeto (respect), personalismo (relating personally), familismo (family values), and machismo (maleness), which she incorporated into the songwriting activities.

Schwantes et al. (2011) reported on the process of creating one song by one of the groups of Mexican farmworkers. In their study, the farmworker community was grieving the loss of two friends who were killed in a car accident. The therapist facilitated a program that focused on creating and recording a song that described the events of the accident. Using the corrido song form, a culturally relevant means of sharing stories of important events, the CoMT program enabled group participation, bonding, and an opportunity to share their community's story of grief and loss. The song contained detailed descriptions of the events, for example 'A van rolled over with 14 men on board, four times it turned'. The farmworkers were encouraged to take active involvement such as by changing, adding, or deleting lyrics, and singing the song acapella. In keeping with CoMT practices, the musical strengths of the various group members were identified and each was assigned a role in the performance and recording of the song. They later shared their story with the local community and used the composed songs to educate the community about seatbelt safety.

Affordance and appropriation through songwriting

With the concept of affordance and appropriation in mind (DeNora, 2000), I suggest that songwriting offers opportunities to afford and appropriate. Through creating the song and then recording, sharing, or performing it, songwriters have possibilities to use songwriting as a resource for wellbeing. Songwriting can be a resource for identity and emotional work; creating songs together with others allows opportunities to connect with others and construct one's own identity. Tuastad and O'Grady (2013) discuss their separate programs in prison contexts. They suggest that prisoners 'can actively reconfigure their identities through music' (p. 213). Their programs, which draw heavily on creating and performing songs, enable prisoners to reconnect 'with parts of their identities' that are not about being a prisoner (p. 213). In creating songs, the prison inmates are using the songwriting experience to construct an identity of being a musician/songwriter. For prison inmates, songwriting can be used as a temporary escape from prison life. Tuastad and O'Grady understand this use of songwriting and performing as 'music as a freedom practice' (2013, p. 221).[9] Songs, like art in general, have societal permission to be a vehicle to express views and tell stories that might otherwise be considered taboo or inappropriate in other contexts. In this way, songwriting affords song-writers the freedom to express themselves in an environment where freedom is denied.

Critical points in the songwriting process and levels of depth

Throughout the interviews and in the available literature, there was very little discussion about the critical points in the songwriting process. Bolger's study identified two distinct phases in her collaborative CoMT projects. The first phase she labeled the 'hangout period', which, as the name suggests, is a period of time where the therapist spends time with the community she is about to begin working with. This could include activities such as sharing a meal, playing football, or just 'hanging out'. The format and duration of the hangout period differs between con-texts, but she asserts that the time should be sufficiently long to allow the therapist to build relationships with the communities and those she will be working directly with. For example, she found that it took her three months to build relationships with the drop-in group, several weeks with the therapeutic camp participants, and a single evening for the share home group. Bolger argues that this preliminary work leads to greater chances of buy-in – the motivation to invest oneself in the songwriting project. The initial phases of contact – especially the first session – were considered critical to the success or failure of the song-writing process even when a hangout period was not a feature of the program. One music therapist who works with youth in child welfare contexts commented:

> The beginning, the first meeting is so important, it may be the most important moment. You can make a lot of mistakes along the way, but if they don't have trust in you then you can't do anything with them.

Conversely, other music therapists view the critical points as occurring during the lyric creation stage of songwriting. This is where insight occurs and where songwriters feel validated as their lyrics and the messages they express are acknowledged by the songwriter himself, the therapist, and any others who are present during the lyric creation activity.

The role of songwriting and the music

Songwriting activities afford many people the opportunity to discover their musical and non-musical capabilities. Appropriating the musick-ing experiences afforded by songwriting, songwriters are able to discover and develop musical skill. As CoMT demystifies the songwriting process as not being something only especially talented people can achieve, the songwriters emerge as lyricists and (with the emergence of inexpensive music software) as composers of aesthetically appealing songs. Feelings of pride and accomplishment are derived from these discoveries which flow through to self-esteem and wellbeing.

In addition to this discovery, songwriting in CoMT settings addresses the issue of access to musical participation. As CoMT supports the songwriters to develop new musical skills and gain mastery over the craft of creating original songs, it equips these songwriters with the musical skills necessary for ongoing access to music participation. Acquisitions of such skills increases possibilities for these people to continue to participate in musical activities once the therapist ceases to have input. In Tuastad's (Tuastad & O'Grady, 2013) work with prison inmates and ex-inmates, participation in music activities was examined across three contexts: within the prison, in the early stages after prison release within a community culture center, and self-initiated musical activities post prison release. Band activities facilitated by the therapist included songwriting, recording, performance, and jamming. The men expressed that music was a central part of their personal development –motivation, mastery, confirmation, self-image, and self-esteem – and that the process enabled them gain skills that could be used beyond the prison setting. This study clearly illustrates how songwriting within a CoMT setting can bridge inmate settings to ex-inmate settings, enabling them to engage in personal and community music participation.

Songwriting within CoMT, like FMT, may be viewed as a form of social action. Here, songwriting can function to tell an individual, collective, or societal story. As songs may communicate core messages embedded in people's stories, the process of identifying, acknowledging, and then synthesizing this into lyrics and expressed in music allows people to make public a commitment to instituting change. In a Norwegian CoMT project with children and adolescents registered in the child welfare system, Krüger and Stige (2014) found that through playing in a band, writing songs, and then performing them at a revue, the young people were contributing to the human rights issue of participation. In particular, through the process of creating songs and music, and then talking about their music participation with people (adults) outside the CoMT setting, the adolescents addressed issues of stigma and lack of dialogue with adults. Their music became a focus for showing that 'I am more than just a problem child' (p. 10). Similarly, their study found that musicking (which included songwriting experiences) enabled them to structure their personal and communal stories.

Songwriting within CoMT perspectives assists people to develop their relationships with music and with others involved in creating songs (Bolger, 2014). In Tuastad's study (Tuastad & O'Grady, 2013), social interaction was the third main category that was constructed as a result of the interviews with ex-inmates. Tuastad found that songwriting, rehearsing, and performing allowed for collaboration, solidarity, empathy, and care to emerge between participants. Through the musicking experiences, participants developed musical, individual, and social skills, including an awareness of listening to others and offering positive as well as constructive feedback.

Music plays an interesting function within the community music therapist's songwriting approach. Unlike its function in outcome- and experience-oriented approaches, music is not a 'thing' that sits apart from context and, as has been reiterated several times already in this chapter, is a situated event and activity (Stige, 2002). Rather than playing a specific role of enhancing the expressive potential of the lyrics, the music plays a pivotal role in bonding and bridging within and between communities. Within communities, the style of music may represent or reflect the group's identity, thereby serving to strengthen bonds. When playing their song creations together, it is the groove potential of music that engenders this feeling of being together in a musical space, a place where the musical frameworks for participation allow the songwriters to take risks (Aigen, 2002). Conversely, bridging between communities can occur during the songwriting process as the music is the core reason for being there, and the various individuals are drawn to work collaboratively to create an aesthetically pleasing musical product.

It is the notion of affordance and appropriation that determines music's role in the songwriting process. The ways people will use music in the songwriting process to enhance wellbeing may differ between people. Such contrasts in appropriation are evident in Bolger's (2014) work with young people. Studying the use of music-making (which included a strong emphasis on songwriting) in three different contexts highlighted how songwriting was appropriated in multiple ways to serve the needs of people in each context. For the young people in the drop-in group, musicking experiences were appropriated to connect young people residing in the public housing estate, and primarily to develop musical skills. They were appropriating the musicking songwriting experiences as a 'training ground to prepare the young people for future life experiences' (p. 86). In contrast to the drop-in group, the therapeutic camp appropriated the musicking experiences to explore the meaning and experience of being part of a week-long camp. In the therapeutic camp group there was less of an emphasis on developing music skills, but the musical strengths of different group members as beatboxers, singers, and rap artists contributed significantly to the style of the song being developed. For some group members, this contribution of their musical capacity was their primary way of participating in the songwriting process, and for others it was a way to explore a new musical experience – as a rapper, a singer, or otherwise.

The role of the therapist and the songwriter

Because the community music therapist is grounded in ecological thinking, her role during the songwriting process goes beyond merely being a therapist (in the more traditional sense as outlined in Chapters 12 and 13). Within the ecological perspective, the therapist serves to use the songwriting process to promote health and healing at the individual level and at the microsystem, mesosystem, exosystem, and macrosystem levels – it concerns the relationships between the songwriters and their communities, a relational practice (Stige, 2003/2012). At the individual level, the therapist's role is to support the songwriter so that he is able to experience a meaningful songwriting process. This may entail assisting the songwriter to build musical skills that will prepare him for musical activities beyond the context of the therapist–songwriter dyad. The therapist is always considering what personal, interpersonal, and musical skills can be shaped or strengthened to increase the likelihood that engagement in community-based musical activities are successful. Skills in playing music, creating lyrics, constructing musical accompaniments that (a) match the lyrics of the songs, and/or (b) reflect the songwriter's musical identity address the much-needed musical skills. Further, the therapist provides musical experiences that assist in building skills about collaborative musicking. Group songwriting also demands the ability to work collaboratively with others, listen to and be open to others' suggestions, be empowered to offer ideas, and to share one's own musical self with others. The therapist's role is to model such behaviors, at times 'teach' the songwriter specific instrumental skills and the craft of songwriting, offer supportive but constructive feedback on contributions, and provide opportunities to practice creating and playing songs with others. While there is an element of music education to this process, the therapist is actually considering how developing certain skills will increase access to and participation in music arenas that were otherwise inaccessible.

Going beyond the individual to the microsystem and the mesosystem, the therapist's role shifts to bridging the individual with these surrounding systems. Songwriting within small groups (microsystems) were facilitated when Bolger (2014) shared her musical expertise and provided the songwriters access to musical equipment that they otherwise might not have been able to use. She indicated that her role was also to ensure the young songwriters had realistic expectations of their musical skills, to reduce the risk of setting them up for ridicule and rejection when taking their songs out to the wider community. She also viewed her role as facilitator of the collaborative process and to keep the songwriters focused on task completion – the song creations.

Fostering the right conditions for creativity is another important component impacting the success of a CoMT songwriting process. As the women in O'Grady's (2011) study were working collaboratively with community musicians and artists, it was important for the female prisoners to feel safe and to trust in the process – particularly as trust and safety was not a given in the prison setting. For the women to tell their stories, the therapist's role is to create a safe space where the artists and women are encouraged to be non-judgmental toward themselves and others. The therapist needs to guide the artists so that the songwriters are presented with opportunities to succeed.

For a songwriting process to flourish, the therapist's role is to ensure that there is a health-promoting relationship between the songwriter and the community. This includes creating an environment that gives space for those who may have never had opportunities to access community music-making. To achieve this, the role of the therapist in the songwriting process is to reject the expert-directed approach and replace it with a participatory approach whereby the therapist allows the songwriters to express their needs, have a voice, and take responsibility for the direction of the songwriting process. At the same time, the therapist has a responsibility to facilitate negotiations with communities to ensure that attitudes and assumptions which may otherwise inhibit participation are addressed (Stige, 2003/2012). In this sense, the therapist's role is one of 'a resourceful collaborator, project-coordinator, consultant, mentor, and coach' (Stige, 2003/2012, p. 413). For example, if a songwriter has mobility issues (e.g. using a wheelchair), then the therapist might consult with staff at a recording studio to ensure that there is ample access if the songwriter chooses to record his song. Similarly, if a songwriter has levels of performance anxiety that are in part a symptom of his mental illness, the therapist may work with the stage staff to identify strategies that may minimize anxiety for the songwriter and increase the potential for him to have a satisfying performance of his song.

The role of the songwriter in the songwriting process is as a participant and collaborator. As the songwriting process encourages active participation and empowerment, the songwriter must share in the process, take responsibility for decisions, and follow through on actions needed to complete the songwriting task. The songwriter's role is, at the very least, to provide lyrical material – either in the form of ideas, a story, or fully formed lyrics – and provide some of the musical vision as to how these lyrics can be transformed into a song.

Some songwriters who are already feeling empowered often drive the creative process, with the therapist following the songwriter's lead. Conversely, those who are less active require more support from the therapist to ensure the process moves along. The role of the songwriter is inextricably linked with that of the therapist; as one interviewee stated, it is an 'interplay between the two based on each person's strengths, experience, and comfort with the creative process'.

The role of the artifact

Artifacts afford an important role in CoMT practices because of the extent to which they are performed in different contexts. Performance, in the broadest sense of the word, is integral to CoMT practice because of its focus on 'human development through action and the performance of relationships' (Stige & Aarø, 2012). The performance of a group-composed song within the setting in which it was created serves to bond the group members, allowing them to relate to one another through the groove of music (Aigen, 2002). Moreover, there are arenas where songwriters perform on stage to a wider audience. In these situations, performance can only have meaning when there is a 'relationship between performer, spectator, and the space in which it all meets' (Elefant, 2010, p. 207). As will be clearly outlined in this section, performance offers possibilities to support the individual (Baker, 2013d; O'Grady, 2009, 2011), as well as the relational and community levels of change within microsystem, mesosystem, and exosystem (Bolger, 2014; O'Grady, 2009).

Songs created during CoMT may serve political and activist functions. The notion that people are seen as something different to their 'label' contributes to combating stigma and chairing public perceptions and attitudes (Krüger & Stige, 2014). For this to transpire, the song needs to be shared in some form beyond the setting in which it was created. As public audiences observe the songwriters performing their songs, there is an increased understanding of 'the plight of the performers'. Viewing the songwriters through a different lens has the potential to affect social change and strengthen social connectedness (O'Grady et al., 2014, p. 4). For example, one interviewee in the study suggests that performing songs can contribute to a sense of social collective identity, which has flow-on effects to creating a collective power that challenges the community's assumptions. The interviewee suggested that group songs created by adolescents become important after they are created because the whole group identifies with the content of the song, and it subsequently affords a role that expresses the whole group's social collective identity. Conjointly, in sharing the song with a wider community, the songwriters feel empowered to state that they do not want to be treated differently to other adolescents. In reference to a particular song titled 'Ordinary', the messages the young people were communicating were that they viewed themselves as ordinary young people and that 'it's totally okay'. The interviewee states:

> I think that the song says something about okay, 'it's okay to be adolescent in the institution', 'we don't have to be ashamed of this', 'it's totally okay', 'we, like everybody else, want to have a life as normal people and you guys out there, listen to us because this is our message'. There's a kind of empowering process to use the song to tell the world okay, we are like everybody else. Don't treat us differently because we want to be like you.

The wider distribution of songs may take several forms: public performances (O'Grady, 2011), performances for family (Aasgaard, 2002), performances for peers (Bolger, 2014), performances for policy makers (O'Grady, 2011), and performances via public media (Aasgaard, 2002). Within these arenas, people are being seen and heard – not only may they share their experiences of, for example, prison life, homelessness, or discrimination, but they are also being seen and heard as talented musicians who have acquired the capacity to engage in meaningful community musical engagements.

At the individual level, performing self-composed songs enhances pride and ownership of the material (Baker, 2013d), increases the significance of the song for the songwriters (Baker, 2013d), and becomes a public acknowledgment of the musical skills they have acquired (O'Grady et al., 2014). When professional musicians either collaborate with the songwriters in the performance of the song or perform the songwriters' songs independently, songwriters experience enhanced self-worth (Baker, 2013d). Uptake of their music by professional musicians offers unsolicited feedback that they are worthy musicians attracting attention from other musicians. This places them as equals with respect to musical contributions and serves to boost self-esteem and strengthen their musical identity.

Baker (2013d) suggests, however, that therapists should be cautious about allowing songwriters to perform their songs to unknown public audiences when:

1. the songwriters have a life-long experience of being judged,
2. the songwriters have insufficient inner resources to manage the performance context,
3. the songwriters are not well supported by the context (e.g. when degree of audience support is unreliable or unknown),
4. performing in public is outside the songwriters' comfort zone, and
5. audiences may not relate to or understand the significance of the song for the songwriter.

Resource-oriented music therapy

Theoretical frameworks, aims, and objectives

ROMT is an approach to music therapy that incorporates belief and principles derived from empowerment and human rights theory, positive psychology, and feminist theory (Rolvsjord, 2010). The principle concern of ROMT is to enable people to participate to their fullest potential and wishes, particularly for those who have been excluded from participating for health or social reasons. The therapist works to support and facilitate empowerment through engendering hope, self-determination, and community inclusion. According to Solli (2014), ROMT aligns with contemporary recovery-oriented practices that are aimed at improving health, strength, and capabilities, rather than treating disorders. There is a focus on enabling people to directly, constructively, and actively engage with the world within which they live (Rolvsjord, 2010). While ROMT grounds itself in context-oriented thinking, it differs from CoMT in that it also focuses on music therapy as a psychotherapeutic practice (Rolvsjord, 2010; Schwabe, 2005).

ROMT is informed by empowerment theory. Psychological empowerment (Renblad, 2003) comprises three dimensions: (1) interpersonal dimensions (self-esteem, self-efficacy, locus of control), (2) interactional dimensions (capacity and skills to influence the environment), and (3) behavioral dimensions (acting through community participation) (Renblad as cited in Rolvsjord, 2010). Feminist influences are also present in ROMT because of the focus on empowerment and equality. Procter

(2002) argues that music therapy can be a medium whereby people are enabled and empowered to experience themselves and their potentials through music-making experiences. Their capacity to participate goes beyond merely their individual resources to include the social, cultural, and economic resources available to them (Rolvsjord, 2010). To achieve this, there is a need to focus on bringing awareness of and strengthening existing resources as well as developing new resources (Procter, 2002).

ROMT begins by working with a person at the individual level, assisting him to acquire knowledge, skills, and competence needed for experiences beyond the music therapeutic context (Rolvsjord, 2010; Solli, 2014). Once these have been acquired, ROMT can move beyond the treatment setting to a community setting. In these situations, the therapist may play a role in connecting the person in recovery with community-based music activities (Solli, 2014).

In line with CoMT perspectives, affordance and appropriation are of relevance, where music is the resource that can be taken and used (DeNora, 2000) rather than the therapist's actions affecting change. ROMT embeds principles of positive psychology into its approach. Here, positive emotions are fostered, there is an emphasis on resilience and coping with negative emotional experiences, and this occurs through a strengthening of resources and potentials. These principles fit with the discussions on broaden-and-build theory (Chapter 13) whereby strengthening positive emotions through resource building can 'undo' enduring negative emotions and build resilience and overall wellbeing.

A key principle of ROMT is the focus on collaboration – a shared responsibility between the therapist and the person working toward improved health and wellbeing. Such a collaborative process is also a feature of CoMT and FMT and is connected with empowerment philosophy. Having a voice in the decision-making process correlates with a decrease in psychological and somatic symptoms and stress, and a reduction in helplessness, by exchanging dependency with interdependency (Rolvsjord, 2010). Rolvsjord suggests that such collaboration is characterized by:

1. Equality (shared responsibility to work but with different roles, consciously striving for equal rights, counteracting oppressive power relations),
2. Mutuality (engagement, equally shared responsibility and affective responsiveness, interdependency),
3. Participation in a collaborative activity (communal and/or political activity) so that decision-making is not about holding power but rather having the opportunity to exert influence and make one's voice heard.

Aligned with the contextual model described at the beginning of this chapter, ROMT promotes viewing a person not in isolation, but within interpersonal, structural, societal, and cultural contexts. So even though ROMT may work in a one-to-one setting, the person is always considered as an entity beyond his individual self.

Rolvsjord (2010) is very clear about the aims underpinning ROMT. There is a focus on achieving mastery, self-esteem, and self-efficacy through establishing a person's belief in his own capabilities. Mastery leads to possibilities for artistic participation, enablement, and the building of social capital.

Models

There have been very few published articles where researchers have employed songwriting within a ROMT framework. However, evidence of its wide use was apparent in the language of interviewees – the phrase 'resource-oriented' was frequently mentioned in descriptions of practitioners' approaches, often alongside language depicting empowerment. As described by interviewees, songwriting within a ROMT perspective (referred to here as resource-oriented songwriting or ROS) usually avoids parody and approaches where many of the lyrical or musical structures are predefined. This is largely due to the philosophy of identifying and developing resources – in this case, musical resources. Interviewees also suggested that song parody was experienced as artificial and minimized the feelings of ownership that are needed to feel fully resourced. As mastery, self-esteem, and self-efficacy are primary aims of ROS, structuring songwriting approaches that promote ownership are considered integral. One interviewee relayed how a young woman had created her own melody that she considered underscored the songwriter's text. It was when the young woman sang her song that there was a notable change in the quality of her voice – 'it had more strength'. Such an increase in inner strength may not have transpired from creating a parody, where full ownership of a song creation may not be experienced.

Viega (2013) suggests that songwriting is a means of mobilizing and activating self-healing, a process whereby people have the possibility to identify and connect with internal resources. Internal resources in songwriting can be acknowledged in several ways. Sometimes, a songwriter arrives with his own lyrics or poems (Aasgaard, 2002; Rolvsjord, 2005), ready to collaborate on the creation of music that expresses his songs' messages. At other times, the songwriter brings pre-existing music resources such as playing a musical instrument, singing, or previous experience in creating songs (Rolvsjord, 2005). In almost all cases, a songwriter will bring with him a musical identity, an understanding of a certain genre of music, including the various musical forms, typical rhythms, and instrumentation. These resources can be acknowledged, nurtured, and further developed. A case study of Marco, a man with severe and enduring mental illness, discovered that creating rap was a resource he could harness to find meaning, hope, and motivation in his life (Solli, 2014). Music afforded him positive participatory experiences that served to combat his battle 'with the dark forces' (p. 8). In sessions with the music therapist, Marco would collaboratively musick through free-style rapping. The lyrical material comprised present issues interspersed with prewritten lyrical material. Despite Marco's severe illness and incapacity to function in other areas of his life, his musical skills and resources were of a surprisingly high level.

Empowerment is embedded throughout the ROS process. Through the element of choice, songwriters are empowered to decide on song content, specific lyrics, musical style, instrumentation, and other musical content (Solli, 2014). Through narrative songwriting – telling their story and sharing their musical identities – their lyrics and music give them a voice. Empowerment is then fostered in deciding what happens to the song post-creation. Will it be recorded? Will it be performed? And if so, who is the audience?

Collaboration is also integral to the success of the ROS experience. The process is characterized by the therapist and songwriter interacting musically with lyrics and music, and working together to create a song imbued with meaning. Sharing in the ensuing musical interactions, the songwriter has possibilities for health musicking and creating musical experiences and songs that can afford health benefits. Musical affordances are connected not only to the music and lyrics, but also to the social phenomenon as embodied in the therapist–songwriter interactions. As one interviewee states:

> Songs are a very social common phenomenon that people recognize, and they may have lots of ideas about how a song is used in social life. So many people connect with songs – possibilities of shaping identity. . . . So I think there's some affordances with this aspect of songwriting, but the main thing is how it's actually performed, how it's an interaction between two or more people and how they make use of these potential affordances to make it afford something for them.

Rolvsjord (2005) describes the case of Emma, a young woman who was an inpatient in a psychiatric hospital. Her song creations played a role in strongly connecting her to her own identity. Through her songs, Emma told the story of her life, her experienced trauma, her feelings, her hopes, and her wishes. She described the songs as 'pieces of her, and they all have to be there' (p. 118). So the more than 30 songs she created became a resource for capturing her life experiences. She 'used' these songs in difficult situations, a health resource to remind her that these difficult situations pass. Similarly, for Marco (Solli, 2014) rapping afforded musicking by connecting him with his identity. In addition, he used the songwriting process to experience himself as a musician, music producer, music technician, as well as in the music management roles of performance manager, distributer, and music promoter. Solli (2014) asserts that by engaging in these activities Marco experiences a sense of agency as he chooses, initiates, acts out, and accomplishes music-focused activities.

Self-esteem and self-efficacy were identified as primary aims of ROMT. Within the ROS process, self-esteem and self-efficacy are derived from creating a song that holds aesthetic value for society. The creation of a product allows for musical resources to be highlighted, especially when recorded, and relistening to the song at different moments can serve to maintain or further build self-esteem. Similarly, when songs are shared with others, positive feedback and a sense of support can flow between the audience and the songwriter (Baker, 2013c, 2013d). For example, an interviewee reported how there were several musicians amongst nursing and other health staff at the hospital where she worked. They often offered positive feedback as songwriters shared their material with them. Such experiences build self-esteem, self-efficacy, and thus resilience.

Critical points in the songwriting process and levels of depth

Authors practicing within ROMT frameworks have not written about when the critical points in the songwriting process occur. Some music therapists I interviewed reported that the critical points occurred when a true collaboration became apparent, where there was a feeling of mutuality and equality in the participation. So the critical point was not determined by a certain phase in the songwriting process, but when the qualities of the interactions and participations transformed into a strong collaborative relationship. As one interviewee stated:

> On some occasions, it is the process of creating the song that is important, whereas on other occasions it is how the song is used after it's created that gives it its power.

The songwriter's own identification and an acknowledgment of resources were also a key point in the songwriting process, and again, these could occur at any point during the ROS process. They sometimes occurred as the songwriter identified musical resources such as being able to create lyrics and music in his chosen musical style or being able to sing or play the instrumental accompaniments. Resources were also related to personal traits such as being courageous enough to share painful stories, to acknowledge inner strengths, and to identify strategies for using their songs as a health resource. In the case of Marco, his rap skills and knowledge of rap artists were far more advanced than that of the therapist. He used his resources as a rap expert to instruct the therapist on playing styles such as rap drum rhythms and beatboxing rhythms into the microphone. Solli illustrates, however, in this case there was a mutual sharing of resources between the therapist and Marco, where the two musicians were aware of each other's expertise and used this to afford mutuality in their relationships.

One interviewee argued the importance of the refinement process – where small changes to the lyrics and/or music are discussed. It is therapeutically important that the song is perceived as 'good enough' by the songwriter, otherwise the song is not truly finished. Such a process of refinement offers the songwriter the opportunity to be empowered – to make changes that are most reflective of his identity, story, and message.

The levels of depth achieved in ROS may be substantially deeper when compared with CoMT, mainly because of the emphasis on the psychotherapeutic process (Rolvsjord, 2010) and the inherent difference between individual- and group-focused work. One example is Rolvsjord's (2005) case of Emma, a young woman who had been abused by her father and was receiving music therapy as an inpatient in a psychiatric hospital. As mentioned earlier, the 30-plus songs she created told the story of her life. What Rolvsjord intimated, however, was that Emma had managed to create something she viewed as beautiful from her traumatic experiences. Indeed the wounds she revealed in her songs illustrate the level of depth that was achieved – an insight-oriented process that led to transformative experiences.

The role of songwriting and the music

Songwriting with ROMT takes on a number of different roles. At the broadest level, it can be considered a useful musical interactive experience that allows opportunities for therapeutic 'collaborative' experiences with others (Rolvsjord, 2005). The focus of creating a song through collaboration suggests that the therapist and songwriter work together in a meaningful and effective way to ensure that the song is completed. Therefore, this structure has the potential to provide emotional relational experiences that Rolvsjord suggests are inherent in any musical interaction. However, within therapeutic songwriting 'these are explicated within the song product' (Rolvsjord, 2005, p. 102). In a second case, Rolvsjord (2010) discussed how songwriting was used with a young woman to address her life challenges. Songwriting offered the young woman an opportunity to communicate with the therapist and others, and to interact with them in a way that was meaningful and helpful for her. The process was a medium for interactional experiences.

Songwriting as a process offers songwriters opportunities to experience positive emotions, explore their strengths, and experience pleasure, joy, and mastery (Rolvsjord, 2010, p. 5). Creating a product that highlights one's musical and personal skills is one of the biggest strengths of songwriting (see Chapter 2). Showcasing one's own song creation boosts esteem and communicates the songwriter's capacity to contribute to cultural capital. In many ways, this form of achievement demonstrates a creativity that many would argue exceeds that of merely playing a musical instrument. And songwriters experience pleasure and joy in recognizing their creative mastery and sharing it with others.

The role of music within the songwriting process is regarded as much less about the music itself and more about its subjective and contextualized use (Rolvsjord, 2010). Rolvsjord suggested that music and health share 'a two-way relationship'. She proposed that good health may enable possibilities for participating in creating music, and in reverse, music creation provides possibilities for health-enhancing experiences.

Role of the therapist and the songwriter

Rolvsjord (2010) outlines a range of unique and essential roles that the music therapist brings to the music therapy experience, many of which I suggest may be present when therapist and songwriter collaborate on songwriting. Adapting Rolvsjord's essential features of ROMT, I propose that the therapist should:

1. focus on the songwriters' strengths and potentials rather than on their weaknesses and impairments,
2. collaborate with the songwriters about the aim of the songwriting experience and how they may work together on the song product,
3. acknowledge the songwriters' musical identity and bring this in to the songwriting experience, and
4. foster positive emotions through the song creation process.

The therapist's role is also to engage the songwriter in musicking and use these musicking experiences to listen to the songwriter's expressions, attune to his emotional expressions, and respond empathically (Rolvsjord, 2010).

To communicate her interest in and support the evolution of a collaborative relationship, the music therapist may offer the songwriter a range of suggestions for melodies and accompaniments to choose from. These suggestions may have been created by the therapist outside of the songwriting session, and when the therapist presents these possibilities to the songwriter for consideration, she communicates her 'care' and willingness to collaborate. As one interviewee states:

> If I had a client's lyrics just laying around in my office, sometimes I would have an idea that I would try out even if the client wasn't there. I think the first times I did that I thought 'oh dear am I doing too much here, should I wait and see, am I taking the song from them', but I think over the years when I use songwriting it seems that it was usually a good thing for the client also to see that someone could actually think about their song after the session and to go back and say that I have this suggestion for you.

However, the therapist's interest and support need to be carefully balanced with possibilities for the songwriter to insert his own identity into the song. The therapist can address this need for ownership by leaving some 'unfinished' sections or allowing space for the songwriter to suggest changes.

Some practitioners who work with young people use the music mixing and editing process to increase an 'artist's' involvement in the process and empower him to discover his own strengths and reach his fullest potential (Viega, 2013). Here, the role of the therapist is of a fan, a supportive listener, and a music producer who can create the conditions for the songwriter to identify his positive internal resources (Viega, 2013). As Aigen (2005b) states, 'I am here to help you make music rather than I am here to change you, fix you, control you, or heal you' (p. 120). In Solli's (2014) work, the songwriter and therapist dyad epitomize equality of collaboration. Solli and songwriter Marco alternated roles between musician and music studio operator, discussing together how to combine musical elements to create the feel of the song that Marco had in mind.

Like the therapist, the songwriter has a role in bringing his own resources – personal and musical – to the experience and in using them within the collaborative creative activity. The songwriters have knowledge of song forms related to their culture, knowledge about how songs can be used in different ways and different contexts, and a musical identity and connection with music that can be utilized as a resource to create songs. For example, a songwriter will often have opinions about what his song should sound like, and as the therapist offers suggestions, there can be a narrowing down process until the music created resembles something akin to what is in the songwriter's mind.

Role of the artifact

> It is how the song is used after it's created that gives it its power. (Statement by an interviewee)

While the process of creating a song undoubtedly has power to utilize and strengthen resources, according to many interviewees and as alluded to in the literature in ROMT the artifact is equally, if perhaps not more, important than its creation. The meaning of a song and its affordances are linked according to interpersonal feelings of mastery, pride in the creation of an art that reflects the person's capabilities to engage in artistic creation. By possessing a copy of the song (either an audio recording or a lyric sheet), the songwriter can be reminded of his inner resources and use this as a means of boosting esteem during low moments in his life.

From the relational perspective, sharing the song with others also affords possibilities for receiving feedback from them about either the story expressed in the song or its artistry. Sharing can take the form of providing audio copies of song creations to family and friends or, more increasingly, through live performance of the songs. In the case of Marco (Solli, 2014), as part of his therapy process he created an album of songs, which he shared with other inpatients at the psychiatric hospital. The songs were played through the hospital system and functioned as an avenue to socialize with others.

Performance is also a starting point for those in recovery to begin to connect with the outside world. Marco (Solli, 2014) had prepared a performance of one of his rap songs at a concert at the hospital. On this occasion, he was the solo 'supporting act' for a professional band employed to play at the hospital event. Marco informally interacted with the band members prior to the commencement of the concert. Quite unexpectedly, the lead singer of the band invited Marco to freestyle rap during the last song of the set. He successfully 'jammed' with

Table 14.1 Salient features of context-oriented models of songwriting

	Feminist music therapy	Community music therapy	Resource-oriented music therapy
Premise	1. Systems are patriarchal and are a source of oppression 2. Class systems create division and are a source of oppression 3. Identity, personality, and behavior are partly socially constructed	1. Health implies ecological wholeness, including the capacity to partake in social and cultural activities 2. Musicking is a social process that creates opportunities to transform communities, create social capital, and promote health 3. Music practices can be empowering for individuals and communities 4. Music affordance and appropriation are individual and context-dependent	1. Health and wellbeing is associated with: empowerment and human rights, strengthening resources, positive psychology, feminist theory 2. A person's health must be viewed within interpersonal, structural, societal, and cultural contexts
Outcomes/ objectives of songwriting	1. Combat oppression 2. Cultivate culture of openness to and appreciation of difference 3. Sociopolitical transformation 4. Independence, empowerment 5. Identification, rejection, and replacement of internalized socially constructed beliefs and values	1. To create a healthy environment 2. Social justice and equitable distribution of resources 3. Stimulate health-promoting relationships 4. Reduce barriers to participation 5. Challenge community attitudes that exclude the disadvantaged 6. Cultivate musical communities	1. Individual treatment with focus on context 2. Affordances and appropriation 3. Mastery, self-esteem, self-efficacy 4. Identifying and strengthening (musical) identity 5. Artistic participation, enablement, and the building of social capital

(continued)

Table 14.1 (continued)

	Feminist music therapy	Community music therapy	Resource-oriented music therapy
Approach	1. Process-oriented and problem-oriented 2. Non-directive 3. Emergent/organic process 4. Emphasis on increasing awareness and understanding, and later rejection and replacement of internalized messages 5. Empowerment, collaboration, mutual/equal relationships	1. Non-predetermined 2. Songwriter-driven (not therapist-driven) 3. Emphasis on cultural musical practices (musicking) 4. Emphasis on empowerment, collaboration 5. Performative practices	1. Non-predetermined 2. Collaboration that is equal, mutual, and participatory 3. One-to-one setting but with a view to the broader context 4. Musical affordances are connected to the music structures and the social phenomenon 5. Create a song of aesthetic social value

Songwriting models	*Songwriting as therapy*
	1. Feminist individual songwriting
	  – create lyrics and music to give voice to an individual's story and embed feminist principles into song creations
	  – replace unhealthy internalized messages with healthy ones
	  – empower and increase independence
	2. Feminist focused song parody
	  – identify feminist issues embedded in pre-existing songs and rewrite to voice rights to equality
		1. Methods are more framed as influencing perspectives
		2. Participatory, collaborative, not expert-driven
		3. Resource-oriented
		4. Ecological
		5. Performative
		6. Sociopolitical, empowerment
		7. Culture-centered
			1. Resource-oriented songwriting with focus on identifying and extending resources
			2. Transforming poem into song
			3. Narrative songwriting
			4. Creating songs that reflect musical identity

3. Feminist group songwriting
   - create lyrics and music to give voice to a group's collective story
   - foster collaborative, respectful, supportive relationships
   - organic process

Critical points in the process	1. Identification, rejection, and replacement of internalized socially constructed messages 2. Building trust through creation of authentic lyrics 3. Committing to change through carefully worded lyrics	1. Hangout period 2. Trust and safety 3. Lyric creation phase 4. Performance	1. Establishment of an equal and mutual collaboration 2. Identification and an acknowledgment of resources 3. Song refinement process
Levels of depth	1. Reconstructive and transformative	1. Not specifically focused on, as songwriting is a more cultural practice. Likely to be supportive activities-oriented or insight-oriented/re-educative.	1. Likely to be supportive activities-oriented or insight-oriented/re-educative. Can go deeper than CoMT due to the emphasis on psychotherapeutic processes.
Emphasis	1. Identifying, discussing, rejecting and reconstructing internalized messages	1. Collaboration 2. Musicking 3. Performing	1. Collaboration 2. Musicking 3. Performing

(continued)

Table 14.1 (continued)

	Feminist music therapy	Community music therapy	Resource-oriented music therapy
Role of songwriting	1. Give voice to silenced, internalized messages 2. Create a story about experiences of oppression and/or actions/beliefs that free people from oppression 3. Create songs that have the potential to function as political activism	1. Context for musicking 2. Gain mastery of songwriting craft 3. Develop musical, individual, and social skills 4. Motivation to collaborate 5. Social action, address attitudes and assumptions	1. Provides opportunities for therapeutic collaborative/emotional relational experiences 2. Leads to a song product with continued therapeutic potential – both personal, interpersonal, and sociopolitical
Role of music	1. Heighten the expression of emotion attached to the story 2. Express the songwriter's authentic self 3. Convey struggles/tensions between the self vs societial views	1. Musicking is the aim, music the means 2. Bonding and bridging, groove potential 3. Group identity	1. As a health resource
Role of music therapist	1. Create conditions that foster an egalitarian relationship 2. Challenge (when appropriate) societal views embedded in pre-existing songs 3. Support, validate, respect, and understand experiences of oppression	1. Activist and advocate 2. Willingness to listen to and acknowledge songwriters' voices 3. Resourceful collaborator, project coordinator, consultant, mentor, coach 4. Facilitate the development of health relationships in the community	1. Guide songwriter toward identification of strengths and resources 2. Fan, 3. Supportive listener, 4. Collaborator 5. Music producer 6. Create the conditions to discover resources and create music

	4. Guide songwriters to embed positive beliefs into song creations or express pain, anger, or sadness associated with oppression 5. Advocate for equality		
Role of songwriter	1. Actively contribute to song creation 2. Share story authentically 3. Engage in decision-making and action	1. Collaborator, participator, narrator, activist (where appropriate) 2. Drive or participate in the process depending upon degree of empowerment experienced 3. Contribute lyrical material and provide musical vision	1. Bringing his own resources – personal and musical – for use in creative process 2. Provide story or fully developed lyrics 3. Provide guidance on music creation to reflect music identity and expression of story
Role of artifact	1. Tangible record of healthy messages 2. Recordings or public performances are a form of political and social activism 3. Shift focus from a purely individual challenge to societal challenge	1. Performance and recordings have individual, relational and community benefits 2. Pride, ownership, public acknowledgment, motivation, renewed confidence 3. Has sociopolitical functions 4. Challenges attitudes and assumptions	1. Symbol of inner resources available 2. Mastery and pride 3. Relational possibilities through sharing songs (via recordings or performance)

the professional musicians. This is a clear example of how the song creations were afforded for health purposes.

Conclusion

This chapter described the perspectives and models of songwriting
relevant to music therapists practicing in context-oriented models.
Table 14.1 provides a comparison of the salient features of feminist-
oriented, CoMT-oriented, and resource-oriented perspectives.

15

Songwriting as an Integral Practice

As I alluded to in the introductory chapter, the main aim of this research was to expand and deepen our understanding of the potential of songwriting to transform the lives of people across the lifespan. I was particularly motivated to construct concrete, descriptive, and clear perspectives that could assist the clinician to make choices about what method and model of songwriting would most aptly meet the needs of the people engaging in therapy. I wanted to offer flexible methods and models as context is everything in music therapy practice. While I am typically averse to assigning concepts and perspectives in boxes or categories because of the danger that this might lead to rigid application (the antithesis of what I hoped for), I believed at the outset (and still believe) that being able to be more specific in naming what we do and why we do it will enhance music therapy discourse, improve our reporting of the use of songwriting in research, and will assist in determining what methods, models, and practices are most efficacious to address a broad range of goals and purposes in diverse contexts .

As a consequence of my early music therapy experiences in private industry, I have always been a believer in evidence-based practice, a need to justify the financial investment that service users or stakeholders commit to. It might be a human right to have access to good healthcare, but this does not always follow through with action In an increasingly budget conscious world where we are competing with other service providers for an ever-shrinking pool of money, value for money is paramount in many (but fortunately not all) clinical contexts. If clinicians are better able to name what they do in their research irrespective of the lens through which they view songwriting and how they locate themselves, other researchers have a better chance of replicating and adapting the described methods and models as needed.

The expected outcome will be an increased body of research evidence. This is not to say that practice has to be dictated by the rigid songwriting protocols used in research, but it does lay important foundational work in illustrating what impact songwriting might have in enhancing the lives of the people we encounter in our workplace. I hope that people reading this text will begin to label what they do and how they think about songwriting in their research and clinical practice, so that in years to come I will be reading research papers that describe the songwriting method or models in terms such as sung imaginal dialogue, feminist focused song parody, narrative songwriting, contingency songwriting, rap over pre-composed music, and so on. I also hope that practitioners and researchers will be more reflexive about their own practice, are more aware of the potential for songwriting to impact health across diverse populations, and are more conscious of the environmental and socio-cultural factors that guide intervention choices.

As I bring together the models into an overarching framework, I want to reiterate Bruscia's (2014) ideas of integral thinking and not the 'functional fixedness' of only seeing things in one way, through a single lens (p. 227). When approaching songwriting practice, I have explored multiple perspectives so that the therapist can make reflexive choices. As Bruscia so aptly asserts, to be integral is to think about our songwriters' contexts, needs, goals, strategies, level of directedness, the role of music in songwriting, the therapist's role, the songwriter's role, and the depth of practice needed to ensure that we are meeting the needs of our songwriters. This is how I have approached the analysis of the in-depth interviews that informed this work. To this end, I offer this overview of the models and encourage you to open yourself to multiple possibilities (Figure 15.1).

Therapeutic songwriting is a form of music therapy experience that actively engages the songwriter or songwriters in a process of creating lyrics and/or music within the context of a therapeutic relationship. The process may be predominantly lyric-centered (parody, strategic songwriting, FITB, rapping over pre-composed music), music-centered (mash-ups, pastiche, hodge podge, and original songwriting), or involve a more or less equal focus on the two components (rapping over original music, song collage, improvised song creations). Further, the refining, recording, performing, and sharing of the songs may bolster the therapy process. It is important to be aware that performing and sharing songs with others may not always be in the best interests of the songwriter.

The songwriting process may operate at the supportive level, insight/process-oriented level, or reach a deeper transformative level, depending upon therapeutic context, the health and emotional stability of the

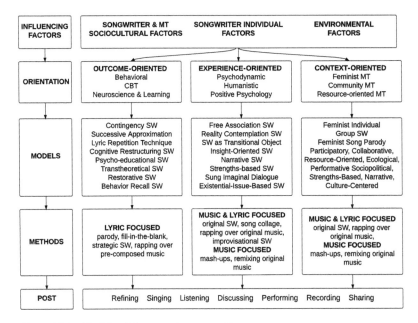

Figure 15.1 Models of therapeutic songwriting

songwriter, and the orientation of the therapist or organization involved in the songwriter's care. Further, the songwriting method may be therapist-directed, client-directed, or collaborative. Many factors impact the therapist's choice of model and method of songwriting, including the songwriter's individual characteristics (gender, age, sociocultural background, physical health status, cognitive abilities, personality, psychological and emotional wellbeing, and musical skills), and the environmental considerations of the organization (orientation, brief versus long-term therapy, scheduling, and the clinician's position within the hierarchy of care).

Songwriting has a different meaning, purpose, outcome, and experience when viewed through different philosophical or psychological lenses, even though the overarching methods of practice appear similar at first glance. A good outcome, experience, and purpose may be predetermined or unfold organically and may:

1. be measured by a positive change in behavior or thinking,
2. be experienced as an enhanced understanding and recognition of the true self,
3. provide recognition of the meaning and purpose in life,

4. provide a sense of empowerment and independence,
5. provide access to community musical participation,
6. create awareness and extension of inner resources, or
7. result in an increased sense of personal and/or musical identity.

While afforded little attention in the literature, the role that music plays in the songwriting process is significant. In some outcome-oriented contexts it provides the framework for treatment, it increases songwriters' investment in the process, or can function as a mnemonic aid. For those engaging in experience-oriented approaches, music allows for the expression of musical identity, complex or contradictory emotions, and the creation of a socially and aesthetically acceptable artistic product. Music offers possibilities to express oneself symbolically, access the unconscious, express the juxtaposition of order and chaos, or hold and contain the songwriter. Within context-oriented perspectives, music has a role in bonding and bridging communities at various ecological levels, in providing health musicking opportunities, in expressing a sociocultural or group identity, and as a health resource.

This work is a follow-up text to the first book dedicated to exploring songwriting as a method (Baker & Wigram, 2005). It is clear that a considerable number of practices and perspectives have emerged and that the field continues to rapidly change. As I reflect on my own process in undertaking the research and consider how it has shaped my thinking, not only about songwriting but more broadly about music therapy practice, I am struck by how open I have become to understanding, appreciating, and embracing such diverse ways of thinking about songwriting. I have been moved by the many stories shared of songwriting's use in numerous contexts, from seemingly incompatible orientations and with diverse clinical (and non-clinical) populations. I hope that this book will also open you to new ways of thinking, understanding, and approaching songwriting practice.

Notes

1 Introduction, Research Focus, and Approach

1 Bruscia subsequently revised this term to 'Ecological-oriented' (Bruscia, 2014).

2 Songwriting: A Coming of Age

1 Given that this book is designed to facilitate songwriting with a range of different people – patients, community participants, students, residents, inmates, families, clients – and within various contexts and therapy orientations, I have chosen to adopt the word 'songwriter' to denote the person or group of people who actively construct the song. For sake of clarity and consistency, I have also chosen to generally refer to songwriters as males and music therapy clinicians as females, except when referring to specific clinical case studies.

2 It is important to highlight here that in some orientations, verbal processing is not a key component to the songwriting process (see the subsection 'Music-centered songwriting' in Chapter 13).

3 Environmental Factors

1 Also referred to as ward atmosphere, ward milieu, and ward culture.

5 Individual Factors

1 A tendency to speak rapidly and frenziedly.
2 It is important to note that from a music-centered perspective songs can contain these elements and intrinsically create meaning from the chaos. Songwriting provides intrinsic benefits for those who have a stream of conscious by containing those thoughts and making meaning from them within the metaphoric language.
3 Reality-based creativity involves *novel but real-world* possibilities, such as a novel move in a game of chess or a novel sequence of notes in a musical composition. Imaginative creativity describes creativity that is purely imaginative, such as telling a story of an event that was impossible or painting a picture of an object that could never exist (Craig & Baron-Cohen, 1999).
4 The reader is encouraged to refer to Baker and Krout's (2009) publication to review the lyrics and accompanying chords of the two songs.
5 'Readiness for change' is a term that refers to a person's state of being emotionally ready to explore and commit to change.

9 Songwriting Methods That Emphasize Lyric Creation

1 It is important to point out that many of the strengths and limitations of the methods discussed in Chapters 9–11 – which originated from interviewees' perspectives and the literature – are not contextualized in terms of orientation. While this is a limitation of these chapters, as perspectives will undoubtedly differ depending upon the background of the interviewee expressing the views, I felt it was important to try to separate out methods from models of songwriting. Models are addressed in Chapters 12–14.

2 For clarity, the pronoun 'she' has been used to indicate the therapist and 'he' to denote that the material is referring to the songwriter (client).

3 The group composition differs from session to session because the groups are open to anyone who chooses to attend.

10 Songwriting Methods That Emphasize Lyric and Music Creation

1 Note that this approach isn't synchronous in the true sense of the word, because the music is not created at the same time as the rap lyrics. However, the rap lyrics are created in-the-moment, and potentially in a single 'take', rather than using time to think through the lyrics, edit, rewrite, rearrange, and so on before testing them out with music (as is the case in the asynchronous approach).

11 Songwriting Methods That Emphasize Music Creation

1 Halo traction is the term used for the process of immobilizing the upper body and cervical spine with a traction device. The device consists of a metal ring around the head, held in place with pins screwed into the skull. A supporting frame is attached to the ring and to a body jacket or vest to provide immobilization.

12 Outcome-Oriented Models of Songwriting

1 For a more detailed description of the theories and approaches, please refer to Baker and Roth (2004).

13 Experience-Oriented Models of Songwriting

1 Note that the word 'client' is used here in line with the psychodynamic literature and to differentiate between other psychodynamic methods and songwriting.

2 It should be noted that current psychodynamic approaches center around non-interpretative, non-verbal interaction between the client and therapist, and the experience as a whole. There is less emphasis on making the unconscious conscious.

3 At the time the authors undertook the analysis for this study, Seligman's PERMA theory on human flourishing (Seligman, 2011) had not yet been published, and therefore they applied their research to Seligman's theory that was current at the time.

4 It is important to acknowledge the work of Randi Rolvsjord (2010), who developed a theory to support her Resource Oriented Music Therapy (ROMT) approach. Her approach incorporates strengths-based theories relevant to songwriting (Rolvsjord, 2005). In my personal communication with Rolvsjord, she concluded that ROMT belongs more squarely in the next chapter – Context-Oriented Models of Songwriting. Songwriting within ROMT methods are described in the next chapter.

14   Context-Oriented Models of Songwriting

1 It's important to note that feminist approaches are not only relevant to women – society as a whole is informed by ingrained gender roles that identify women as 'less than'. These impact both women and men.

2 My suggested term.

3 While this text has previously referred to the therapist as female and the songwriter as male for reasons of literary flow, here I have chosen to refer to both songwriter and clinician as female because all the cases of feminist music therapy that I have encountered in the body of literature and from interviews were with women. This is not to suggest, however, that feminist issues of power or oppression cannot be addressed with male songwriters, but rather that examples have not yet been documented.

4 My term.

5 However, for some songwriters, this level of transformation may never be achieved.

6 Tony Attwood is a world leader in the field of Asperger's syndrome.

7 Several definitions of empowerment exist, but are beyond the needs of this book. Readers are encouraged to refer to Rolvsjord's (2004, 2010) article on empowerment in music therapy for in-depth discussions.

8 Their program also drew on other music therapy methods.

9 Note that songwriting was only a small component of Tuastad's work.

References

Aasgaard, T. (2002). *Song creations by children with cancer: Process and meaning.* Doctoral Dissertation. Aalborg, Denmark: Aalborg University.

Aasgaard, T. (2005). Assisting children with malignant blood disease to create and perform their own songs. In F. A. Baker & T. Wigram (Eds.), *Songwriting: Methods, techniques and clinical applications for music therapy clinicians, educators and students* (pp. 154–179). London: Jessica Kingsley Publishers.

Abad, V. (2003). A time of turmoil: Music therapy interventions for adolescents in a paediatric oncology ward. *Australian Journal of Music Therapy, 20,* 20–37.

Abrams, B. (2014). Humanistic approaches. In B. Wheeler (Eds.), *Music therapy handbook* (pp. 148–160). New York: Guilford Press.

Adams, K. (2008). Aspects of the music/text relationship in rap. *Music Theory Online, 14*(2). Retrieved from http://mto.societymusictheory.org/issues/mto. 08.14.2/mto.08.14.2.adams.html. Accessed 17 October 2014.

Adrienne, J. K. (2006). A feminist sociology of professional issues in music therapy. In S. Hadley (Ed.), *Feminist perspectives in music therapy* (pp. 41–62). Gilsum, NH: Barcelona Publishers.

Aigen, K. (1991). Creative fantasy, music and lyric improvisation with a gifted acting out boy. In K. Bruscia (Ed.), *Case studies in music therapy* (pp. 109–126). Gilsum, NH: Barcelona Publisher.

Aigen, K. (2002). *Playing in the band: A qualitative study of popular music styles as clinical improvisation.* New York: Nordoff-Robbins Center for Music Therapy, Steinhardt School of Education New York University.

Aigen, K. (2005a). *Music-centered music therapy.* Gilsum, NH: Barcelona.

Aigen, K. (2005b). *Playin' in the band: A qualitative study of popular music styles as clinical improvisation.* Gilsum, NH: Barcelona.

Aigen, K. (2008). The religious dimensions of popular music and their implications for music therapy. *The British Journal of Music Therapy, 22*(1), 24–34.

Amir, D. (2006). Awakening the "wild woman": Feminist music therapy with Israeli women who suffered trauma in their lives. In S. Hadley (Ed.), *Feminist perspectives in music therapy* (pp. 267–290). Gilsum, NH: Barcelona.

Ansdell, G. (2002). Community music therapy and the winds of change: A discussion paper. In C. B. Kenny & B. Stige (Eds.), *Contemporary voices of music therapy: Communication, culture, and community* (pp. 109–142). Oslo: Unipub forlag.

Ansdell, G. (2004). Rethinking music and community: Theoretical perspectives in support of community music therapy. In M. Pavlicevic & G. Ansdell (Eds.), *Community music therapy* (pp. 65–90). London: Jessica Kingsley Publishers.

Ansdell, G. (2010). Belonging through musicking. In B. Stige, G. Ansdell, C. Elefant, & M. Pavlicevic (Eds.), *Where music helps: Community music therapy in action and reflection* (pp. 41–59). Aldershot: Ashgate.

Antonovsky, A. (1987). *Unraveling the mystery of health: How people manage stress and stay well.* San Francisco: Jossey-Bass Publishers.

Asakawa, K. (2010). Flow experience, culture, and well-being: How do autotelic Japanese college students feel, behave, and think in their daily lives? *Journal of Happiness Studies, 11*(2), 205–223. doi:10.1007/s10902-008-9132-3

Austin, D. (2008). *The theory and practice of vocal psychotherapy: Songs of the self.* London: Jessica Kingsley Publishers.

Baird, A., & Samson, S. (2014). Music evoked autobiographical memory after severe acquired brain injury: Preliminary findings from a case series. *Neuropsychological Rehabilitation, 24*(1), 125–144.

Baker, F. A. (2005). Working with impairments in pragmatics through song writing with traumatically brain injured patients. In F. A. Baker & T. Wigram (Eds.), *Songwriting: Methods, techniques and clinical applications for music therapy clinicians, educators and students* (pp. 134–153). London: Jessica Kingsley Publishers.

Baker, F. A. (2013a). Music therapists' perceptions of the group factors impacting on the therapeutic songwriting process, *Music Therapy Perspectives, 31*(2), 137–143.

Baker, F. A. (2013b). The environmental conditions that support or constrain the therapeutic songwriting process. *Arts in Psychotherapy, 40*(1), 230–238. doi. org/10.1016/j.aip.2013.02.001

Baker, F. A. (2013c). The ongoing life of participant-composed songs within and beyond the clinical setting. *Musicae Scientiae, 17*(1), 40–56. doi:10.1177/1029864912471674

Baker, F. A. (2013d). Front and center stage: Participants performing songs created during music therapy. *Arts in Psychotherapy, 40*(1), 20–28.

Baker, F. A. (2013e). What about the music? Music therapists' perspectives of the role of music in the therapeutic songwriting process. *Psychology of Music.* doi:10.1177/0305735613498919

Baker, F. A. (2013f). An investigation of the sociocultural factors impacting on the therapeutic songwriting process. *Nordic Journal of Music Therapy, 23*(2), 123–151. doi:10.1080/08098131.2013.783094

Baker, F. A., & Jones, C. (2005). Holding a steady beat: Stabilising the behaviours of newly arrived young refugee students. *British Journal of Music Therapy, 19*(2), 67–74.

Baker, F. A., & Ballantyne, J. (2013). "You've got to accentuate the positive": Group songwriting to promote a life of enjoyment, engagement and meaning in aging Australians. *Nordic Journal of Music Therapy, 22*(1), 7–24. doi:10.1080/08098131.2012.678372

Baker, F. A., Dingle, G., & Gleadhill, L. (2012). "Must be the ganja" (Eminem 2009): Rap music in drug and alcohol rehabilitation. In S. Hadley & G. Yancey (Eds.), *Therapeutic uses of rap and hip-hop* (pp. 319–334). New York: Brunner-Routledge.

Baker, F. A., Gleadhill, L., & Dingle, G. A. (2007). Music therapy and emotional exploration: Exposing substance abuse clients to the experiences of non-drug induced emotions. *Arts in Psychotherapy, 34*, 321–330.

Baker, F. A., & Jones, C. (2006). The effect of music therapy services on classroom behaviours of newly arrived refugee students in Australia – A pilot study. *Emotional and Behavioural Difficulties, 11*(4), 249–260. doi:10.1080/13632750601022170

Baker, F. A., Kennelly, J., & Tamplin, J. (2005a). Songwriting to explore identity change and sense of self-concept following traumatic brain injury. In F. A. Baker & T. Wigram (Eds.), *Songwriting: Methods, techniques and clinical applications for music therapy clinicians, educators and students* (pp. 116–133). London: Jessica Kingsley Publishers.

Baker, F. A., Kennelly, J., & Tamplin, J. (2005b). Themes in songs written by patients with traumatic brain injury: Differences across the lifespan. *Australian Journal of Music Therapy, 16*, 25–42.

Baker, F. A., Kennelly, J., & Tamplin, J. (2005c). Themes within songs written by people with traumatic brain injury: Gender differences. *Journal of Music Therapy, 42*(2), 111–122.

Baker, F. A., Kennelly, J., & Tamplin, J. (2005d). Adjustment to TBI through song writing: Reviewing the past and looking to the future. *Brain Impairment, 6*(3), 205–211.

Baker, F. A., & Krout, R. (2009). Songwriting via Skype: An on-line music therapy intervention to enhance social skills in an adolescent diagnosed with Aspergers. *British Journal of Music Therapy, 23*(2), 3–14.

Baker, F. A., & MacDonald, R. A. R. (2013a). Flow, identity, achievement, satisfaction and ownership during therapeutic songwriting experiences with university students and retirees. *Musicae Scientiae, 17*(2), 129–144.

Baker, F. A., & MacDonald, R. A. R. (2013b). Students' and retirees' experiences of creating personally meaningful songs within a therapeutic context. *Arts & Health, 35*(1), 67–82. doi.org/10.1080/17533015.2013.808254

Baker, F. A., & MacDonald, R. A. R. (in press). Shaping identities through therapeutic songwriting. In R. A. R. MacDonald, D. Miell, & D. Hargreaves (Eds.), *The Oxford handbook of musical identities*. Oxford: Oxford University Press.

Baker, F. A., & Roth, E. (2004). Neuroplasticity and recovery: Training models and compensatory strategies in music therapy. *Nordic Journal of Music Therapy, 13*(1), 20–32.

Baker, F. A., Silverman, M. J., & MacDonald, R. A. R. (submitted for publication). Reliability and validity of the Meaningfulness of Songwriting Scale (MSS) with adults on acute psychiatric and detoxification units. *Journal of Music Therapy*.

Baker, F. A., & Tamplin, J. (2006). *Music therapy in neurorehabilitation: A clinician's manual*. London: Jessica Kingsley Publishers.

Baker, F. A., & Wigram, T. (Eds.). (2005). *Songwriting: Methods, techniques and clinical applications for music therapy clinicians, educators and students*. London: Jessica Kingsley Publishers.

Baker, F. A., Wigram, T., Stott, D., & McFerran, K. (2008). Therapeutic songwriting in music therapy: Part 1. Who are the therapists, who are the clients, and why is songwriting used? *Nordic Journal of Music Therapy, 17*(2), 105–123.

Baker, F. A., Wigram, T., Stott, D., & McFerran, K. (2009). Therapeutic objectives underpinning songwriting with different clinical populations: Comparing the literature with practice. *Nordic Journal of Music Therapy, 18*(1), 32–56.

Ballou, M., Hill, M., & West, C. (2007). *Feminist therapy: Theory and practice*. New York: Springer.

Barba, H. N. (2005). *Songwriting and self discovery: A heuristic study grounded in the arts and supported by the theories of Carl Jung and James Hillman*. Doctoral Dissertation. Cincinnati, OH: Union Institute and University.

Baron-Cohen, S., Ring, H. A., Bullimore, E. T., Wheelwright, S., Ashwin, C., & Williams, C. (2000). The amygdala theory of autism. *Neuroscience and Biobehavioral Review, 24*, 3, 355–384.

Bäuml, J., Fröböse, T., Kraemer, S., Rentrop, M., & Pitschel-Walz, G. (2006). Psychoeducation: A basic psychotherapeutic intervention for patients with schizophrenia and their families. *Schizophrenia Bulletin, 32*(S1), S1–S9. doi:10.1093/schbul/sbl017

Beck, A. T. (1976). *Cognitive therapies and emotional disorders*. New York: New American Library.

Bentham, J. (1978). *The principles of morals and legislation*. Buffalo: Prometheus.

Beutler, L. E., Malik, M., Alimohamed, S., Harwood, T. M., Telebi, N., & Wong, E. (2004). Therapist variables. In N. J. Lambert (Ed.), *Bergin and Garfield's handbook of psychotherapy and behavior change* (pp. 227–306). New York: John Wiley & Sons.

Bogner, D., Brewin, C., & Herlihy, J. (2010). Refugees' experiences of home office interviews: A qualitative study on the disclosure of sensitive personal information. *Journal of Ethnic and Migration Studies, 36*(3), 519–535.

Bolger, L. (2014). Understanding and articulating the process and meaning of collaboration in participatory music projects with marginalized young people and their supporting communities. Unpublished Doctoral Dissertation. Melbourne: The University of Melbourne.

Bonde, L. O. (2007). Music as metaphor and analogy. *Nordic Journal of Music Therapy, 16*(1), 60–81.

Borling, J. (2011). Music therapy and addition: Addressing essential components in the recovery process. In A. Meadows (Ed.), *Developments in music therapy practice: Case study perspectives* (pp. 334–349). Gilsum, NH: Barcelona Publishers.

Bradt, J. (1997). Ethical issues in multicultural counselling: Implications for the field of music therapy. *Arts in Psychotherapy, 24*(2), 137–143.

Brodsky, W. (1989). Music therapy as an intervention for children with cancer in isolation rooms. *Music Therapy, 8*(1), 17–34.

Bronfenbrenner, U. (1979). *The ecology of human development: Experiments by nature and design*. Cambridge, MA: Harvard University Press.

Bruscia, K. E. (1987). *Improvisational models of music therapy*. Springfield, IL: C.C. Thomas.

Bruscia, K. E. (1998). *Defining music therapy* (2nd ed.). Gilsum, NH: Barcelona Publishers.

Bruscia, K. E. (2011). *Ways of thinking in music therapy*. Sears distinguished lecture series. American Music Therapy Association's National Conference, 18 November 2011.

Bruscia, K. E. (2014). *Defining music therapy* (3rd ed.). Gilsum, NH: Barcelona Publishers.

Burns, D. S., Robb, S. L., & Haase, J. E. (2009). Exploring the feasibility of a therapeutic music video intervention in adolescents and young adults during stem-cell transplantation. *Cancer Nursing, 32*(5), E8–E16.

Burns, G. W. (2001). *100 healing stories using metaphors in therapy*. New York: John Wiley & Sons.

Campbell, M., Fitzpatrick, R., Haines, A., Kinmonth, A. L., Sandercock, P., Speigelhalter, D., & Tyrer, P. (2000). Framework for design and evaluation of complex interventions to improve health. *British Medical Journal, 321*, 694–696.

Carr, A. (2013). *Positive psychology: The science of happiness and human strengths*. Hobken, NJ: Taylor & Francis.

Castonguay, L. G., Constantino, M. J., & Holtforth, M. G. (2006). The working alliance: Where are we and where should we go? *Psychotherapy, 43*(3), 271–279.

Cicerone, K., Levin, H., Malec, J., Stuss, D., & Whyte, J. (2006). Cognitive rehabilitation interventions for executive function: Moving from bench to bedside in patients with traumatic brain injury. *Journal of Cognitive Neuroscience, 18*(7), 1212–1222.

Clark, L. F. (1993). Stress and the cognitive-conversational benefits of social interaction. *Journal of Social and Clinical Psychology, 12*(1), 25–55.

Clements-Cortes, A. (2009). *Episodes of relationship completion through song: Case studies of music therapy research in palliative care.* Saarbrucken: VDM Verlag.

Clifton, D. O., & Nelson, P. (1992). *Soar with your strengths.* New York: Dell.

Colley, A. (2008). Young people's musical taste: Relationship with gender and gender-related traits. *Journal of Applied Social Psychology, 38*(8), 2039–2055.

Cook, K. F., Molton, I. R., & Jensen, M. P. (2011). Fatigue and aging with a disability. *Archives of Physical Medicine & Rehabilitation, 92*(7), 1126–1133.

Corbin, J., & Strauss, A. (2008). *Basics of qualitative research* (3rd ed.). Los Angeles/London/New Delhi/Singapore: Sage.

Cordobés, T. K. (1997). Group songwriting as a method for developing group cohesion for HIV-seropositive adult patients with depression. *Journal of Music Therapy, 34*(1), 46–67.

Corey, G. (2013). *Theory and practice of counseling and psychotherapy.* Belmont, CA: Brooks/Cole.

Craig, J., & Baron-Cohen, S. (1999). Creativity and imagination in Autism and Aspergers Syndrome. *Journal of Autism & Developmental Disorders, 29*(4), 319–326.

Csikszentmihalyi, M. (1990). *Flow: The psychology of optimal experience.* New York: Harper & Row.

Csikszentmihalyi, M. (1997). *Creativity: Flow and the psychology of discovery and invention.* New York: HarperCollins Publishers.

Csikszentmihalyi, M. (2000). Flow. In A. E. Kazdin (Ed.), *Encyclopedia of psychology* (Vol. 3, pp. 381–382). New York: Oxford University Press.

Curtis, S. L. (1997). *Singing subversion, singing soul: Women's voices in feminist music therapy.* Doctoral Dissertation. Canada: Concordia University. Retrieved from http://search.proquest.com/docview/304389436?accountid=14723, ProQuest Dissertations & Theses (PQDT) database.

Curtis, S. L. (2006). Feminist music therapy: Transforming theory, transforming lives. In S. Hadley (Ed.), *Feminist perspectives in music therapy* (pp. 227–244). Gilsum, NH: Barcelona.

D'Zurilla, T. J., & Nezu, A. M. (2007). *Problem-solving therapy: A positive approach to clinical intervention* (3rd ed.). New York: Springer.

Dalton, J. H., Elias, M. J., & Wandersman, A. (2001). *Community psychology: Linking individuals and communities.* London: Wadsworth.

Dalton, T. A. (2012). *My life is changing* (CD). Lake Worth, FL: MT Space Publishing. Retrieved from CD Baby website: http://www.cdbaby.com/cd/tomdalton17

Dalton, T. A., & Krout, R. E. (2005). Development of the Grief Process Scale through music therapy songwriting with bereaved adolescents. *The Arts in Psychotherapy, 32*(2), 131–143.

Dalton, T. A., & Krout, R. E. (2006). The grief song-writing process with bereaved adolescents: An integrated grief model and music therapy protocol. *Music Therapy Perspectives, 24*(2), 94–107.

Dalton, T. A., & Krout, R. E. (2014). Integrative songwriting. In B. E. Thompson & R. A. Neimeyer (Eds.), *Grief and the expressive arts: Practices for creating meaning* (pp. 222–225). New York: Brunner-Routledge.

Day, T. (2005). Giving a voice to childhood trauma through therapeutic songwriting. In F. A. Baker & T. Wigram (Eds.), *Songwriting: Methods, techniques and clinical applications for music therapy clinicians, educators and students* (pp. 86–100). London: Jessica Kingsley Publishers.

Day, T., Baker, F. A., & Darlington, Y. (2009a). Participants' experiences of the song writing process and the on-going meaning of their song creations following completion of a music therapy program. *Nordic Journal of Music Therapy, 18*(2), 133–149.

Day, T., Baker, F. A., & Darlington, Y. (2009b). Beyond the therapy room: Women's experiences of "going public" with song creations. *British Journal of Music Therapy, 23*(1), 19–26.

De Backer, J., & Van Camp, J. (2003). The case of Marianne: Repetition and musical form in psychosis. In S. Hadley (Ed.), *Psychodynamic music therapy: Case studies* (pp. 273–297). Gilsum, NH: Barcelona Publishers.

DeNora, T. (1999). Music as a technology of the self. *Poetics, 27*, 31–56.

DeNora, T. (2000). Music in everyday life. Cambridge: Cambridge University Press.

DeNora, T. (2003). *After Adorno. Rethinking music sociology.* Cambridge: Cambridge University Press.

DeNora, T. (2011). *Music-In-Action: Selected essays in sonic ecology.* Surrey: Ashgate.

Derrington, P. (2005). Teenagers and songwriting: Supporting students in a mainstream secondary school. In F. A. Baker & T. Wigram (Eds.), *Songwriting: Methods, techniques and clinical applications for music therapy clinicians, educators and students* (pp. 68–81). London: Jessica Kingsley Publishers.

Derrington, P. (2011). Working with secondary-aged students who have complex emotional and behavioural difficulties. In A. Oldfield, J. Tomlinson, P. Derrington, & J. Strange (Eds.), *Music therapy in schools* (pp. 195–211). London: Jessica Kingsley Publishers.

Diamond, G. M., Rochman, D., & Amir, O. (2010). Arousing primary vulnerable emotions in the context of unresolved anger: "Speaking about" versus "speaking to". *Journal of Counseling Psychology, 57*(4), 402–410. doi:10.1037/a0021115

Dileo, C., & Magill, L. (2005). Songwriting with oncology and hospice adult patients from a multicultural perspective. In F. A. Baker & T. Wigram (Eds.), *Songwriting: Methods, techniques and clinical applications for music therapy clinicians, educators and students* (pp. 226–245). London: Jessica Kingsley Publishers.

Dilts, S. (2012). *Models of the mind: A framework for biopsychosocial psychiatry.* Hoboken, NJ: Taylor and Francis.

Dingle, G. A., Baker, F. A., & Gleadhill, L. M. (2008). Can music therapy engage patients in group cognitive behaviour therapy for substance abuse treatment? *Drug and Alcohol Review, 27*, 190–196.

Dixon, R. A., & Backman, L. (1999). Principles of compensation in cognitive neurorehabilitation. In D. T. Stuss & G. Winocur (Eds.), *Cognitive neurorehabilitation* (pp. 59–72). New York: Cambridge University Press.

Duxbury, J. A., Bjorkdahl, A., & Johnson, S. (2006). Ward culture and atmosphere. In D. Richter & R. Whittington (Eds.), *Violence in mental health settings: Causes, consequences, and management* (pp. 273–291). New York: Springer Science–Business Media.

Dwyer, O. (2007). Would you like to write your own song. *Voices: A World Forum for Music Therapy, 17*(2). https://normt.uib.no/index.php/voices/article/view/494

Edvardsson, J. D., Sandman, P. O., & Holriz Rasmusen, B. (2005). Sensing an atmosphere of ease: A tentative theory of supportive care settings. *Scandinavian Journal of Caring Sciences, 19*, 344–353. http://dx.doi.org/10.1111/j.1471-6712. 2005.00356.x

Egan, G. (2014). *The skilled helper: A problem-management and opportunity-development approach to helping* (10th ed.). Belmont, CA: Brooks/Cole.

Eklund, M., & Hansson, L. (2001). Perceptions of the real and the ideal ward atmosphere among trainees and staff before and after the introduction of a new work rehabilitation model. *European Psychiatry, 16*, 299–306. http://dx.doi. org/10.1016/S0924.9338.01.00582.x

Elefant, C. (2010). Giving voice: Participatory action research with a marginalized group. In B. Stige, G. Ansdell, C. Elefant, & M. Pavlicevic (Eds.), *Where music helps: Community music therapy in action and reflection* (pp.199–215). Surrey: Ashgate.

El Haj, M., Clément, S., Fasotti, L., & Allain, P. (2013). The effects of music on auto-biographical verbal narration in Alzheimer's disease. *Journal of Neurolinguistics, 26*(6), 691–700.

Elliott, D. J. (1995). *Music matters: A new philosophy of music education.* New York: Oxford University Press.

Ellis, A. (1987). The impossibility of achieving consistently good mental health. *American Psychologist, 42*(4), 364–375.

Environment. (2011). *Oxford English Dictionary* (3rd ed.). Online version March 2012. Retrieved from http://www.oed.com/view/Entry/63089

Erkkilä, J. (2011). Punker, Bassgirl, and Dingo-man: Perspectives on adolescents music therapy. In A. Meadows (Ed.), *Developments in music therapy practice: Case study perspectives* (pp. 198–214). Gilsum, NH: Barcelona Publishers.

Erkkilä, J., Gold, C., Fachner, J., Ala-Ruona, E., Punkanen, M., & Vanhala, M. (2008). The effect of improvisational music therapy on the treatment of depression: Protocol for a randomised controlled trial, *BMC Psychiatry, 8*, 50. doi:10.1186/1471-244X-8-50

Esparza, D. E. (2001). Therapeutic metaphors and clinical hypnosis. *Hypno-gensis*, 1–5. Retrieved from http://www.hypnosis.co.uk. Accessed 5 December 2013.

Evans, M. (2014). Introduction. In M. Evans, C. Hemmings, M. Henry, H. Johnstone, S. Madhok, A. Plomien, & S. Wearing (Eds.), *Sage handbook of feminist theory* (pp. xviii–xxvi). Los Angeles, London, New Delhi, Singapore, Washington: Sage.

Ferguson, R. M. (2006). *The effect of music therapy songwriting on the identification and utilization of short-term coping strategies by caregivers of loved ones with Alzheimer's disease.* Master of Music Dissertation. Tallahassee, FL: Florida State University.

Ficken, T. (1976). The use of songwriting in a psychiatric setting. *Journal of Music Therapy, 13*(4), 163–172.

Fischer, R. G. (1991). Original song drawings in the treatment of a developmentally disabled, autistic young man. In K. Bruscia (Ed.), *Case studies in music therapy* (pp. 359–371). Gilsum, NH: Barcelona Publishers.

Flaherty, A. W. (2005). Frontotemporal and dopaminergic control of idea generation and creative drive. *The Journal of Comparative Neurology, 493*, 147–153. doi:10.1002/cne.20768

Flaherty, A. W. (2011). Brain illness and creativity: Mechanisms and treatment risks. *Maladie Cérébrale et Créativité: Mécanismes et Risques du Traitement, 56*(3), 132–143.

Foucault, M. (1982/1988). Technologies of the self. In L. H. Martin, H. Gutman, & P. H. Hutton (Eds.), *Technologies of the self* (pp. 16–50). London: Tavistock Publications.

Fouche, S., & Torrace, K. (2011). Crossing the divide: Exploring identities within communities fragmented by gang violence. In A. Meadows (Ed.), *Developments in music therapy practice: Case study perspectives* (pp. 215–229). Gilsum, NH: Barcelona Publishers.

Fredrickson, B. L. (2001). The role of positive emotions in positive psychology: The broaden-and-build theory of positive emotions. *American Psychologist, 56*, 218–226.

Freed, B. S. (1987). Songwriting with the chemically dependent. *Music Therapy Perspectives, 4*, 13–18.

Friis, S. (1986). Characteristics of a good ward atmosphere. *Acta Psychiatrica Scandanavica, 74*, 573–581. http://dx.doi.org/10.1111/j.1600-0447.1986.tb06270.x

Frisch, A. (1990). Symbol and structure: Music therapy for the adolescent psychiatric patient. *Music Therapy, 9*(1), 16–34.

Frisch Hara, A. (2012). RAP (Requisite, Ally, Protector) and the desperate contemporary adolescent. In S. Hadley & G. Yancey (Eds.), *Therapeutic uses of rap and hip-hop* (pp. 3–25). New York: Brunner-Routledge.

Frosh, S. (2012). *A brief introduction to psychoanalytic theory*. New York: Palgrave Macmillan.

Gabbard, G. O. (2010). *Long-term psychodynamic psychotherapy* (2nd ed.). Arlington, VA: American Psychiatric Publishing.

Gaucher, D., Wood, J. V., Stinson, D. A., Forest, A. L., Holmes, J. G., & Logel, C. (2012). Perceived regard explains self-esteem differences in expressivity. *Personality and Social Psychology Bulletin, 38*(9), 1144–1156. doi:10.1177/0146167212445790

Glassman, L. R. (1991). Music therapy and bibliotherapy in the rehabilitation of traumatic brain injury: A case study. *The Arts in Psychotherapy, 18*(2), 149–156.

Gleadhill, L. M. (2014). *The stories we haven't told: The lived experience of music used in therapy for bereaved parents*. Doctoral Dissertation. Brisbane, Australia: The University of Queensland.

Goldstein, M. J., Bednar, R. L., & Yandell, B. (1978). Personal risk associated with self-disclosure, interpersonal feedback, and group confrontation in group psychotherapy. *Small Group Behavior, 9*(4), 579–587.

Goldstein, S. L. (1990). A songwriting assessment for hopelessness in depressed adolescents: A review of the literature and a pilot study. *Arts in Psychotherapy, 17*(2), 117–124.

Grant, J. G., & Cadell, S. (2009). Power, pathological worldviews, and the strengths perspective in social work. *Families in Society, 90*(4), 425–430.

Greenberg, L. S., & Malcolm, W. (2002). Resolving unfinished business: Relating process to outcome. *Journal of Consulting and Clinical Psychology, 70*(2), 406–416. doi:10.1037/0022-006X.70.2.406

Greenwald, B. D., & Ripley, D. L. (2009). Fatigue. In A. Cristian (Ed.), *Medical management of adults with neurologic disabilities* (pp. 129–137). New York: Demos Medical Publishing, LLC.

Greitemeyer, T. (2009). Effects of songs with prosocial lyrics on prosocial thoughts, affect, and behavior. *Journal of Experimental Social Psychology, 45,* 186–190.

Griffin, J. (1986). *Well-being: Its meaning, measurement, and moral importance.* Oxford: Clarendon Press.

Grocke, D., Bloch, S., Castle, D., Thompson, G., Newton, R., Stewart, S., & Gold, C. (2014). Group music therapy for severe mental illness: A randomized embedded-experimental mixed methods study. *Acta Psychiatrica Scandinavica,* 130(2), 144–153. doi:10.1111/acps.12224/abstract

Grocke, D., Bloch, S., & Castle, D. (2009). The effect of group music therapy on quality of life for participants living with a severe and enduring mental illness. *Journal of Music Therapy, 46*(2), 90–104.

Grocke, D., & Castle, D. (2012). Music, music therapy and schizophrenia. In D. Hargreaves, D. Miell, & R. MacDonald (Eds.), *Musical imaginations* (pp. 399–413). London: Oxford University Press.

Grolnick, S. (1990). *The work & play of Winnicott.* New Jersey: Aronson.

Grotstein, J. S. (1992). The enigmatic relationship of creativity to mental health and psychopathology. *American Journal of Psychotherapy, 46*(3), 405–421.

Gurung, R. A. R. (2010). Cultural influences on health. In K. D. Keith (Ed.), *Cross-cultural psychology: Contemporary themes and perspectives* (pp. 259–273). Hoboken, NJ: Wiley-Blackwell.

Hadley, S. (1996). A rationale for the use of songs with children undergoing bone marrow transplantation. *Australian Journal of Music Therapy, 7,* 16–27.

Hadley, S. (Ed.). (2006). *Feminist perspectives in music therapy.* Gilsum, NH: Barcelona.

Hadley, S. (2013). Feminist music therapy. In K. Kirkword (Ed.), *Dictionary of Music Therapy* (p. 47). New York: Routledge.

Hakomäki, H. (2013). *Storycomposing as a path to a child's inner world: A collaborative music therapy experiment with a child co-researcher.* Doctoral Dissertation. Jyväskylä, Finland: University of Jyväskylä.

Haldane, M., & Frangou, S. (2004). New insights help define the pathophysiology of bipolar affective disorder: Neuroimaging and neuropathology findings. *Progress in Neuropsychopharmacology and Biological Psychiatry, 28,* 943–960.

Hammel-Gormley, A. (1995). *Singing the songs: A qualitative study of music therapy with individuals having psychiatric illness as well as histories of childhood sexual abuse.* Doctoral Dissertation. New York: New York University.

Happe, S. (2003). Excessive daytime sleepiness and sleep disturbances in patients with neurological diseases: Epidemiology and management. *Drugs, 63,* 2725–2737.

Harris, R. (2006). Embracing your demons: An overview of Acceptance and Commitment Therapy, *Psychotherapy in Australia, 12*(4), 2–8.

Hatcher, J. (2004). *I am your son: Therapeutic songwriting with a man living with complex trauma.* Masters Dissertation. Ottowa, Canada: Simon Fraser University.

Hays, P. A. (2008). *Addressing cultural complexities in practice: Assessment, diagnosis, and therapy* (2nd ed.). Washington, DC: American Psychological Association.

Heath, B., & Lings, J. (2012). Creative songwriting in therapy at the end of life and in bereavement. *Mortality, 17*(2), 106–118. doi:10.1080/13576275.2012.673381

Henderson, H. (1991). Improvised song stories in the treatment of a thirteen year old girl from the Xhosa tribe in South Africa. In K. Bruscia (Ed.), *Case studies in music therapy* (pp. 207–217). Gilsum, NH: Barcelona Publishers.

Hilliard, R., & Justice, J. (2011). Songs of faith in end of life care. In A. Meadows (Ed.), *Developments in music therapy practice: Case study perspectives* (pp. 582–594). Gilsum, NH: Barcelona Publishers.

Hong, I. S., & Choi, M. J. (2011). Songwriting oriented activities improve the cognitive functions of the aged with dementia. *The Arts in Psychotherapy, 38*(4), 221–228. doi:10.1016/j.aip.2011.07.002

Hoyt, T., Pasupathi, M., Smith, B. W., Yeater, E. A., Kay, V. S., & Tooley, E. (2010). Disclosure of emotional events in groups at risk for posttraumatic stress disorder. *International Journal of Stress Management, 17*(1), 78–95. doi:10.1037/a0017453

Hudson-Smith, G. (1991). The song-writing process: A woman's struggle against depression and suicide. In K. Brusica (Ed.), *Case studies in music therapy* (pp. 479–496). Gilsum, NH: Barcelona Publisher.

Huppert, J. D. (2009). The building blocks of treatment in cognitive-behavioral therapy. *Israel Journal of Psychiatry Related Sciences, 46*(4), 245–250.

Hurtado, A. (2010). Multiple lenses: Multicultural feminist theory. In H. Landrine & N. F. Russo (Eds.), *Handbook of diversity in feminist psychology* (pp. 29–54). New York: Springer.

Iliya, Y. A. (2015). Music therapy as grief therapy for adults with mental illness and complicated grief. *Death Studies, 39*(3), 173–184. doi:10.1080/07481187.2014.946623.

Janata, P., Tomic, S. T., & Rakowski, S. K. (2007). Characterization of music-evoked autobiographical memories. *Memory, 15*, 845–860.

John, D. (1992). Towards music psychotherapy. *British Journal of Music Therapy, 6*(1), 10–12.

Johnsdøttir, V. (2011). *Music caring within the framework of early intervention: The lived experience of a group of mothers of young children with special needs, participating in a music therapy group.* Doctoral Dissertation. Aalborg, Denmark: Aalborg University.

Jones, C., Baker, F. A., & Day, T. (2004). From healing rituals to music therapy: Bridging the cultural divide between therapist and young Sudanese refugees. *Arts in Psychotherapy, 31*, 89–100.

Jones, J. D. (2005). A comparison of songwriting and lyric analysis techniques to evoke emotional change in a single session with people who are chemically dependent. *Journal of Music Therapy, 42*(2), 94–110.

Jørgensen, C. R. (2004). Active ingredients in individual psychotherapy: Searching for common factors. *Psychoanalytic Psychology, 21*(4), 516–540. doi:10.1037/0736-9735.21.4.516

Jörgensen, K. N., Römma, V., & Rundmo, T. (2009). Associations between ward atmosphere, patient satisfaction and outcome. *Journal of Psychiatric and Mental Health Nursing, 16*, 113–120. http://dx.doi.org/10.1111/j.1365-2850.2008.01333.x

Judde, S., & Rickard, N. (2010). The effect of post-learning presentation of music on long-term word-list retention. *Neurobiology of Learning and Memory, 94*(1), 13–21.

Jung, C. G. (1966). On the relation of analytical psychology to poetry. In H. Read, M. Fordham, G. Adler, & W. McGuire (Eds.), *The collected works of C. G. Jung* (Vol. 15, pp. 65–83). London: Routledge & Kegan Paul.

Jung, C. G. (1971). Psychological types. In H. Read, M. Fordham, G. Adler, & W. McGuire (Eds.), *The collected works of C. G. Jung* (Vol. 6, pp. 3–7). London: Routledge & Kegan Paul.

Kearns, M. C., Edwards, K. M., Calhoun, K. S., & Gidycz, C. A. (2010). Disclosure of sexual victimization: The effects of Pennebaker's emotional disclosure paradigm on physical and psychological distress. *Journal of Trauma & Dissociation, 11*(2), 193–209. doi:10.1080/15299730903502979

Kennelly, J. (1999). Don't give us: Providing music therapy to an adolescent boy in the bone marrow transplant unit. In R. R. Pratt & D. Erdonmez Grocke (Eds.), *Music Medicine 3*, (pp. 228–235). Melbourne: University of Melbourne.

Klauer, K. C., & Musch, J. (2003). Affective priming: Findings and theories. In K. C. Klauer & J. Musch (Eds.), *The psychology of evaluation: Affective processes in cognition and emotion* (pp. 7–50). Mahwah, NJ: Erlbaum.

Klein, C. M., & Silverman, M. J. (2012). With love from me to me: Using songwriting to teach coping skills to caregivers of those with Alzheimer's and other dementias. *Journal of Creativity in Mental Health 7*(2), 153–164.

Koelsch, S. (2013). Striking the chord in the brain: Neurophysiological correlates of music-evoked positive emotions. In T. Cochrane, B. Fantini, & K. R. Scherer (Eds.), *The emotional power of music: Multidisciplinary perspectives on musical arousal, expression, and social control* (pp. 547–605). Oxford: Oxford University Press.

Koenig, H. G. (1998). Religious attitudes and practices of hospitalized medically ill older adults. *International Journal of Geriatric Psychiatry, 13*, 213–224.

Koenig, H. G., McCullough, M. E., & Larson, D. B. (2001). *Handbook of religion and health*. Oxford and New York: Oxford University Press.

Kolb, B., & Gibb, R. (1999). Neuroplasticity and recovery of function after brain injury. In D. T. Stuss & G. Winocur (Eds.), *Cognitive neurorehabilitation* (pp. 9–25). New York: Cambridge University Press.

Kowski, J. (2003). Growing up alone: Analytical music therapy of children with parents treated within a drug and substance abuse program. In S. Hadley (Ed.), *Psychodynamic music therapy: Case studies* (pp. 87–103). Gilsum, NH: Barcelona Publishers.

Krippner, S., & Feinstein, D. (2008). A mythological approach to transpersonal psychotherapy. *ReVision, 30*(1/2), 18–31.

Krout, R. E. (2005). The music therapist as singer–songwriter: Applications with bereaved teenagers. In F. A. Baker & T. Wigram (Eds.), *Songwriting: Methods, techniques and clinical applications for music therapy clinicians, educators and students* (pp. 212–229). London: Jessica Kingsley Publishers.

Krout, R. E. (2011). Our path to peace: Songwriting-based brief music therapy with bereaved adolescents. In A. Meadows (Ed.), *Developments in music therapy practice: Case study perspectives* (pp. 230–247). Gilsum, NH: Barcelona Publishers.

Krüger, V., & Stige, B. (2014). Between rights and realities – Music as a structuring resource in child welfare everyday life: A qualitative study. *Nordic Journal of Music Therapy*. First published online 5 March 2014. doi:10.1080/08098131.2014.890242

Krupnick, J. L., Sotsky, S. M., Simmens, S., Moyer, J., Elkin, I., Watkins, J., & Pilkonis, P. A. (1996). The role of the therapeutic alliance in psychotherapy and pharmacotherapy outcome: Findings in the National Institute of Mental Health Treatment of Depression Collaborative Research Program. *Journal of Consulting and Clinical Psychology, 64*(3), 532–539.

Krupp, L. B. (2004). *Fatigue in multiple sclerosis: A guide to diagnosis and management*. New York: Demos Medical Publishing.

Larson, R. (1995). Secrets in the bedroom: Adolescents' private use of media. *Journal of Youth and Adolescence, 24*(5), 535–550.

Laudet, A. B. (2003). Attitudes and beliefs about 12-step groups among addiction treatment clients and clinicians: Toward identifying obstacles to participation. *Substance Use and Misuse, 38*(14), 2017–2047.

Laungani, P. D. (2007). *Understanding cross-cultural psychology.* London: Sage.

Ledger, A. (2001). Song parody for adolescents with cancer. *Australian Journal of Music Therapy, 12,* 21–27.

Ledley, D. R., Marx, B. P., & Heimberg, R. G. (2010). *Making cognitive-behavioral therapy work* (2nd ed.). New York: Guildford Publications.

Lee, C. (2013). Music-centered music therapy. In K. Kirkword (Ed.), *Dictionary of Music Therapy* (p. 89). New York: Routledge.

Lee, J. (2007). Music therapy with a woman who was hurt by a cowboy. *Canadian Journal of Music Therapy, 13*(1), 30–37.

Lee, P. L., Lan, W., Wang, C. L., & Chiu, H. Y. (2008). Helping young children to delay gratification. *Early Childhood Education Journal, 35*(6), 557–564. doi: 10.1007/s10643-008-0240-9

Levitt, H., Korman, Y., & Angus, L. (2000). A metaphor analysis in treatments of depression: Metaphor as a marker of change in counseling. *Psychology Quarterly, 13*(1), 10–23.

Lightstone, A. (2012). Yo, can ya flow! Research findings on hip-hop aesthetics and rap therapy in an urban youth shelter. In S. Hadley & G. Yancy (Eds.), *Therapeutic uses of rap and hip-hop* (pp. 211–251). New York: Brunner-Routledge.

Lindberg, K. A. (1995). Songs of healing: Songwriting with an abused adolescent. *Music Therapy, 13*(1), 93–108.

Lorber, J. (2005). *Gender inequality: Feminist theories and politics* (3rd ed.). Los Angeles: Roxbury.

Lukens, E. P., & McFarlane, W. R. (2004). Psychoeducation as evidence-based practice: Considerations for practice, research, and policy. *Brief Treatment and Crisis Intervention, 4*(3), 205–225.

MacDonald, R. A. R., Miell, D., & Hargreaves, D. J. (Eds.). (2002). *Musical identities.* Oxford: Oxford University Press.

MacDonald, S., & Viega, M. (2012). Hear our voices: A music therapy songwriting program and the message of the Little Saints through the medium of rap. In S. Hadley & G. Yancy (Eds.), *Therapeutic uses of rap and hip-hop* (pp. 153–171). New York: Brunner-Routledge.

Magyar-Moe, J. L. (2012). Principles of positive psychology. In W. T. O'Donoghue & J. E. Fischer (Eds.), *Cognitive behavior therapy: Core principles for practice* (pp. 353–375). Hoboken, NJ: John Wiley & Sons.

Malone, L. A., & Vogtle, L. K. (2010). Pain and fatigue consistency in adults with cerebral palsy. *Disability & Rehabilitation, 32*(5), 385–391.

Marade, A. A., Gibbons, J. A., & Brinthaupt, T. M. (2007). The role of risk-taking in songwriting success. *The Journal of Creative Behavior, 41*(2), 125–149. doi:10.1002/j.2162-6057.2007.tb01285.x

Markus, H. R., & Hamedani, M. G. (2007). Social-cultural psychology: The dynamic interdependence among self systems and social systems. In S. Kitaysm & D. Cohen (Eds.), *Handbook of cultural psychology* (pp. 3–38). New York: Guilford Press.

Marley, B. (1974). No woman no cry. Track from *Natty Dread Album.* New York: Island Records.

Maslow, A. H. (1943). A theory of human motivation. *Psychological Review, 50*(4), 370–396. Retrieved from http://psychclassics.yorku.ca/Maslow/motivation. htm

Maslow, A. H. (1962). *Toward a psychology of being.* New York: Van Nostrand.

Maslow, A. H. (1971). *Farther reaches of human nature.* New York: Viking Press (Esalen Series).

May, R., & Yalom, I. (1995). Existential psychotherapy. In R. J. Corsini & D. Wedding (Eds.), *Current psychotherapies* (5th ed., pp. 1–38). Adelaide, Australia: F. E. Peacock Publishers.

Mayers, K. S. (1995). Songwriting as a way to decrease anxiety and distress in traumatized children. *The Arts in Psychotherapy, 22*(5), 495–498.

McFerran, K. (2011). Moving out of your comfort zone: Group music therapy with adolescents who have misused drugs. In A. Meadows (Ed.), *Developments in music therapy practice: Case study perspectives* (pp. 248–267). Gilsum, NH: Barcelona Publishers.

McFerran, K., Baker, F. A., Patton, G. C., & Sawyer, S. M. (2006). A retrospective lyrical analysis of songs written by adolescents with anorexia nervosa. *European Eating Disorders Review, 14*(6), 397–403.

McFerran, K., & Teggelove, T. (2011). Music therapy with young people in schools: After the Black Saturday Fires. *Voices: A World Forum for Music Therapy, 11*(1). https://normt.uib.no/index.php/voices/article/view/285/442

McNair, L. D. (1996). African American women and behavior therapy: Integrating theory, culture, and clinical practice. *Cognitive and Behavioral Practice, 3,* 337–349.

Menon, V., & Levitin, D. J. (2005). The rewards of music listening: Response and physiological connectivity of the mesolimbic system. *NeuroImage, 28,* 175–184.

Merrill, T. (2006). Power and voice in the institutional setting: A journey toward activating a feminist music therapy approach. In S. Hadley (Ed.), *Feminist perspectives in music therapy* (pp. 187–204). Gilsum, NH: Barcelona.

Meyer, L. B. (1956). *Emotion and meaning in music.* Chicago: University of Chicago Press.

Miller, B. L., Cummings, J., Mishkin, F., Boone, K., Prince, F., Ponton, M., & Cotman, C. (1998). Emergence of artistic talent in frontotemporal dementia. *Neurology, 51,* 978–982.

Mion, L. C. (2009). Establishing a therapeutic hospital environment: The patient perspective. *Geriatric Nursing, 30*(4), 268–271. http://dx.doi.org/10.1016/j. gerinurse.2009.06.004

Nagayama Hall, G. C. (2001). Psychotherapy research with ethnic minorities: Empirical, ethical, and conceptual issues. *Journal of Consulting and Clinical Psychology, 69*(3), 502–510. doi:10.1037//0022-006X.69.3.502

Navas, E. (2009). Remix: The bond of repetition and representation. In S. Sonvilla-Weiss (Ed.), *Mashup culture* (pp. 157–178). New York: SpringerWien.

Neimeyer, R. A. (2000). *Lessons of loss: A guide to coping.* Melbourne, Australia: Centre for Grief Education.

Nezu, A. M., & Maguth Nezu, C. (2012). Problem solving. In W. T. O'Donoghue & J. Fischer (Eds.), *Cognitive behavior therapy: Core principles of practice* (pp. 159–182). Hoboken, NJ: Wiley.

Noy, P. (1966). The psychodynamic meaning of music, Part I. *Journal of Music Therapy, 3,* 126–135.

Nudo, R. J., Barbay, S., & Kleim, J. A. (2000). Role of neuroplasticity in functional recovery after stroke. In H. S. Levin & J. Graffman (Eds.), *Cerebral reorganisation of function after stroke* (pp. 168–200). New York: Oxford University Press.

Nussbaum, M. (1992). Human functioning and social justice: In defense of Aristotelian essentialism. *Political Theory, 20*, 202–246.

O'Brien, E. (2012). "Morphine Mamma": Creating original songs using rap with women with cancer. In S. Hadley & G. Yancy (Eds.), *Therapeutic uses of rap and hip-hop* (pp. 335–350). New York: Brunner-Routledge.

O'Callaghan, C. (2005). Song writing in threatened lives. In C. Dileo & J. V. Loewy (Eds.), *Music therapy at the end of life* (pp. 117–127). Cherry Hill, NJ: Jeffrey Books.

O'Grady, L. (2009). *Therapeutic potentials of creating and performing music with women in prison: A qualitative case study.* Doctoral Dissertation. Melbourne: The University of Melbourne.

O'Grady, L. (2011). The therapeutic potentials of creating and performing music with women in prison: A qualitative case study. *Qualitative Inquiries in Music Therapy* (pp. 123–152). Gilsum, NH: Barcelona Publishers.

O'Grady, L., & McFerran, K. (2006). Birthing feminist community music therapy: The progeny of Community Music Therapy practice and Feminist Music Therapy Theory. In S. Hadley (Ed.), *Feminist perspectives in music therapy* (pp. 63–80). Gilsum, NH: Barcelona Publishers.

O'Grady, L., Rolvsjord, R., & McFerran, K. (2014). Women performing music in prison: An exploration of the resources that come into play, *Nordic Journal of Music Therapy*. First published 28 March 2014. doi:10.1080/08098131.2013.87 7518

Okuda, A. M., Runco, M. A., Berger, D. E. (1991). Creativity and the finding and solving of real-world problems. *Journal of Psychoeducational Assessment, 9*(1), 45–53. doi:10.1177/073428299100900104

Oldfield, A., & Franke, C. (2005). Improvised songs and stories in music therapy diagnostic assessments at a unit for child and family psychiatry: A music therapist's and a psychotherapist's perspective. In F. A. Baker & T. Wigram (Eds.), *Songwriting: Methods, techniques and clinical applications for music therapy clinicians, educators and student* (pp. 25–46). London: Jessica Kingsley Publishers.

Olney, M. F., & Kim, A. (2001). Beyond adjustment: Integration of cognitive disability into identity. *Disability & Society, 16*, 563–583.

O'Neil, D. (2005). How can a strengths approach increase safety in a child protection context? *Children Australia, 30*(4), 28–32.

Oxford Concise Medical Dictionary. (2010). 8th ed. Oxford: Oxford University Press. e-ISBN: 9780191727016

Oxford Dictionary of English. (2010). 3rd ed. Edited by A. Stevenson. Oxford: Oxford University Press.

Pahari, N., Tripathi, S. K., Maity, T., Gupta, B., Bagchi, C., & Nondal, D. K. (2012). Evaluation and analysis of adverse drug reactions of second generation antipsychotics in a psychiatry out-patient department. *International Journal of Pharmacy & Pharmaceutical Sciences, 4*, 158–162.

Pavlicevic, M., & Ansdell, G. (2004) *Community music therapy.* London: Jessica Kingsley Publishers.

Pennebaker, J. W. (1997). Writing about emotional experiences as a therapeutic process. *Psychological Science, 8*(3), 162–166.

Pennebaker, J. W., Mayne, T. J., & Francis, M. E. (1997). Linguistic predictors of adaptive bereavement. *Journal of Personality and Social Psychology, 72*, 863–871.

Perilli, G. G. (1991). Integrated music therapy with a schizophrenic woman. In K. Bruscia (Ed.), *Case studies in music therapy* (pp. 403–416). Gilsum, NH: Barcelona Publishers.

Perren, F., & Fekaris, D. (1978). I will survive. From the album *Love Tracks*. London: Polydor.

Polkinghorne, D. E. (2001). The self and humanistic psychology. In K. J. Schneider, J. F. T. Bugental, & J. F. Pierson (Eds.), *The handbook of humanistic psychology: Leading edges in theory, research, and practice* (pp. 81–100). Thousand Oaks, CA: Sage.

Priestley, M. (1994). *Essays on analytical music therapy*. Phoenixville, PA: Barcelona Publishers.

Prigatano, G. P. (1999). Motivation and awareness in cognitive neurorehabilitation. In D. T. Stuss & G. Winocur (Eds.), *Cognitive neurorehabilitation* (pp. 240–251). New York: Cambridge University Press.

Privette, G. (1983). Peak experience, peak performance, and flow: A comparative analysis of positive human experiences. *Journal of Personality and Social Psychology, 45*(6), 1361–1368.

Privette, G. (2001). Defining moments of self-actualization: Peak performance and peak experience. In K. J. Schneider, J. F. T. Bugental, & J. Fraser Pierson (Eds.), *The handbook of humanistic psychology: Leading edges in theory, research, and practice* (pp. 160–182). Thousand Oaks, CA: Sage.

Prochaska, J. O., Norcross, J. C., & DiClemente, C. C. (1994). *Changing for good: The revolutionary program that explains the six stages of change and teaches you how to free yourself from bad habits*. New York: W. Morrow.

Prochaska, J. O., & Velicer, W. F. (1997). The transtheoretical model of health behavior change. *American Journal of Health Promotion, 12*(1), 38–48.

Prochaska, J. O., Velicer, W. F., Rossi, J. S., Goldstein, M. G., Marcus, B. H., Rakowski, W., Fiore, C., Harlow, L. L., Redding, C. A., Rosenbloom, D., & Rossi, S. R. (1994). Stages of change and decisional balance for 12 problem behaviors. *Health Psychology, 13*, 39–46.

Procter, S. (2002). Empowering and enabling – Music therapy in nonmedical mental health provision. In C. Kenny & B. Stige (Eds.), *Contemporary voices in music therapy* (pp. 95–108). Oslo: Unipub Forlag.

Procter, S. (2004). Playing politics: Community music therapy and the therapeutic redistribution of musical capital for mental health. In M. Pavlicevic & G. Ansdell (Eds.), *Community music therapy* (pp. 214–230). London: Jessica Kingsley Publishers.

Procter, S. (2011). Reparative musicking: Thinking on the usefulness of social capital theory within music therapy, *Nordic Journal of Music Therapy, 20*(3), 242–262. doi:10.1080/08098131.2010.489998

Purdon, C. (2006). Feminist music therapy with abused teen girls. In S. Hadley (Ed.), *Feminist perspectives in music therapy* (pp. 205–226). Gilsum, NH: Barcelona.

Putnam, R. D. (2000). *Bowling alone*. New York: Simon and Schuster.

Putnam, R. D., & Feldstein, L. M. (2003). *Better together: Restoring the American community*. New York, London: Simon & Schuster.

Reitman, A. D. (2011). *Songs in group psychotherapy for chemical dependence*. Gilsum, NH: Barcelona Publishers.

Renblad, K. (2003). *Empowerment. A question about democracy and ethics in everyday life*. Stockholm: Institute of Education Press.

Rickson, D., & Watkins, W. G. (2003). Music therapy to promote prosocial behaviours in aggressive adolescent boys – A pilot study. *Journal of Music Therapy, 40*(4), 283–301.

Robb, H. (2002). Practicing rational emotive behavior therapy and religious clients. *Journal of Rational-Emotive & Cognitive-Behavior Therapy, 20*(3/4), 169–200.

Robb, S. L. (1996). Techniques in song writing: Restoring emotional and physical well being in adolescents who have been traumatically injured. *Music Therapy Perspectives, 14*(1), 30–37.

Robb, S. L., Burns, D. S., Stegenga, K. A., Haut, P. R., Monahan, P. O., Meza, J., & Haase, J. E. (2014, 15 March). Randomized clinical trial of therapeutic music video intervention for resilience outcomes in adolescents/young adults undergoing hematopoietic stem cell transplant. *Cancer,* 909–915. doi.10.1002/cncr.28355.

Robb, S. L., & Ebberts, A. G. (2003). Songwriting and digital video production interventions for pediatric patients undergoing bone marrow transplantation, part I: An analysis of depression and anxiety levels according to phase of treatment. *Journal of Pediatric Oncology Nursing, 20*(1), 2–15.

Roberts, M. (2006). I want to play and sing my story: Home-based songwriting for bereaved children and adolescents. *Australian Journal of Music Therapy, 17*, 18–34.

Roberts, M. (2008). *A content analysis of song lyrics written by bereaved pre-adolescent (7–12 year old) children during individual music therapy*. Master's Dissertation. Melbourne: The University of Melbourne.

Rogers, C. (1959). A theory of therapy, personality and interpersonal relationships as developed in the client-centered framework. In S. Koch (Ed.), *Psychology: A study of a science, 3, formulations of the person and the social context* (pp. 184–256). New York: McGraw-Hill.

Rogers, C. (1961). *On becoming a person*. Boston, MA: Houghton Mifflin.

Rogers, C. R. (1986). A client-centered/person-centered approach to therapy. In I. Kutash & A. Wolf (Eds.), *Psychotherapist's casebook* (pp. 197–208). San Francisco, CA: Jossey-Bass.

Rolvsjord, R. (2001). Sophie learns to play her tears: A case study exploring the dialectics between didactic and psychotherapeutic music therapy practices. *Nordic Journal of Music Therapy, 10*(1), 77–85.

Rolvsjord, R. (2004). Therapy as empowerment: Clinical and political implications of empowerment philosophy in mental health practices of music therapy. *Nordic Journal of Music Therapy, 13*(2), 99–111.

Rolvsjord, R. (2005). Collaborations on songwriting with clients with mental health problems. In F. A. Baker & T. Wigram (Eds.), *Songwriting: Methods, techniques and clinical applications for music therapy clinicians, educators and students* (pp. 101–118). London: Jessica Kingsley Publishers.

Rolvsjord, R. (2010). *Resource-oriented music therapy in mental health care*. Gilsum, NH: Barcelona Publishers.

Rolvsjord, R., & Stige, B. (2015). Concepts of context in music therapy. *Nordic Journal of Music Therapy, 24*(1), 44–66. First published online 12 December 2013. doi:10.1080/08098131.2013.861502

Romer, N., Ravitch, N. K., Tom, K., Merrell, K. W., & Wesley, K. L. (2011). Gender differences in positive social-emotional functioning. *Psychology in the Schools, 48*(10), 958–970. doi:10.1002/pits.20604

Røssberg, J. I., Melle, I., Opjordsmoen, S., & Friis, S. (2006). Patient satisfaction and treatment environment: A 20-year follow-up study from an acute psychiatric ward. *Nordic Journal of Psychiatry, 60,* 176–180. http://dx.doi.org/10.1080/08039480600583894

Ruud, E. (1997). Music and the quality of life. *Nordic Journal of Music Therapy, 6,* 86–97. doi:10.1080/08098139709477902

Ruud, E. (2010). *Music therapy: A perspective from the humanities.* Gilsum, NH: Barcelona.

Sadnovik, N. (2014). The birth of a therapeutic recording studio: Addressing the need of the hip hop generation on an adult inpatient psychiatric unit. In W. Magee (Ed.), *Music technology in therapeutic and health settings* (pp. 247–262). London: Jessica Kingsley Publishers.

Salimpoor, V. N., Benovoy, M., Longo, G., Cooperstock, J. R., & Zatorre, R. J. (2009). The rewarding aspects of music listening are related to degree of emotional arousal. *PLoS ONE, 4*(10), e7487.

Särkämö, T., Tervaniemi, M., Laitinen, S., Forsblom, A., Soinila, S., Mikkonen, M., Autti, M., Silvennoinen, H. M., Erkkilä, J., Laine, M., Peretz, I., & Hietanen, M. (2008). Music listening enhances cognitive recovery and mood after middle cerebral artery stroke. *Brain, 131*(3), 866–876.

Schaefer, H., & Martin. P. L. (1969). *Behavioral therapy.* New York: McGraw-Hill.

Schmidt, J. A. (1983). Songwriting as a therapeutic procedure. *Music Therapy Perspectives, 1*(2), 4–7.

Schneider, K. J., & Krug, O. T. (2010). *Existential-humanistic therapy.* Washington, DC: American Psychological Association.

Schooler, C. (2007). Culture and social structure: The relevance of social structure to social psychology. In S. Kitaysm & D. Cohen (Eds.), *Handbook of cultural psychology* (pp. 370–388). New York: Guilford Press.

Schultz, D., & Schultz, S. (2009). *Theories of personality* (9th ed.). Belmont, CA: Wadsworth, Cengage Learning.

Schwabe, C. (2005). Resource-Oriented Music Therapy – The development of a concept. *Nordic Journal of Music Therapy,* 14:1, 49–56. doi:10.1080/08098130509478125

Schwantes, M. (2011). *Music therapy's effects on Mexican migrant farmworkers' levels of depression, anxiety, and social isolation: A mixed methods randomized control trial utilizing participatory action research.* Doctoral Dissertation. Aalborg, Denmark: Aalborg University.

Schwantes, M., Wigram, T., McKinney, C., Lipscomb, A., & Richards, C. (2011). The Mexican "corrido" and its use in a music therapy bereavement group. *Australian Journal of Music Therapy, 22,* 2–23.

Seligman, M. E. P. (2002). *Authentic happiness: Using the new positive psychology to realize your potential for lasting fulfillment.* New York: Simon and Schuster.

Seligman, M. E. P. (2011). *Flourish: A visionary new understanding of happiness and well-being.* New York: First Free Press.

Seligman, M. E. P., & Csikszentmihalyi, M. (2000). Positive psychology: An introduction. *American Psychologist, 55,* 5–14.

Shapiro, N. (2005). Sounds in the world: Multicultural influences in music therapy in clinical practice and training. *Music Therapy Perspectives, 23*(1), 29–35.

Shechtman, Z. (1990). Promoting a therapeutic classroom climate through democratic values. *School of Psychology International, 11*, 39–44. doi:10.177/014303 4390111006.

Silber, F., & Hes, J. P. (1995). The use of songwriting with patients diagnosed with Alzheimer's disease. *Music Therapy Perspectives, 13*(1), 31–34.

Silverman, M. J. (2003). Contingency songwriting to reduce combativeness and non-cooperation in a client with schizophrenia: A case study. *The Arts in Psychotherapy, 30*, 25–33.

Silverman, M. J. (2009). The use of lyric analysis in contemporary music therapy: Descriptive results of songs and objectives for clinical practice. *Music Therapy Perspectives, 21*(1), 55–67.

Silverman, M. J. (2011a). The effect of songwriting on knowledge of coping skills and working alliance in psychiatric patients: A randomized clinical effectiveness study. *Journal of Music Therapy, 48*(1), 103–122.

Silverman, M. J. (2011b). Effects of music therapy on change and depression on clients in detoxification. *Journal of Addictions Nursing, 22*, 185–192. doi:10.310 9/10884602.2011.616606

Silverman, M. J. (2011c). Effects of music therapy on change readiness and craving in patients on a detoxification unit. *Journal of Music Therapy, 48*(4), 509–531. doi:10.1111/j.1360-443.1993.tb00820.x

Silverman, M. J. (2012). Effects of group songwriting on depression and quality of life in acute psychiatric inpatients: A randomized three group effectiveness study. *Nordic Journal of Music Therapy, 22*(2), 131–148. doi:10.1080/08098131. 2012.709268

Silverman, M. J. (2013). Effects of family-based educational music therapy on acute care psychiatric patients and their family members: An exploratory mixed-methods study. *Nordic Journal of Music Therapy, 23*(2), 99–122. doi:10. 1080/08098131.2013.783097

Sirgy, M. J., & Wu, J. (2009). The pleasant life, the engaged life, and the meaningful life: What about the balanced life? *Journal of Happiness Studies, 10*, 183–196.

Sloan, S., & Ponsford, J. (2012). Managing cognitive problems following TBI. In J. Ponsford (Ed.), *Traumatic brain injury: Rehabilitation for everyday adaptive living* (2nd ed., pp. 99–132). Hoboken: Taylor & Francis.

Small, C. (1998). *Musicking: The meanings of performing and listening.* Hanover: University Press of New England.

Smircich, L. (1983). Concepts of culture and organizational analysis. *Administrative Science Quarterly, 28*, 339–358.

Solli, H. P. (2014). Battling illness with wellness: A qualitative case study of a young rapper's experiences with music therapy. *Nordic Journal of Music Therapy.* doi:doi. org/10.1080/08098131.2014.907334. First published online 1 May 2014.

Spitzer, C., Barnow, S., Armbruster, J., Kusserow, S., Freyberger, H. J., & Grabe, H. J. (2006). Borderline personality organization and dissociation. *Bulletin of the Menninger Clinic, 70*(3), 210–221.

Spitzer, M. (2013). Sad flowers: Analyzing affective trajectory in Schubert's "Trockne Blumen". In T. Cochrane, B. Fantini, & K. R. Scherer (Eds.), *The emotional power of music: Multidisciplinary perspectives on musical arousal, expression, and social control* (pp. 7–22). Oxford: Oxford University Press.

Stevens, A. (2006). The archetypes. In R. Papadopoulos (Ed.), *The handbook of Jungian psychology* (pp. 74–93). Hoboken, NJ: Taylor and Francis.

Stige, B. (2002). *Culture-centered music therapy.* Gilsum, NH: Barcelona.

Stige, B. (2003/2012). *Elaborations toward a notion of community music therapy.* Gilsum, NH: Barcelona Publishers.

Stige, B., & Aarø, L. E. (2012). *Invitation to community music therapy.* New York: Routledge.

Stige, B., Ansdell, G., Elefant, C., & Pavlicevic, M. (2010). *Where music helps. Community Music Therapy in action and reflection.* Surrey: Ashgate.

Stige, B., Malterud, K., & Midtgarden, T. (2009). Toward an agenda for evaluation of qualitative research. *Qualitative Health Research, 19*(10), 1504–1516. doi:10.1177/1049732309348501

Stoeber, J. K. (2006). Positive conceptions of perfectionism: Approaches, evidence, challenges. *Personality & Social Psychology Review, 10*(4), 295–319. doi:10.1207/s15327957pspr1004-2

Substance Abuse and Mental Health Services Administration. (1999). *Brief interventions and brief therapies for substance abuse.* Rockville, MD: SAMHSA.

Sylvan, R. (2002). *Traces of the spirit: The religious dimensions of popular music.* New York: New York University Press.

Sylvestre, A., & Merette, C. (2010). Language delay in severely neglected children: A cumulative or specific effect of risk factors? *Child Abuse & Neglect: The International Journal, 34*(6), 414–428.

Tamplin, J. (2006). Song collage technique: A new approach to songwriting. *Nordic Journal of Music Therapy, 15*(2), 177–190.

Tamplin, J., Baker, F. A., Rickard, N., Roddy, C., & MacDonald, R. A. R. (2015). *Nordic Journal of Music Therapy.* doi:10.1080/08098131.2015.1011208. First published online 13 March 2015.

Temple, N. (1996). Transference and countertransference: General and forensic aspects. In C. Cordess and M. Cox (Eds.), *Forensic psychotherapy. Crime, psychodynamics and the offender patient* (pp. 23–47). London: Jessica Kingsley Publishers.

Thompson, R. A., & Miranda, M. (2009). Development of self, relationships, and socioemotional competence. In O. A. Barbarin & B. A. Wasik (Eds.), *Handbook of child development and early education* (pp. 147–171). New York: Guildford Press.

Thompson, S. (2011). *The impact and effect of group music therapy on anxiety, depression, quality of life and coping with women with breast cancer: A mixed methods study.* Doctoral Dissertation. Melbourne: University of Melbourne.

Thompson, S. (2009). Themes and metaphors in songwriting with clients participating in a psychiatric rehabilitation program. *Music Therapy Perspectives, 27*(1), 4–10.

Thompson, T. (2004). Failure-avoidance: Parenting, the achievement environment of the home and strategies for reduction. *Learning and Instruction, 14*(1), 3–26.

Tov, W., & Diener, E. (2007). Culture and subjective well-being. In S. Kitaysm & D. Cohen (Eds.), *Handbook of cultural psychology* (pp. 691–712). New York: Guilford Press.

Tuastad, L., & O'Grady, L. (2013). Music therapy inside and outside prison – A freedom practice? *Nordic Journal of Music Therapy, 22*(3), 210–232.

Twohig, M. P., & Dehlin, J. P. (2012). Skill training. In W. T. O'Donoghue & J. Fischer (Eds.), *Cognitive behavior therapy: Core principles of practice* (pp. 37–73). Hoboken, NJ: Wiley.

Tyler, H. M. (2003). Being Beverely: Music therapy with a troubled eight year old girl. In S. Hadley (Ed.), *Psychodynamic music therapy: Case studies* (pp. 37–51). Gilsum, NH: Barcelona Publishers.

Tyson, E. H., Detchkov, K., Eastwood, E., Carver, A., & Sehr, A. (2012). Therapeutically and socially relevant themes in hip-hop music: A comprehensive analysis of a selected sample of songs. In S. Hadley & G. Yancy (Eds.), *Therapeutic uses of rap and hip-hop* (pp. 99–114). New York: Brunner-Routledge.

Uhlig, S. (2006). *Authentic voices, authentic singing: A multicultural approach to vocal music therapy*. Gilsum, NH: Barcelona Publishers.

Uhlig, S. (2011). From violent rap to lovely blues: The transformation of aggressive behaviour through vocal music therapy. In A. Meadows (Ed.), *Developments in music therapy practice* (pp. 182–197). Gilsum, NH: Barcelona Publishers.

Uhlig, S., & Baker, F. A. (2011). Voicework in music therapy: Pioneers and a new generation. In F. A. Baker & S. Uhlig (Eds.), *Voicework in music therapy: Research and practice* (pp. 25–42). London, Philadelphia: Jessica Kingsley Publishers.

Ulrich, R. S. (1984). View through a window may influence recovery from surgery. *Science, 224*, 420–421.

Unkefer, R. F., & Thaut, M. H. (2002). *Music therapy in the treatment of adults with mental disorders: Theoretical bases and clinical interventions* (2nd ed.). Saint Louis, MO: MMB Music.

Van Der Slot, W. M. A., Nieuwenhuijsen, C., Van Den Berg-Emons, R. J. G., Bergen, M. P., Hilberink, S. R., Stam, H. J., & Roebroeck, M. E. (2012). Chronic pain, fatigue, and depressive symptoms in adults with spastic bilateral cerebral palsy. *Developmental Medicine and Child Neurology, 54*(9), 836–842.

Veltre, V. J., & Hadley, S. (2012). It's bigger than hip-hop: A hip-hop feminist approach to music therapy with adolescent females. In S. Hadley & G. Yancy (Eds.), *Therapeutic uses of rap and hip-hop* (pp. 79–98). New York: Brunner-Routledge.

Viega, M. (2012). The hero's journey in hip-hop and its applications in music therapy. In S. Hadley & G. Yancey (Eds.), *Therapeutic uses of rap and hip-hop* (pp. 57–78). New York: Brunner-Routledge.

Viega, M. (2013). *Loving me and my butterfly wings: A study of hip-hop songs created by adolescents in music therapy*. Doctoral Dissertation. Philadelphia, PA: Temple University.

Viega, M. (in press a). Working with the negative to make a better picture: Exploring hip-hop songs in pediatric rehabilitation. In C. Dileo (Ed.), *Advanced practices in medical music therapy: Case reports*. Cherry Hill, NJ: Jeffrey Books.

Viega, M. (in press b). Sanctify and testify creating hip-hop and rap in music therapy. In C. A. Lee & S. Pun (Eds.), *Creative Explorations and Resources for Music Therapists*. New Braunfels: Barcelona.

Viega, M. (unpublished manuscript). The effects of therapeutic songwriting on hope, anxiety, mood, and motivation for adolescents with adverse childhood experiences: An experimental pilot study. Unpublished study. Philadelphia, PA: Temple University.

Wagner-Moore, L. E. (2004). Gestalt therapy: Past, present, theory, and research. *Psychotherapy: Theory, Research, Practice, Training, 41*(2), 180–189. doi:10.1037/0033-3204.41.2.180

Wheeler, B. (1983). A psychotherapeutic classification of music therapy practice: A continuum of Procedures. *Music Therapy Perspectives, 1*(2), 8–12.

Whitehead-Pleaux, A., Robinson, B., Hardy, S., Oswanski, L., Forinash, M., Hearns, M., Anderson, N., & York, E. (2012). Lesbian, gay, bisexual, transgender, and questioning: Best practices in music therapy. *Music Therapy Perspectives, 30*(2), 158–166.

Whitehead-Pleaux, A., & Spall, L. (2014). Innovations in medical music therapy: The use of electronic music technologies in a pediatric burn hospital. In W. Magee (Ed.), *Music technology in therapeutic and health settings* (pp. 133–148). London: Jessica Kingsley Publishers.

Wiemer, H. J. (2014). Schizophrenia: Speech therapy. In S. Richman (Ed.), *CINAHL Rehabilitation Guide* (pp. 1–18). Ipswich, MA: EBSCO Publishing.

Wigram, T. (2005). Songwriting methods – Similarities and differences: Developing a working model. In F. A. Baker & T. Wigram (Eds.), *Songwriting: Methods, techniques and clinical applications for music therapy clinicians, educators and students* (pp. 252–279). London: Jessica Kingsley Publishers.

Wilber, K. (2000). *Integral psychology: Consciousness, spirit, psychology, therapy.* Boston: Shambhala.

Wilber, K. (2006). *Integral spirituality: A startling new role for religion in the modern and postmodern world.* Boston, MA: Integral Books.

Wilson, K. G., Flynn, M. K., Bordieri, M., Nassar, S., Lucas, N., & Whiteman, K. (2012). Acceptance and cognitive behavior therapy. In W. T. O'Donoghue & J. Fischer (Eds.), *Cognitive behavior therapy: Core principles of practice* (pp. 377–398). Hoboken, NJ: Wiley.

Winnicott, D. W. (1965). *The maturational process and the facilitating environment: Studies in the theory of emotional development.* New York: International UP Inc.

Winnicott, D. W. (1999). *Playing and reality.* First published 1971. London: Tavistock Publications; London: Pelican Books.

Worden, J. W. (2008). *Grief counseling and grief therapy.* New York: Springer.

Worthington, A., & Melia, Y. (2006). Rehabilitation is compromised by arousal and sleep disorders: Results of a survey of rehabilitation staff. *Brain Injury, 20,* 327–332.

Yalom, I. (1980). *Existential psychotherapy.* New York: Basic Books.

Yalom, I. D. (1995). *The theory and practice of group psychotherapy* (4th ed.). New York: Basic Books.

Yalom, I. D., & Leszcz, M. (2005). *The theory and practice of group psychotherapy.* New York: Basic Books.

Yontef, G. (1993). *Awareness, dialogue, and process.* Gouldsboro, ME: The Gestalt Journal Press.

Zettle, R. D. (2005). The evolution of a contextual approach to therapy: From comprehensive distancing to ACT. *International Journal of Behavioral Consultation and Therapy, 1*(2), 77–89.

Zimmerman, M. A. (2000). Empowerment theory. Psychological, organizational, and community levels of analyses. In J. Rappaport & E. Seidman (Eds.), *Handbook of community psychology* (pp. 43–63). New York: Kluwer Academic/Plenum Publishers.

Zollo, P. (1997). *Songwriters on songwriting* (Expanded ed.). Cincinnati, OH: Da Capo Press.

Index

CPSIA information can be obtained
at www.ICGtesting.com
Printed in the USA
LVHW041127021218
598984LV00015B/793